Learning Node.js

Second Edition

Addison-Wesley Learning Series

Visit **informit.com/learningseries** for a complete list of available publications.

The **Addison-Wesley Learning Series** is a collection of hands-on programming guides that help you quickly learn a new technology or language so you can apply what you've learned right away.

Each title comes with sample code for the application or applications built in the text. This code is fully annotated and can be reused in your own projects with no strings attached. Many chapters end with a series of exercises to encourage you to reexamine what you have just learned, and to tweak or adjust the code as a way of learning.

Titles in this series take a simple approach: they get you going right away and leave you with the ability to walk off and build your own application and apply the language or technology to whatever you are working on.

  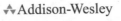

Learning Node.js

Second Edition

Marc Wandschneider

✦ Addison-Wesley

Boston • Columbus • Indianapolis • New York • San Francisco • Amsterdam • Cape Town
Dubai • London • Madrid • Milan • Munich • Paris • Montreal • Toronto • Delhi
Mexico City • São Paulo • Sidney • Hong Kong • Seoul • Singapore • Taipei • Tokyo

Learning Node.js, Second Edition

Copyright © 2017 Pearson Education, Inc.

ISBN-13: 978-0-134-66370-8

ISBN-10: 0-134-66370-5

Library of Congress Control Number: 2016956520

Printed in the United States of America

1 16

Trademarks

Warning and Disclaimer

Special Sales

For information about buying this title in bulk quantities, or for special sales opportunities (which may include electronic versions; custom cover designs; and content particular to your business, training goals, marketing focus, or branding interests), please contact our corporate sales department at corpsales@pearsoned.com or (800) 382-3419.

For government sales inquiries, please contact governmentsales@pearsoned.com.

For questions about sales outside the U.S., please contact intlcs@pearson.com.

Visit us on the Web: informit.com/aw

Editor
Mark Taber

Project Manager
Dhayanidhi

Copy Editor
Warren Hapke

Indexer
Cheryl Lenser

Technical Reviewer
Gustavo Moreira

Cover Designer
Chuti Prasertsith

❖

Much love to Tina, for simply being there.

❖

Contents at a Glance

Contents

Acknowledgments

I'd like to thank all the Marks at Pearson (it's a common name, it seems) who have helped me make this book and other projects a reality. The copy editors have been brilliant and helpful.

A huge debt of gratitude is due to Gustavo Moreira for his excellent technical and style reviews.

And finally, much love to Tina, for making it all worthwhile.

About the Author

Marc Wandschneider is a software developer who has spent much time working on scalable web applications and responsive mobile apps. A graduate of McGill University's School of Computer Science, he spent five years at Microsoft, developing and managing developers on the Visual Basic, Visual J++, and .NET Windows Forms teams. As a Software Developer/Architect at SourceLabs, he built the SWiK open source Wiki platform and then co-founded Adylitica in Beijing. He currently works for Google in London. He authored *PHP and MySQL LiveLessons and Core Web Application Development with PHP and MySQL*.

Introduction

Welcome to *Learning Node.js*. Node.js is an exciting platform for writing applications of all sorts, ranging from powerful web applications to simple scripts you can run on your local computer. The project has grown from a reasonably small software package managed by one company into a production-quality system governed by a Technical Steering Committee (TSC) and has a sizeable following in the developer community. In this book, I teach you more about it and why it is special, then get you up and writing Node.js programs in short order. You'll soon find that people are rather flexible with the name of Node.js and will refer to it frequently as just Node or even node. I certainly do a lot of that in this book as well.

Why Node.js?

Node.js has arisen for a couple of primary reasons, which I explain next.

The Web

In the past, writing web applications was a pretty standard process. You have one or more servers on your machine that listen on a *port* (for example, *80* for HTTP), and when a request is received, it forks a new process or a thread to begin processing and responding to the query. This work frequently involves communicating with external services, such as a database, memory cache, external computing server, or even just the file system. When all this work is finally finished, the thread or process is returned to the pool of available servers, and more requests can be handled.

It is a reasonably linear process, easy to understand and straightforward to code. There are, however, a couple of disadvantages that continue to plague the model:

1. Each of these threads or processes carries some overhead with it. On some machines, PHP and Apache can take up as much as 10–15MB per process. Even in environments where a large server runs constantly and forks threads to process the requests, each of these carries some overhead to create a new stack and execution environment, and you frequently run into the limits of the server's available memory.

2. In most common usage scenarios where a web server communicates with a database, caching server, external server, or file system, it spends most of its time sitting around doing nothing and waits for these services to finish and return their responses. While it is sitting there doing nothing, this thread is effectively blocked from doing anything else. The resources it consumes and the process or thread in which it runs are entirely frozen waiting for those responses to come back.

Only after the external component has finally sent back its response will that process or thread be free to finish processing, send a response to the client, and then reset to prepare for another incoming request.

So, although it's pretty easy to understand and work with, you do have a model that can be quite inefficient if your scripts spend most of their time waiting for database servers to finish running a query—an extremely common scenario for many modern web applications.

Many solutions to this problem have been developed and are in common use. You can buy ever bigger and more powerful web servers with more memory. You can replace more powerful and feature-rich HTTP servers such as Apache with smaller, lightweight ones such as *lighttpd* or *nginx*. You can build stripped-down or reduced versions of your favorite web programing language such as PHP or Python (indeed, for a time, Facebook took this one step further and built a system that converts PHP to native C++ code for maximal speed and optimal size). Or you can throw more servers at the problem to increase the number of simultaneous connections you can accommodate.

New Technologies

Although the web developers of the world have continued their eternal struggle against server resources and the limits on the number of requests they can process, a few other interesting things have happened in the world.

JavaScript, that old (meaning 1995 or so) language that came to be known mostly (and frequently reviled) for writing client-side scripts in the web browser, has become hugely popular. Modern versions of web browsers are cleaning up their implementations of it and adding new features to make it more powerful and less quirky. With the advent of client libraries for these browsers, such as jQuery, script.aculo.us, or Prototype, programming in JavaScript has become fun and productive. Unwieldy APIs have been cleaned up, and fun, dynamic effects have been added.

At the same time, a new generation of browser competition has erupted, with Google's Chrome, Mozilla's Firefox, Apple's Safari, and Microsoft's Edge all vying for the crown of browser king. As part of this, all these companies are investing heavily in the JavaScript portion of these systems as modern web applications continue to grow ever-more dynamic and script-based. In particular, Google Chrome's V8 JavaScript runtime is particularly fast and also open sourced for use by anybody.

With all these things in place, the opportunity arose for somebody to come along with a new approach to network (web) application development. Thus, the birth of Node.js.

What Exactly Is Node.js?

In 2009, a fellow named Ryan Dahl was working for Joyent, a cloud and virtualization services company in California. He was looking to develop push capabilities for web applications, similar to how Gmail does it, and found most of what he looked at not quite appropriate. He eventually settled on JavaScript because it lacked a robust input/output (I/O) model (meaning he could write his own new one), and had the fast and fully programmable V8 runtime readily available.

Inspired by some similar projects in the Ruby and Python communities, he eventually took the Chrome V8 runtime and an event-processing library called *libev* and came up with the first versions of a new system called *Node.js*. The primary methodology or innovation in Node.js is that it is built entirely around an event-driven, nonblocking model of programming. In short, you never (well, rarely) write code that blocks.

If your web application—in order to process a request and generate a response—needs to run a database query, it runs the request and then tells Node.js what to do when the response returns. In the meantime, your code is free to start processing other incoming requests or, indeed, do any other task it might need, such as cleaning up data or running analyses.

Through this simple change in the way the application handles requests and work, you are able to easily write web servers that can handle hundreds, if not thousands, of requests simultaneously on machines without much processing or memory resources. Node runs in a single process, and your code executes largely in a single thread, so the resource requirements are much lower than for many other platforms.

This speed and capacity come with a few caveats, however, and you need to be fully aware of them so you can start working with Node with your eyes wide open.

First and foremost, the new model is different from what you may have seen before and can sometimes be a bit confusing. Until you've wrapped your brain fully around some of the core concepts, some code you see written in Node.js can seem a bit strange. Much of this book is devoted to discussing the core patterns many programmers use to manage the challenges of the asynchronous, nonblocking way of programming that Node uses and how to develop your own.

Another limitation with this model of programming is that it really is centered around applications that are doing lots of different things with lots of different processes, servers, or services. Node.js truly shines when your web application is juggling connections to databases, caching servers, file systems, application servers, and more. The flip side of this, however, is that it's actually not necessarily an optimal environment for writing compute servers that are doing serious, long-running computations. For these, Node's model of a single thread in a single process can create problems if a given request is taking a ton of time to generate a complicated password digest or processing an image. In situations in which you're doing more computationally intensive work, you need to be careful how your applications use resources or perhaps even consider farming those tasks out to other platforms and run them as a service for your Node.js programs to call.

Node.js's path to adulthood has been a somewhat rocky one—the 0.x series of Node.js lingered for quite a while, releasing often but seemingly not making much progress, and some grew impatient with the governance of the project. This caused a schism in late 2014, with a group of people forking the open sourced code and creating io.js, a new version of node with the goals of being more open and transparent and responsive to the developer community. Fortunately, this break did not last long, and within nine months, Joyent agreed to hand over guidance of Node.js to the Technical Steering Committee (TSC) in autumn 2015.

Today, however, the platform is quite stable and predictable, and has adopted *semantic versioning*, where your versionsversion numbers have the format *major.minor.patchlevel*. In this model you only make breaking API changes with major version number changes, add features in minor version number changes, and can update and fix anything necessary in patch-level changes. Each major version is developed for 18 months and then supported for another 12 months after that, meaning you have 2.5 years of use for each version. After that, you'll need (and definitely want) to migrate to the latest version to be sure you're getting the latest features and most secure version of the software).

To help you keep track of and manage all of these updates, the developers have taken to labeling portions of the system with different degrees of *stability*, ranging from *Unstable* to *Stable* to *Locked*. Changes to *Stable* or *Locked* portions of the runtime are rare and involve much community discussion to determine whether the changes will generate too much pain. As you work your way through this book, we point out which areas are less stable than others and suggest ways you can mitigate the dangers of changing APIs. Newer versions of Node.js have introduced the concept of *Deprecated* APIs. If part of Node.js is becoming too difficult to maintain and is not heavily used, or otherwise doesn't make sense to continue supporting, it will (again, after much community discussion) be marked as *Deprecated* and not included in the next major version update. This gives developers plenty of time to move to alternatives (of which there are always going to be dozens).

The good news is that Node.js already has a large and active user community and a bunch of mailing lists, forums, and user groups devoted to promoting the platform and providing help where needed. A simple Internet search will get you answers to 99 percent of your questions in a matter of seconds, so never be afraid to look!

Who Is This Book For?

I wrote this book under the assumption that you are comfortable programming computers and are familiar with the functionality and syntax of at least one major programming language such as Java, C/C++, PHP, or C#. Although you don't have to be an expert, you've probably moved beyond "Learn X in Y days" level tasks.

If you're like me, you have probably written some HTML/CSS/JavaScript and thus have "worked with" JavaScript, but you might not be intimately familiar with it and have just largely templated heavily off code found on blog posts or mailing lists. Indeed, because of its clunky UI and frustrating browser mismatches, you might even frown slightly at the mere mention of JavaScript. Fear not—by the end of the first section of this book, distasteful memories of the language will be a thing of the past and, I hope, you'll be happily writing your first Node.js programs with ease and a smile on your face!

I also assume that you have a basic understanding of how web applications work: browsers send HTTP requests to a remote server; the server processes each request and sends a response with a code indicating success or failure, and then optionally some data along with that response (such as the HTML for the page to render or perhaps JavaScript Object Notation, or JSON, containing data for that request). You've probably connected to database servers in the past, run queries, and waited for the resulting rows, and so on. When I start to describe concepts beyond these in the samples and programs, I explain and refresh everybody's memory on anything new or uncommon.

How to Use this Book

This book is largely tutorial in nature. I try to balance out explanations with code to demonstrate it as much as possible and avoid long, tedious explanations of everything. For those situations in which I think a better explanation is interesting, I might point you at some resources or other documentation to learn more if you are so inclined (but it is never a necessity).

The book is divided into four major sections:

Part 1. **Learning to Walk**—You start installing and running Node, take another look at the JavaScript language and the extensions used in V8 and Node.js, and then write your first application.

Part 2. **Learning to Run**—You start developing more powerful and interesting application servers in this part of the book, and I start teaching you some of the core concepts and practices used in writing Node.js programs.

Part 3. **Breaking Out the Big Guns**—In this section, you look at some of the powerful tools and modules available to you for writing your web applications, such as help with web servers and communication with database servers.

Part 4. **Getting the Most Out of Node.js**—Finally, I close out the book by looking at a few other advanced topics such as ways in which you can run your applications on production servers, how you can test your code, and how you can use Node.js to write command-line utilities as well!

As you work your way through the book, take the time to fire up your text editor and enter the code, see how it works in your version of Node.js, and otherwise start writing and developing your own code as you go along. You develop your own little photo sharing application as you work through this book, which I hope provides you with some inspiration or ideas for things you can write.

Download the Source Code

Source code for most of the examples and sample projects in this book can be found at *github.com/marcwan/LearningNodeJS*. You are highly encouraged to download it and play along, but don't deny yourself the opportunity to type in some of the code as well and try things out.

The GitHub code has some fully functioning samples and has been tested to work on Mac, Linux, and Windows with the latest versions of Node.js. If new updates of Node require updates to the source code, I will put changes and notes there, so please be sure to pull down new versions every few months. Sadly, my code is not perfect, and I always welcome bug reports and pull requests!

If you have any questions or problems with the code in this book, feel free to go to *github.com/marcwan/LearningNodeJS* and add an issue; they'll be monitored and answered reasonably quickly.

Part I

Learning to Walk

1

Getting Started

In this chapter, you dive right into things and install Node.js on your machine and make sure it is working correctly before moving further into the language and writing networked applications. By the end of this chapter, you should have Node set up and running on your computer, have entered a few small test programs to play around with it, and know how to use the built-in Node debugger.

Installing Node.js

Let's begin by looking at installation on Windows. Mac and Linux users should feel free to skip ahead to the appropriate subsection, unless you have both types of machine.

Installation on Windows

To install Node.js on a Windows machine, you can use the handy installer provided on the *nodejs.org* website. Visit the Download page and then download the Windows Installer *(.msi)* for either 32 bits or 64 bits, depending on what platform you are running. I show the installation for Windows 10/64-bit.

After you download the MSI, double-click it. You should see a setup program similar to that shown in Figure 1.1.

Figure 1.1   Windows Setup Installer

Read and accept the License Agreement and then click Install. The install is pretty quick and painless, and a few seconds later, you can click Finish to complete the installation.

Verifying the Installation

To test the installation of the Node software, you can use the Windows command prompt cmd.exe (if you are using PowerShell, that also works just fine). If you are not familiar with the command prompt, you can launch it by going to Start / Run and then typing cmd, as shown in Figure 1.2.

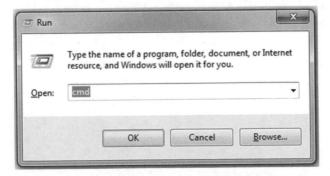

Figure 1.2   Launching the Windows command prompt

You then see a command interpreter, such as in Figure 1.3. If you want to learn more about using the command prompt, search the Internet for help using the phrases "Learning to use Windows cmd.exe" or "Getting Started with PowerShell" (if you are running Windows 7 or later) for more information.

Figure 1.3   The Windows command prompt

To make sure Node was installed properly, type `node --version` in the command window. You should see the output as in Figure 1.4.

Figure 1.4   Verifying that Node is installed correctly. Check the version number

The command prompt window should print out the version number of Node you just installed a few seconds ago (don't worry if the number in Figure 1.4 doesn't match what you see—indeed, I'd be surprised if it did!). If you do not see a version number or if instead you see the output saying that "'node' is not recognized as an internal or external command" (see Figure 1.5), something has gone wrong and you should do the following:

- Look in Control Panel / Programs and see whether the installation is actually completed. If not, try the install again, and pay a bit closer attention to what happens. Perhaps something has gone wrong and there will be an error message.

- Look in `Program Files\nodejs` and make sure `node.exe` is actually there. If it is not, try installing again (uninstall the old version first, if necessary).

- Make sure that `node.exe` is in your `PATH` environment variable. In the command prompt, Windows has a list of directories in which you can search when you type in the name of a program. You can view this by simply typing `path` in the command prompt window. It should show something similar to that in Figure 1.6. In particular, look at the two highlighted directory names at the end. Something very similar to both of these should be in your `PATH`.

- If `Program Files\nodejs` and `Users\..\AppData\..\npm` are not in your `PATH` but these folders definitely do exist, you can add them to your `PATH` manually by adding them to your `PATH` environment variable. You do this in the System Control Panel window. Click on Advanced System Settings and then Environment Variables. Then add the path of the NPM folder (it is in something like C:\Users\UserName\Local\npm) to the PATH under User Variables for *Username* and also add the path to the Node.js folder (it is in something like C:\Program Files\nodejs) to the PATH under System Variables. Note that the NPM folder might be in Username\Remote\npm instead of Username\Local\npm, depending on how your computer is configured.

Figure 1.5   Node is not recognized as an internal or external command

Figure 1.6   Checking your PATH environment variable

After confirming you have node.exe installed and working, you can start writing JavaScript.

Installation on the Mac

Although it's always possible to build the Node.js software directly from the source code, it's become sufficiently complex over the last few years that I no longer recommend it and, indeed, just use the package installers provided on the nodejs.org website. I'll demonstrate this now. If you are extremely keen on building from source, head over to the official Node.js GitHub repository at *github.com/nodejs/node* and find the instructions there.

Using the PKG Installer

By far the quickest way to install Node.js on your Apple Mac computer running OS X is to download and run the Node PKG installer available from the nodejs.org website.

After you download the installer, double-click it, and you should see something similar to what is shown in Figure 1.7. I tend to use just the default installation because I want all the components, and the default path (`/usr/local/bin`) is what I want. I recommend you do the same here.

Figure 1.7   Running the Mac PKG installer for Node.js

When the installation is complete, you should see something similar to what is shown in Figure 1.8. As the package installer explains, it is important to make sure that `/usr/local/bin` is in your PATH environment variable. You can open the Terminal.app program (go to `/Applications/Utilities`, and launch Terminal). In the terminal window, type

```
echo $PATH
```

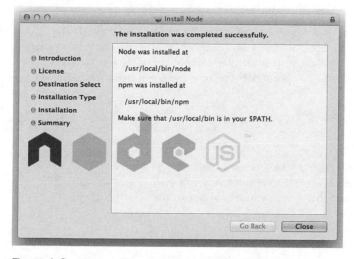

Figure 1.8   Make sure your path is set up correctly

On my machine, the output is

/usr/bin:/bin:/usr/sbin:/sbin:**/usr/local/bin**:/Users/marcw/bin:/usr/local/git/bin

You can see that /usr/local/bin is indeed here in the PATH. If it is not, you should edit your ~/.bash_profile file (it's okay to create this file if it does not exist) and add

PATH=${PATH}:/usr/local/bin

Close the terminal window, launch another, and verify that /usr/local/bin is now in your PATH. You should be able to type

```
node --version
npm --version
```

and see something like

```
client:LearningNode marcw$ node --version
v6.3.1
client:LearningNode marcw$ npm --version
3.10.3
```

Don't worry if the version number above doesn't match what you have on your computer.

After confirming you have the node program installed and working, you can start writing JavaScript.

Installation on Linux

Installing Node.js

Although I used to build Node.js on Linux from source in the past, this has become sufficiently complex over the last few years that I've switched to just using the prebuilt binary packages provided on the nodejs.org website. For those super keen on building from the source code, head on over to *github.com/nodejs/node* for instructions on how to do this.

First, go to the nodejs.org website and download the appropriate tarball (archive package ending in *.tar.xz*) for your platform listed under "Linux Binaries".." This will leave you with a file of the form *node-vX.Y.Z-linux-x64.tar.xz*. This archive contains everything in the right place, so basically we just need to copy it to an appropriate location and use it from there. Here is what I usually do:

```
marcw@hostname:~$ cd ~/bin
marcw@hostname:~$ tar xz ~/Downloads/node-vX.Y.Z-linux-x64.tar.xz
marcw@hostname:~$ PATH=$PATH:~/bin/node-vX.Y.Z-linux-x64
```

If ~/bin does not exist, I create it first. It will become a hassle to type in the PATH=... line every time you start a new terminal, so you should actually edit your .bash_profile file (or the equivalent for your current shell) and include that line in there.

When you are done, you should be able to just enter

```
node --version
npm --version
```

and get output somewhat similar to

```
marcw@hostname:~$ node --version
v6.3.1
marcw@hostname:~$ npm --version
3.10.3
```

Running Node.js and "Hello World!"

There are two primary ways to use Node.js on your machines: by using the Node shell or by saving JavaScript to files and running those.

The Node Shell

The first way you will run Node.js is the Node shell, which is frequently called the *Node REPL*—REPL stands for *Read-Eval-Print-Loop*. It's a great way to quickly test things in Node. If you don't remember exactly how a function should be used, you can just quickly use the REPL and type in something to see what happens.

To launch the Node shell, you simply type `node` in whatever shell you are using:

```
marcw@hostname:~$ node
>
```

The `>` is all the response you get. You can immediately start typing in some code:

```
> console.log("Hello World!");
Hello World!
undefined
>
```

The first line of the output is the result of the code you just executed. In this case, you use the Node global variable `console` and its `log` function to print out `Hello World!` (see the next chapter for more information on `console` and other globals). The output of this statement is, predictably, `Hello World!`, which is printed for you.

The last line of the output is always the *resulting value* of the preceding statement. Every statement, function call, or expression has a value associated with it, which is printed out in the Node shell for you. If there is no evaluated expression value or the called function does not return any particular value, the special value `undefined` is returned instead.

To exit the REPL, you simply press Ctrl+D (same on Windows).

If you ever see three dots (...) in the Node REPL, that means it is expecting more input from you to complete the current expression, statement, or function. If you do not quite understand why it is giving you the ellipsis, you can just type .break (with the period) to get out of it:

```
> function () {
... }
... what?
... .break
>
```

Editing and Running JavaScript Files

The other option for running Node.js code is to simply use your favorite text editor to write JavaScript code into a file and then run that code via the command line using the node command.

To demonstrate this, save the following to a file called hello.js:

```
/**
 * Let's be sociable.
 */
console.log("Hello World!");
```

Now, you can execute this file from the command line with

```
node hello.js
```

And you should see this output:

```
Hello World!
```

Because you are not in the Node shell, you don't get any information on the return values of the code executed.

Your First Web Server

You're ready to write something a bit more interesting now and create a little web server. Fortunately, Node makes this task extremely easy. Enter and save the following into a file called web.js:

```
var http = require("http");

function process_request(req, res) {
    var body = 'Thanks for calling!\n';
    var content_length = body.length;
    res.writeHead(200, {
        'Content-Length': content_length,
        'Content-Type': 'text/plain'
    });
    res.end(body);
```

```
}
```

```
var s = http.createServer(process_request);
s.listen(8080);
```

To run it, simply type

```
node web.js
```

Your computer now has a web server running on port 8080. To test it, you can use the command-line program `curl`, which most Mac and Linux machines have preinstalled (Windows users, see "Downloading from the Web on Windows"). (You also can just type `http://localhost:8080` into a web browser, but you won't see the response codes there unless you open a debug console).

```
curl -i http://localhost:8080
```

You should now see something similar to the following:

```
HTTP/1.1 200 OK
Content-Length: 20
Content-Type: text/plain
Date: Tue, 15 Feb 2013 03:05:08 GMT
Connection: keep-alive

Thanks for calling!
```

Downloading from the Web on Windows

By default, Windows does not ship with any command-line utilities to get the contents of a URL. Because it's such a useful thing to do, I highly recommend you download cURL (I just refer to it as `curl` from now on) or `wget` for Windows.

Curl:

You can download the Windows binaries for `curl` by visiting ***http://curl.haxx.se/download.html***, and looking there for the "Win32—Generic" section (don't worry if you're running 64-bit windows—this works just fine).

Download one of the highlighted binaries, preferably one with support for SSL and SSH (if it redirects you to another page, download the binary "Download WITH SUPPORT SSL"), unpack it, and put `curl.exe` somewhere in your PATH or user directory. To launch it in the command prompt or PowerShell, just type

```
C:\Users\Mark\curl --help
```

Wget:

If you cannot get `curl` working on your Windows machine, `wget` is a great alternative. You can download it from https://www.gnu.org/software/wget/.

It works basically the same as `curl`, but with some slightly different command-line arguments. To learn more, view the help:

```
C:\Users\Mark\wget --help
```

Node.js provides a lot of powerful functionality right out of the box, and in the first line of the preceding program, you use one of these built-in modules—the *http* module, which allows your program to act as a web server. The `require` function includes this module, and you have the variable `http` to refer to it.

The `createServer` function takes only one argument, and that is a function that will be called each and every time somebody makes a connection to your server. You pass the `process_request` function you wrote earlier, which is called with two parameters: an object representing the incoming request (a `ServerRequest` object) and another for the pending response (of type `ServerResponse`). Once the server is created, you tell it to start listening for incoming requests on a particular port—here, you use *8080*—when you launch the program.

The `-i` switch you passed to `curl` earlier tells it to print out the headers along with the response. This lets you learn a little bit more about what exactly Node is doing for you.

You can see that the `200 (OK)` response you passed to the `ServerResponse#writeHead` function is returned in the HTTP response headers, and you also see the content length and types are both represented. Node.js, by default, also indicates that HTTP connections to its server are `keep-alive`, which allows multiple requests on the same network connection; you don't need it for most of the examples early in this book.

To stop the server from running, you simply press Ctrl+C. It is smart enough to clean up everything and shut down properly.

Debugging Your Node.js Programs

Now you can rewrite the preceding web server, but this time get a little careless and introduce a smelling pistake—misspell `body.length`, as follows—and put it into a file called `debugging.js`:

```
var http = require("http");

var s = http.createServer(function (req, res) {
    var body = 'Thanks for calling!\n';
    var content_length = body.lengtth;
    res.writeHead(200, {
        'Content-Length': content_length,
        'Content-Type': 'text/plain'
    });
    res.end(body);
});

/**
 * Now run the server, listening on port 8080
 */
s.listen(8080);
```

You can run this program as before:

```
node debugging.js
```

Now, when you connect to *http://localhost:8080*, you'll probably see something like this:

```
client:~ marcw$ curl -i localhost:8080
HTTP/1.1 200 OK
Content-Length: undefined
Content-Type: text/plain
Date: Tue, 30 Oct 2012 04:42:44 GMT
Connection: keep-alive
```

You no longer get the "Thanks for calling!" message, and you can see that the Content-Length header is not what you expected.

For a trivial program like this, the error is pretty easy to figure out, but in a bigger program, it can be hard to determine what exactly has gone wrong. To help with this issue, Node.js includes a debugger right in the node program. To use it, you just add the debug flag before the name of your program:

```
node debug debugging.js
```

You should see something like the following:

```
client:Chapter01 marcw$ node debug debugging.js
< debugger listening on port 5858
connecting... ok
break in debugging.js:1
  1 var http = require("http");
  2
  3 function process_request(req, res) {
debug>
```

You use a few key commands in the Node debugger:

- cont—Continue running.
- next—Step over the next statement.
- step—Step into the next statement (if possible; otherwise, just step over).
- out—Step out of the currently executing function.
- backtrace—Show the current call execution frame or call stack.
- repl—Start the Node REPL to allow you to view variable values and execute code.
- watch(expr)—Add the given expression to the watch list, which is shown whenever you step or move through anything in the debugger.
- list(*n*)—List the *n* lines of source code before and after the currently stopped line in the debugger.

Now, suspecting something might be wrong with the `Content-Length` in the program, you can put a breakpoint on the line `var content_length = body.lengtthlenggth;`, or line 5:

```
debug> setBreakpoint(5)
  1 var http = require("http");
  2
  3 function process_request(req, res) {
  4     var body = 'Thanks for calling!\n';
* 5     var content_length = body.lenggth;
  6     res.writeHead(200, {
debug>
```

Line 5 now has a * next to it to indicate there is a breakpoint. When you start the debugger, the program is stopped at the first line. You can resume execution by using the `cont` command:

```
debug> cont
debug>
```

Now, you go to another terminal window or command prompt and type

```
curl -i http://localhost:8080
```

You should immediately notice two things:

1. The `curl` does not return right away.

2. In your `node` `debug` session, you now see

```
   break in debugging.js:5
     3 function process_request(req, res) {
     4     var body = 'Thanks for calling!\n';
   > 5     var content_length = body.lenggth;
     6     res.writeHead(200, {
     7         'Content-Length': content_length,
```

You can skip over this line:

```
debug> next
break in debugging.js:7
* 5     var content_length = body.lenggth;
> 6     res.writeHead(200, {
  7         'Content-Length': content_length,
  8         'Content-Type': 'text/plain'
  9     });
```

And now start the Node REPL so you can examine some variable values:

```
debug> repl
Press Ctrl + C to leave debug repl
  >
```

Let's look at the values of body and content_length, respectively:

```
> body
'Thanks for calling!\n'
> content_length
>
```

For body, you can see, as expected, that you get a value. But for content_length, which you expect to be 20, you see nothing. You can now see that the code that set its value is wrong and have found the problem!

Finally, you can either just shut down the whole system by pressing Ctrl+D to end the debugger, or you can type cont to continue running the server. Typing cont inside the REPL will not work and results in the following error: "ReferenceError: cont is not defined." You will need to press Ctrl+C to exit the REPL first, and then you can use cont.

Although this introduction to the debugger has been a quite brief, it is worth playing around with; it is quite powerful and very useful. There are, additionally, some other browser-based debuggers being written by Node.js community members, the most promising of which so far is node-inspector. Feel free to search for them and play around with them to see how they can help you.

In a pinch, there is nothing wrong with inserting a simple console.log(variable_name); into your code to have the results printed to the terminal window. It can often be a quick and simple way to get the information you need to track down bugs or problems.

Staying Up-to-Date and Finding Help

As mentioned previously, one of the challenges of working with Node.js is its constant state of change. Although more and more APIs and sections of the product are considered *Stable* or *Locked*, some things are still changing with every new release, and these releases are happening on a weekly basis.

Here are some things you can do to keep up-to-date and not miss out on any important changes or news:

- Join the Node.js mailing list at *http://groups.google.com/group/nodejs*. Many of the core Node developers are on this list and post whenever a new release or change is made.

- If you are on Twitter, follow @nodejs there; you will receive tweets whenever there is a new release or whenever something else important comes along.

- Visit *nodejs.org* on a semiregular basis to make sure you are not falling too far behind.

For help, the nodejs Google group is, of course, invaluable, as is the *nodejs.org* website. Similarly, StackOverflow.com has a very active community helping out with Node-related questions, and you can find many good answers there.

However, I have found that a vast majority of problems are best answered with a simple Internet search. Somebody somewhere has very likely run into the same problem as you and written a blog post or message about it. It is quite rare that I am unable to find the answers with simple searches.

Summary

You should now have Node.js installed on your computer, verified that it is working properly, and even run and debugged a few problems. Now it's time to take a closer look at the JavaScript language.

A Closer Look at JavaScript

Chances are, if you are reading this book, you have worked with JavaScript in the past. Perhaps you have worked on or written a web application that uses HTML, CSS, and JavaScript, and you have written some code to make the client more dynamic and interactive, either directly by manipulating the browser Document Object Model (DOM) or by using a framework such as jQuery or Prototype to hide some of the messier details for you. You might have even found working with JavaScript a reasonably frustrating experience and spent a lot of time fighting the different browsers' incompatibilities, and it is also quite possible that you have never *really* studied the JavaScript language apart from the most basic of language features, looking things up on the fly as you go.

The good news is that modern web browsers are slowly driving a much-needed cleanup of the JavaScript language. Additionally, ECMAScript, which is the specification on which modern implementations are based, is also evolving. The Chrome V8 JavaScript engine itself is also improving and cleaning up many frustrating things about the language and adding important features that are missing or need updating.

So, even if you've already played around with JavaScript in the past, it is probably worth your while to read through this chapter fully and learn about some of the details you might have overlooked or about some of the new features or those changed by V8 and Node.js. Although most of the discussion in this chapter is applicable to standard JavaScript, sometimes I show you something new and improved in Google's V8. For such nonstandard features, I mark them with (**V8 JS**).

Types

This section begins the review of JavaScript by looking at the types the language offers. For much of the discussion in this chapter, I use the Node.js *Read-Eval-Print-Loop* (REPL) to demonstrate how the code works. To help you out, I use **bold** to indicate things that you type into the interpreter.

```
client:LearningNode marcw$ node
>
```

Type Basics

Node.js has a few core types: `number`, `boolean`, `string`, and `object`. The two other types, `function` and `array`, are actually special kinds of `objects`, but because they have extra features in the language and runtime, some people refer to these three—object, function, and array—as *complex types*. The types `null` and `undefined` are also special kinds of `objects` and are also treated specially in JavaScript.

The value `undefined` means that a value has not been set yet or simply does not exist:

```
> var x;
undefined
> x = {};
{}
> x.not_valid;
undefined
>
```

`null`, on the other hand, is an explicit assertion that there "is no value":

```
> var y;
undefined
> y
undefined
> y = null;
null
>
```

To see the type of anything in JavaScript, you use the `typeof` operator:

```
> typeof 10
'number'
> typeof "hello";
'string'
> typeof undefined
'undefined'
> typeof function () { var x = 20; }
'function'
>
```

Constants

While Node.js theoretically supports the `const` keyword extension that some modern JavaScript implementations have implemented, it's still not widely used. For constants, the standard practice is still to just use uppercase letters in variable declarations:

```
> var SECONDS_PER_DAY = 86400;
undefined
> console.log(SECONDS_PER_DAY);
86400
undefined
>
```

Numbers

All numbers in JavaScript are 64-bit IEEE 754 double-precision floating-point numbers. For all positive and negative integers that can be expressed in 2^{53} bits accurately, the `number` type in JavaScript behaves much like integer data types in other languages:

```
> 1024 * 1024
1048576
> 1048576
1048576
> 32437893250 + 3824598359235235
3824630797128485
> -38423538295 + 35892583295
-2530955000
>
```

The tricky part of using the `number` type, however, is that for many numeric values, it is an *approximation* of the actual number. For example:

```
> 0.1 + 0.2
0.30000000000000004
>
```

When performing floating-point mathematical operations, you cannot just manipulate arbitrary real numbers and expect an exact value:

```
> 1 - 0.3 + 0.1 == 0.8
false
>
```

For these cases, you instead need to check if the value is in some sort of approximate range, the size of which is defined by the magnitude of the values you are comparing. (Search the website *stackoverflow.com* for articles and questions on comparing floating-point numbers for good strategies on this.)

For those situations in which you absolutely need to represent 64-bit integer values in JavaScript without any chance of approximation errors, you are either stuck using the `string` type and manipulating these numbers by hand, or you can use one of the available modules for manipulating big integer values. (We'll learn about modules in Chapter 5, "Modules.")

JavaScript is a bit different from other languages in that dividing a number by zero returns the value `Infinity` or `-Infinity` instead of generating a runtime exception:

```
> 5 / 0
Infinity
> -5 / 0
-Infinity
>
```

`Infinity` and `-Infinity` are valid values that you can compare against in JavaScript:

```
> var x = 10, y = 0;
undefined
```

```
> x / y == Infinity
true
>
```

You can use the functions `parseInt` and `parseFloat` to convert strings to numbers:

```
> parseInt("32523523626263");
32523523626263
> parseFloat("82959.248945895");
82959.248945895
> parseInt("234.43634");
234
> parseFloat("10");
10
>
```

If you provide these functions with something that cannot be parsed, they return the special value NaN (not-a-number):

```
> parseInt("cat");
NaN
> parseFloat("Wankel rotary engine");
NaN
>
```

To test for NaN, you must use the `isNaN` function:

```
> isNaN(parseInt("cat"));
true
>
```

Finally, to test whether a given number is a valid finite number (that is, it is not `Infinity`, `-Infinity`, or NaN), use the `isFinite` function:

```
> isFinite(10/5);
true
> isFinite(10/0);
false
> isFinite(parseFloat("banana"));
false
>
```

Booleans

The `boolean` type in JavaScript is both simple and simple to use. Values can either be `true` or `false`, and although you technically can convert values to `boolean` with the `Boolean` function, you almost never need it because the language converts everything to `boolean` when needed, according to the following rules:

1. `false`, 0, empty strings (`""`), NaN, `null`, and `undefined` all evaluate to `false`.

2. All other values evaluate to `true`.

Strings

Strings in JavaScript are sequences of Unicode characters (represented internally in a 16-bit *UCS-2* format) that can represent a vast majority of the characters in the world, including those used in most Asian languages. There is no separate `char` or character data type in the language; you just use a string of length *1* to represent these. For most of the network applications you'll be writing with Node.js, you will interact with the outside world in *UTF-8*, and Node will handle all the details of conversion for you. Except when you are manipulating binary data, your experience with strings and character sets will largely be worry-free.

Strings can be wrapped in single or double quotation marks. They are functionally equivalent, and you are free to use whatever ones you want. To include a single quotation mark inside a single-quoted string, you can use `\'`, and similarly for double quotation marks inside double-quoted strings, you can use `\"`:

```
> 'Marc\'s hat is new.'
'Marc\'s hat is new.'
> "\"Hey, nice hat!\", she said."
'"Hey, nice hat!", she said.'
>
```

To get the length of a string in JavaScript, just use the `length` property:

```
> var x = "cat";
undefined
> x.length;
3
> "cat".length;
3
```

Attempting to get the length of a `null` or `undefined` string throws an error in JavaScript (which helpfully includes a stack trace that can be used to find where exactly the error occurred):

```
> x = null;
null
> x.length;
TypeError: Cannot read property 'length' of null
    at repl:1:2
    at REPLServer.self.eval (repl.js:109:21)
    at rli.on.self.bufferedCmd (repl.js:258:20)
    at REPLServer.self.eval (repl.js:116:5)
    at Interface.<anonymous> (repl.js:248:12)
    at Interface.EventEmitter.emit (events.js:96:17)
    at Interface._onLine (readline.js:200:10)
    at Interface._line (readline.js:518:8)
    at Interface._ttyWrite (readline.js:736:14)
    at ReadStream.onkeypress (readline.js:97:10)
```

To add two strings together, you can use the + operator:

```
> "cats" + " go " + "meow";
'cats go meow'
>
```

If you start throwing other types into the mix, JavaScript converts them as best it can:

```
> var distance = 25;
undefined
> "I ran " + distance + " kilometers today";
'I ran 25 kilometers today'
>
```

Note that this can provide some interesting results if you start mixing expressions a bit too much:

```
> 5 + 3 + " is my favorite number";
'8 is my favorite number'
>
```

If you really want "53" to be your favorite number, you can just prefix it all with an empty string to force the conversion earlier:

```
> "" + 5 + 3 + " is my favorite number";
'53 is my favorite number'
>
```

Many people worry that the concatenation operator + has terrible performance when working with strings. The good news is that almost all modern browser implementations of JavaScript—including Chrome's V8 that you use in Node.js—have optimized this scenario heavily, and performance is now quite good.

String Functions

Many interesting functions are available to manipulate strings in JavaScript. To find the location of a string with another string, use the indexOf function:

```
> "Wishy washy winter".indexOf("wash");
6
>
```

To extract a substring from a string, use the substr or splice function. (The former takes the starting index and length of the string to extract; the latter takes the starting index and ending index.)

```
> "No, they're saying Booo-urns.".substr(19, 3);
'Boo'
> "No, they're saying Booo-urns.".slice(19, 22);
'Boo'
>
```

If you have a string with some sort of separator character in it, you can split that up into component strings by using the `split` function and get an `array` as the result:

```
> "a|b|c|d|e|f|g|h".split("|");
[ 'a',
  'b',
  'c',
  'd',
  'e',
  'f',
  'g',
  'h' ]
>
```

Finally, the `trim` function **(V8 JS)** does exactly what you would expect—removes whitespace from the beginning and end of a string:

```
> '    cat   \n\n\n   '. trim();
'cat'
>
```

Regular Expressions

JavaScript has powerful regular expression support, the full details of which are beyond the scope of this book, but I briefly show how and where you can use them. A certain number of string functions can take arguments that are regular expressions to perform their work. These regular expressions can be entered either in *literal format* (indicated by putting the regular expression between two forward slash [/] characters) or as a call to the constructor of a `RegExp` object:

```
/[aA]{2,}/
new RegExp("[Aa]{2,}")
```

Both of these are regular expressions that match against a sequence of two or more instances of the letter *a* (uppercase or lowercase).

To replace all sequences of two or more *a*'s with the letter *b* on `string` objects, you can use the `replace` function and write either of the following:

```
> "aaoo".replace(new RegExp("[Aa]{2,}"), "b");
'boo'
> "aaoo".replace(/[Aa]{2,}/, "b");
'boo'
>
```

Similar to the `indexOf` function, the `search` function takes a regular expression and returns the index of the first match against it or –1 if no such match exists:

```
> "aaoo".search(/[Aa]{2,}/);
0
> "aoo".search(/[Aa]{2,}/);
-1
>
```

Objects

Objects are one of the core workhorses of the JavaScript language, and something you will use all the time. They are an extremely dynamic and flexible data type, and you can add and remove things from them with ease. To create an object, you can use either of the following, although the latter, known as *object literal syntax*, is almost always preferred nowadays:

```
> var o1 = new Object();
undefined
> var o2 = {};
undefined
>
```

You can also specify the contents of objects using object literal syntax, where you can specify member names and values at initialization time:

```
var user = {
    first_name: "marc",
    last_name: "wandschneider",
    age: Infinity,
    citizenship: "man of the world"
};
```

About JSON

One of the things used quite often in this book (and indeed in all the network and web applications) is JSON, or *JavaScript Object Notation*. This data exchange format gives you all the flexibility of a text-based data format without the hassle that some of the other formats such as XML bring. (To be fair to the latter, JSON does lack some of the validation features of those formats as well, but I still find it infinitely preferable to use.)

JSON is extremely similar to object literal notation with two key differences: whereas, in object literal notation, wrapping the property names in single or double quotation marks is optional, in JSON it is *mandatory*. Furthermore, all strings should be double quoted as follows:

```
// valid object literal notation, INVALID JSON:
var obj = {
    // JSON strings are supposed to use ", not '
    "first_name": 'Marc',
```

```
        // Must wrap property names with double quotes for JSON
        last_name: "Wandschneider"
    }


    // valid JSON and object literal notation:
    var obj = {
        "first_name": "Marc",
        "last_name": "Wandschneider"
    }
```

A nontrivial number of JSON libraries actually accept single-quoted strings, but to be maximally compatible, you should be careful to use double quotation marks whenever you write or generate JSON.

To generate JSON, you mostly use the V8 functions `JSON.parse` and `JSON.stringify`. The former takes a JSON string and converts it to an object (or throws an error if it fails), while the latter takes an object and returns a JSON string representation of it.

When you are writing objects in code, you mostly use object literal notation, but you also work with a lot of JSON in this book as well, so it is important to recognize the difference. I point out whenever JSON is absolutely required.

You can add a new property to your user object by using any of the following methods:

```
> user.hair_colour = "brown";
'brown'
> user["hair_colour"] = "brown";
'brown'
> var attribute = 'hair_colour';
undefined
> user[attribute] = "brown";
'brown'
> user
{ first_name: 'marc',
  last_name: 'wandschneider',
  age: Infinity,
  citizenship: 'man of the world',
  hair_colour: 'brown' }
>
```

If you try to access a property that does not exist, you do not receive an error but instead just get back `undefined`:

```
> user.car_make
undefined
>
```

To remove a property from an object, you can use the `delete` keyword:

```
> delete user.hair_colour;
true
> user
{ first_name: 'marc',
  last_name: 'wandschneider',
  age: Infinity,
  citizenship: 'man of the world' }
>
```

The flexibility of objects in JavaScript makes them quite similar to various associative arrays, hash maps, or dictionaries seen in other languages, but there is an interesting difference: getting the size of an object-as-associative-array in JavaScript is a bit tricky. There are no `size` or `length` properties or methods on `Object`. To get around this, you can write the following:

```
> Object.keys(user).length;
4
```

Note that this uses a nonstandard extension to JavaScript `Object.keys`; although V8 and most modern browsers already support it (older versions of Internet Explorer typically do not).

Arrays

The `array` type in JavaScript is actually a special casing of the `object` type, with a number of additional features that make arrays useful and powerful. To create arrays, you can use either traditional notation or *array literal syntax*:

```
> var arr1 = new Array();
undefined
> arr1
[]
> var arr2 = [];
undefined
> arr2
[]
>
```

As with objects, I almost always prefer the literal syntax version and rarely use the former.

If you use the `typeof` operator on arrays, you get a surprising result:

```
> typeof arr2
'object'
>
```

Because arrays are actually objects, the `typeof` operator just returns that, which is very frequently not what you want! Fortunately, V8 has a language extension to let you test determinatively whether or not something is an array: the `Array.isArray` function:

```
> Array.isArray(arr2);
true
> Array.isArray({});
false
>
```

One of the key features of the `array` type in JavaScript is the `length` property, used as follows:

```
> arr2.length
0
> var arr3 = [ 'cat', 'rat', 'bat' ];
undefined
> arr3.length;
3
>
```

By default, arrays in JavaScript are numerically indexed:

```
// this:
for (var i = 0; i < arr3.length; i++) {
    console.log(arr3[i]);
}
// will print out this:
cat
rat
bat
```

To add an item to the end of an array, you can do one of two things:

```
> arr3.push("mat");
4
> arr3
[ 'cat', 'rat', 'bat', 'mat' ]
> arr3[arr3.length] = "fat";
'fat'
> arr3
[ 'cat', 'rat', 'bat', 'mat', 'fat' ]
>
```

You can specify the index of the element where you want to insert a new element. If this element is past the last element, the elements in between are created and initialized with the value `undefined`:

```
> arr3[20] = "splat";
'splat'
> arr3
[ 'cat', 'rat', 'bat', 'mat', 'fat', , , , , , , , , , , , , , , , 'splat' ]
>
```

To remove elements from an array, you might try to use the `delete` keyword again, but the results may surprise you:

```
> delete arr3[2];
true
> arr3
[ 'cat', 'rat', , 'mat', 'fat', , , , , , , , , , , , , , , , , 'splat' ]
>
```

You see that the value at index 2 still "exists" and has just been set to `undefined`.

To truly delete an item from an array, you probably should use the `splice` function, which takes an index and the number of items to delete. What it returns is an array with the extracted items, and the original array is modified such that they no longer exist there:

```
> arr3.splice(2, 2);
[ , 'mat' ]
> arr3
[ 'cat', 'rat', 'fat', , , , , , , , , , , , , , , , 'splat' ]
> arr3.length
19
```

Useful Functions

There are a few key functions you frequently use with arrays. The `push` and `pop` functions let you add and remove items to the end of an array, respectively:

```
> var nums = [ 1, 1, 2, 3, 5, 8 ];
undefined
> nums.push(13);
7
> nums
[ 1, 1, 2, 3, 5, 8, 13 ]
> nums.pop();
13
> nums
[ 1, 1, 2, 3, 5, 8 ]
>
```

To insert or delete items from the front of an array, use `unshift` or `shift`, respectively:

```
> var nums = [ 1, 2, 3, 5, 8 ];
undefined
> nums.unshift(1);
6
> nums
[ 1, 1, 2, 3, 5, 8 ]
> nums.shift();
1
> nums
[ 1, 2, 3, 5, 8 ]
>
```

The opposite of the string function `split` seen previously is the array function `join`, which returns a string:

```
> var nums = [ 1, 1, 2, 3, 5, 8 ];
undefined
> nums.join(", ");
'1, 1, 2, 3, 5, 8'
>
```

You can sort arrays using the built-in `sort` function, which can be used with the built-in sorting function:

```
> var jumble_nums = [ 3, 1, 8, 5, 2, 1];
undefined
> jumble_nums.sort();
[ 1,  1,  2,  3,  5,  8 ]
>
```

For those cases where the built-in function for it doesn't quite do what you want, you can provide your own sorting function as a parameter:

```
> var names = [ 'marc', 'Maria', 'John', 'jerry', 'alfred', 'Moonbeam'];
undefined
> names.sort();
[ 'John',  'Maria',  'Moonbeam',  'alfred',  'jerry',  'marc' ]
> names.sort(function (a, b) {
        var a1 = a.toLowerCase(), b1 = b.toLowerCase();
        if (a1 < b1) return -1;
        if (a1 > b1) return 1;
        return 0;
    });
[ 'alfred',  'jerry',  'John',  'marc',  'Maria',  'Moonbeam' ]
>
```

To iterate over items in arrays, you have a number of options, including the `for` loop shown previously, or you can use the `forEach` function, as follows:

```
[ 'marc', 'Maria', 'John', 'jerry', 'alfred', 'Moonbeam'].forEach(function (value) {
    console.log(value);
});
marc
Maria
John
jerry
alfred
Moonbeam
```

The `forEach` function is an extension to the JavaScript language that most modern browsers support fully.

Type Comparisons and Conversions

As alluded to previously, for the most part, types in JavaScript behave as you would expect them and as you have seen in other programming languages. JavaScript has both the equality operator == (do the two operands have the same value?) and the precise equality operator === (do the two operands have the same value and are of the same type?):

```
> 234 == '234'
true
> 234 === '234'
false
> 234234.235235 == 'cat'
false
> "cat" == "CAT"
false
> "cat".toUpperCase() == "CAT";
true
```

You also saw that a number of different things evaluate to false, despite being quite different:

```
> '' == false == null == undefined == 0
true
> null === undefined
false
>
```

This saves you some time when doing tasks such as checking arguments to functions:

```
function this_works(param) {
    if (param == null || param == undefined || param == '')
        throw new Error("Invalid Argument");
}

function this_is_better(param) {
    if (!param) throw new Error("Invalid Argument");
}
```

One case where type comparisons can be tricky is if you use object constructors for values instead of just using primitives:

```
> var x = 234;
undefined
> var x1 = new Number(234);
undefined
> typeof x1
'object'
> typeof x
'number'
> x1 == x
true
> x1 === x
false
>
```

The object constructors are functionally equivalent to the primitive types; all the same operations, operators, and functions produce the same results, but the precise equality operator `===` and `typeof` operator produce different results. For this reason, it is recommended to just use the primitive types whenever possible.

Functions

Although it does not look like it at first glance (the name doesn't help either), JavaScript is a *functional* programming language, wherein functions are fully typed objects that can be manipulated, extended, and passed around as data. Node.js takes advantage of this capability, and you will use it extensively in your network and web applications.

Basics

The simplest kind of function is exactly as you would expect:

```
> function hello(name) {
        console.log("hello " + name);
}
undefined
> hello("marc");
hello marc
undefined
>
```

To declare parameters for a function in JavaScript, you simply list them in the parentheses. There is, however, absolutely no checking of these parameters at runtime:

```
> hello();
hello undefined
undefined
> hello("marc", "dog", "cat", 48295);
hello marc
undefined
>
```

If too few parameters are passed into a function call, the resulting variables are assigned the value `undefined`. If too many are passed in, the extras are simply unused.

All functions have a predefined object in the body called `arguments` (that looks and behaves much like an array, but is not really an array—it's actually an object that also has a `length` property). It has all the values that were passed in to this particular function call and gives you greater flexibility on passing in parameters, allowing you can also to do extra checking on the parameter list.

```
function add_two(a, b) {
    return a + b;
}
```

```
function add_n() {
    var sum = 0;
    for (var i = 0; i < arguments.length; i++) {
        sum += arguments[i];
    }
    return sum;
}
```

Indeed, you can go a step further and use it to make your functions more powerful and flexible. Suppose you want to initialize a caching subsystem you wrote. To do this, the function takes a *size* to create the cache with and uses default values for other things such as cache location, expiration algorithm, maximum cache item size, and storage type. You could write the function as follows:

```
function init_cache(size_mb, location, algorithm, item_size, storage_type) {
    ...
}
```

```
init_cache(100, null, null, null, null);
```

However, it would be even cooler if you could have the function be "smart" enough to give you a couple of different ways to call it:

```
function init_cache() {
    var init_data = {
        cache_size: 10,
        location: './tmp',
        algorithm: 'lru',
        item_size: 1024,
        storage_type: 'btree'
    };

    var a = arguments;
    for (var i = 0; i < a.length; i++) {
        if (typeof a[i] == 'object') {
            init_data = a[i];
            break;
        } else if (typeof a[i] == 'number') {
            init_data.cache_size = a[i];
            break;
        } else {
            throw new Error("bad cache init param");
        }
    }

    // etc
}
```

Now you have a number of different ways you can call this function:

```
init_cache();
init_cache(200);
init_cache({ cache_size: 100,
             location: '/exports/dfs/tmp',
             algorithm: 'lruext',
             item_size: 1024,
             storage_type: 'btree'} );
```

Functions in JavaScript do not even need to have names:

```
> var x = function (a, b) {
      return a + b;
}
undefined
> x(10, 20);
30
```

These nameless functions are typically called *anonymous functions*. There is one drawback to fully anonymous functions and that comes in debugging:

```
> var x = function () {
      throw new Error("whoopsie");
}
undefined
> x();
Error: whoopsie
    at x (repl:2:7)
    at repl:1:1
    at REPLServer.self.eval (repl.js:109:21)
    at rli.on.self.bufferedCmd (repl.js:258:20)
```

Anonymous functions do not permit the language engine to tell you what the name of the function is when an exception is thrown. This can make your life a bit more difficult when debugging.

A simple solution and modern extension to the JavaScript language is to simply name the anonymous functions:

```
> var x = function bad_apple() {
      throw new Error("whoopsie");
}
undefined
> x();
Error: whoopsie
    at bad_apple (repl:2:7)
    at repl:1:1
    at REPLServer.self.eval (repl.js:109:21)
    at rli.on.self.bufferedCmd (repl.js:258:20)
```

In complicated programs, having an exact pointer to the location of an error can be a real life-saver. For this reason, some people choose to name all their anonymous functions.

You have already seen an example of anonymous functions in the earlier section "Arrays" when you called the sort function with an anonymous function to do case-insensitive string comparisons. You will use many more of them throughout this book.

Function Scope

Every time a function is called, a new variable scope is created. Variables declared in the parent scope are available to that function, but variables declared within the new scope are not available when the function exits. Consider the following code:

```
var pet = 'cat';

function play_with_pets() {
    var pet = 'dog';
    console.log(pet);
}

play_with_pets();
console.log(pet);
```

It outputs the following:

```
dog
cat
```

Combining this scoping with anonymous functions can be a good way to do some quick or private work with private variables that will disappear when the anonymous function exits. Here's a contrived example to compute the volume of a cone:

```
var height = 5;
var radius = 3;
var volume;

// declare and immediately call anon function to create scope
(function () {
    var pir2 = Math.PI * radius * radius;    // temp var
    volume = (pir2 * height) / 3;
})();

console.log(volume);
```

You will see a number of other common patterns involving functions when you move into Chapter 3, "Asynchronous Programming."

Arrow Functions

One new feature in ECMAScript that has made it into Node.js is a bit of syntactic sugar to make writing anonymous functions a bit easier. Before version 4.4.5 of Node.js, to write an anonymous function, you had to write it as follows:

```
var x = function (a, b) { return a + b; }
```

With the addition of *arrow functions*, however, you can now write anonymous functions in one of two forms:

```
(param1, ..., param n) => { statement list }
(param1, ..., param n) => expression
```

The second of these is actually just a special case of the first and could also be written as:

```
(param1, ..., param n) => { return expression; }
```

Thus, our example expression above could be written as:

```
> var x = (a, b) => a + b;
undefined
> x(4, 5)
9
>
```

Arrow functions also solve a very important problem with object identity (the `this` value), which we will cover in Chapter 3, "Asynchronous Programming," so you'll see us using them quite a lot in our code.

Language Constructs

JavaScript contains nearly all the language operators and constructs you would expect, including most logical and mathematical operators.

The ternary operator is supported:

```
var pet = animal_meows ? "cat" : "dog";
```

Even though numbers are implemented as double-precision floating-point numbers, bitwise operations *are* supported in JavaScript: The `&` (*and*), `|` (*or*), `~` (*inverse*), and `^` (*xor*) operators all work by:

1. First converting the operands into 32-bit integers,

2. Performing the bitwise operation, and

3. Finally, converting the resulting number back to a JavaScript `number`.

In addition to the standard `while`, `do...while`, and `for` loops, JavaScript also supports a new language extension to the `for` loop called the `for...in` loop. This loop is used to get the names of all the keys on an object:

```
> var user = {
        first_name: "marc",
        last_name: "wandschneider",
        age: Infinity,
        occupation: "writer"
};
undefined
> for (key in user) {
        console.log(key);
}
first_name
last_name
age
occupation
undefined
>
```

If you use `for...in` loops on arrays, you'll get the indexes of the elements in the array:

```
> var x = [ 1, 2, 3, 4 ];
undefined
> for (var idx in x) {
        console.log(x[idx]);
}
1
2
3
4
undefined
```

Node.js also supports another recent language extension to JavaScript called the `for...of` loop. This loop is useful for iterating over *values of objects* that are marked as being *iterable*. Arrays (recall these are special types of objects) are all iterable, as are a few other objects that implement the iterable interfaces. While we won't go into iterable objects in detail in this book, you'll run across them in a number of places in Node.js, most notably the `arguments` list we mentioned above for functions:

```
function add_n_iterable() {
    var sum = 0;
    for (x of arguments) {
        sum += x;
    }
    return sum;
}
add_n_iterable(1, 2, 3, 4, 5, 6, 7, 8, 9);
45
```

Classes, Prototypes, and Inheritance

Object-oriented programming in JavaScript is a bit different from other languages in that there is no explicit class keyword or type. Indeed, classes are all declared as functions:

```
function Shape () {
    this.X = 0;
    this.Y = 0;

    this.move = function (x, y) {
        this.X = x;
        this.Y = y;
    }
    this.distance_from_origin = function () {
        return Math.sqrt(this.X*this.X + this.Y*this.Y);
    }
}

var s = new Shape();
s.move(10, 10);
console.log(s.distance_from_origin());
```

Note that when we declare member methods or functions on an object, we will use the standard function keyword syntax, not arrow functions. We'll explain more about why in the next chapter.

The preceding program generates the following output:

```
14.142135623730951
```

You can add as many properties and methods to your classes as you like, at any time:

```
var s = new Shape(15, 35);
s.FillColour = "red";
```

The function that declares the class also serves as its constructor!

There are two problems with this scheme for creating classes, however. First, it seems a bit inefficient to have to carry around the method implementations with every single object (every time you create a new instance of Shape, you are creating the move and distance_from_origin functions from scratch). Second, you might like to extend this class to create circles and squares and have them inherit the methods and properties from the base class without your having to do any extra work.

Prototypes and Inheritance

By default, all objects in JavaScript have a *prototype* object, which is the mechanism through which they inherit properties and methods. Prototypes have been the source of much confusion in JavaScript over the years, often because different browsers use different nomenclature for it and subtly different implementations. Because it is relevant to the interests of this chapter, I demonstrate the model that V8 (and thus Node) uses and that other modern JavaScript implementations seem to be moving toward.

Change the Shape class created earlier so that all inheriting objects also get the X and Y properties, as well as the methods you have declared on it:

```
function Shape () {
}

Shape.prototype.X = 0;
Shape.prototype.Y = 0;

Shape.prototype.move = function (x, y) {
    this.X = x;
    this.Y = y;
}
Shape.prototype.distance_from_origin = function () {
    return Math.sqrt(this.X*this.X + this.Y*this.Y);
}
Shape.prototype.area = function () {
    throw new Error("I don't have a form yet");
}
var s = new Shape();
s.move(10, 10);
console.log(s.distance_from_origin());
```

Run this script and you get the same output as the previous one. Indeed, functionally, apart from potentially being slightly more memory efficient (if you created lots of instances, they would all share the implementations of move and distance_from_origin instead of carrying around their own), it is not that different. You have added a method area that all shapes will have. On the base class, it does not make much sense, so you just have it throw an error.

More importantly, you have set yourself up to extend it quite easily:

```
function Square() {
}

Square.prototype = new Shape();
Square.prototype.__proto__ = Shape.prototype;
Square.prototype.Width = 0;

Square.prototype.area = function () {
    return this.Width * this.Width;
}

var sq = new Square();
sq.move(--5, -5);
sq.Width = 5;
console.log(sq.area());
console.log(sq.distance_from_origin());
```

The code for this new Square class makes use of a new JavaScript language feature seen in V8 and a few other implementations: the __proto__ property. It lets you tell JavaScript that a new class you are declaring should have the base prototype of the specified type, and then you can extend it from there.

You can further extend things with a new class called `Rectangle`, inheriting from the `Square` class:

```
function Rectangle () {
}

Rectangle.prototype = new Square();
Rectangle.prototype.__proto__ = Square.prototype;
Rectangle.prototype.Height = 0;

Rectangle.prototype.area = function () {
    return this.Width * this.Height;
}

var re = new Rectangle();
re.move(25, 25);
re.Width = 10;
re.Height = 5;
console.log(re.area());
console.log(re.distance_from_origin());
```

To convince yourself that things are going smoothly, you can use an operator you have not seen before, `instanceof`:

```
console.log(sq instanceof Square);      // true
console.log(sq instanceof Shape);       // true
console.log(sq instanceof Rectangle);   // false
console.log(re instanceof Rectangle);   // true
console.log(sq instanceof Square);      // true
console.log(sq instanceof Shape);       // true
console.log(sq instanceof Date);        // false
```

Errors and Exceptions

In JavaScript, you traditionally signal errors using an `Error` object and a message. You *throw* this error to signal the error condition:

```
> function uhoh () {
    throw new Error("Something bad happened!");
}
undefined
> uhoh());
Error: Something bad happened!
    at uhoh (repl:2:7)
    at repl:1:1
    at REPLServer.self.eval (repl.js:109:21)
    at rli.on.self.bufferedCmd (repl.js:258:20)
```

You can *catch* this error condition with a `try` / `catch` block as seen in other languages:

```
function uhoh () {
    throw new Error("Something bad happened!");
}

try {
    uhoh();
} catch (e) {
    console.log("I caught an error: " + e.message);
}

console.log("program is still running");
```

The output of this program is:

```
I caught an error: Something bad happened!
program is still running
```

As you see in the next chapter, however, this method of error handling does create some problems with the asynchronous model of programming you will be using in Node.js and thus we won't use it as often as you might expect.

Some Important Node.js Globals

Node.js has a few key global variables that are always available to you.

global

When you write JavaScript in web browsers, you have the `window` object, which acts as a global variable. Any variables or members you attach to it are available anywhere in your application.

Node.js has something similar, called the `global` object. Anything attached to it is available anywhere in your node application:

```
function printit(var_name) {
    console.log(global[var_name]);
}

global.fish = "swordfish";
global.pet = "cat";

printit("fish");  // prints swordfish
printit("pet");    // prints cat
printit("fruit"); // prints undefined
```

console

You have already seen the global variable `console` in Node, as you frequently use the `console.log` function. There are a few other interesting functions on the `console` object, however:

- `warn(msg)`—This function is similar to `log`, but it prints to *stderr* (the standard error output, often given special treatment in shells and scripts).

- `time(label)` and `timeEnd(label)`—The first marks a time stamp, and when you call the second, it prints out the elapsed time since the time function was called.

- `assert(cond, message)`—If `cond` evaluates to `false`, throw an `AssertionFailure` exception with the message provided.

process

The other key global in Node is the `process` global variable, which contains a lot of information and methods that you will see as you work through this book. The `exit` method is one way to terminate your Node.js programs, the `env` function returns an object with current user environment variables, and `cwd` returns the current working directory of the app.

Summary

You took a quick look at the JavaScript language in this chapter, and I hope your knowledge of the language has at least been sharpened a little bit, with some confusing or unknown areas clarified a bit. With this basic knowledge under your belt, you can now begin to look at how Node.js uses the language so effectively to create powerful and speedy applications.

3

Asynchronous Programming

Now that you have a refreshed and updated idea of what JavaScript programming is really like, it's time to get into the core concept that makes Node.js what it is: *nonblocking IO and asynchronous programming*. It carries with it some huge advantages and benefits, which you shall soon see, but it also brings some complications and challenges with it.

The Old Way of Doing Things

In the olden days (2008 or so), when you sat down to write an application and needed to load in a file, you would write something like the following (let's assume you're using something vaguely PHP-ish for the purposes of this example):

```
$file = fopen('info.txt', 'r');
// wait until file is open

$contents = fread($file, 100000);
// wait until contents are read

// do something with those contents
```

If you were to analyze the execution of this script, you would find that it spends a vast majority of its time *doing nothing at all*. Indeed, most of the clock time taken by this script is spent waiting for the computer's file system to do its job and return the file contents you requested. Let me generalize things a step further and state that for most IO-based applications—those that frequently connect to databases, communicate with external servers, or read and write files—your scripts will spend a majority of their time sitting around waiting (see Figure 3.1).

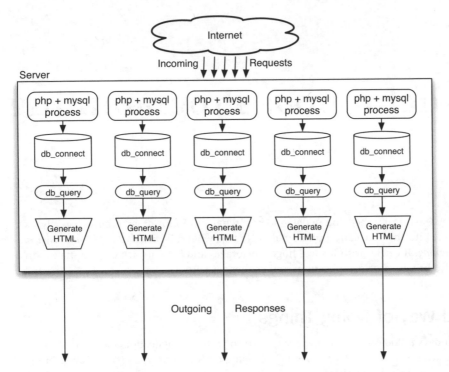

Figure 3.1   Traditional blocking IO web servers

The way your servers process multiple requests at the same time by running many of these scripts in parallel. Modern computer operating systems are great at multitasking, so you can easily switch out processes that are blocked and let other processes have access to the CPU. Some environments take things a step further and use threads instead of processes.

The problem is that for each of these processes or threads, there is some amount of overhead. For heavier implementations using Apache and PHP, I have seen up to 10–15MB of memory overhead per process—never mind the resources and time consumed by the operating system switching that context in and out constantly. That's not even 100 simultaneously executing servers per gigabyte of RAM! Threaded solutions and those using more lightweight HTTP servers do, of course, have better results, but you still end up in a situation in which the computer spends most of its time waiting around for blocked processes to get their results, and you risk running out of capacity to handle incoming requests.

It would be nice if there were some way to make better use of all the available CPU power and available memory so as not to waste so much. This is where Node.js shines.

The Node.js Way of Doing Things

To understand how Node.js changes the method demonstrated in the preceding section into a nonblocking, asynchronous model, first look at the `setTimeout` function in JavaScript. This function takes a function to call and a timeout after which it should be called:

```
setTimeout(() => {
    console.log("I've done my work!");
}, 2000);


console.log("I'm waiting for all my work to finish.");
```

If you run the preceding code, you see the following output:

```
I'm waiting for all my work to finish.
I've done my work!
```

I hope this is not a surprise to you: The program sets the timeout for *2000 ms* (2 seconds), giving it the function to call when it fires, and then continues with execution, which prints out the "I'm waiting…" text. Two seconds later, you see the "I've done…" message, and the program then exits.

Now, look at a world where any time you call a function that needs to wait for some external resource (database server, network request, or file system read/write operation), it has a similar signature. That is, instead of calling `fopen(path, mode)` and waiting, you would instead call `fopen(path, mode, (file_handle) => { ... })`.

Now rewrite the preceding synchronous script using the new asynchronous functions. You can actually enter and run this program with `node` from the command line. Just make sure you also create a file called *info.txt* that can be read.

```
var fs = require('fs');                         // We'll explain this below

var file;
var buf = new Buffer(100000);

fs.open('info.txt', 'r', (err, handle) => {
    file = handle;
});

// fs.read needs the file handle returned by fs.open. But this is broken.
fs.read(file, buf, 0, 100000, null, (err, length) => {
    console.log(buf.toString());
    fs.close(file, () => { /* don't care */ });
});
```

The first line of this code is something you haven't seen just yet: the `require` function is a way to include additional functionality in your Node.js programs. Node comes with a pretty impressive set of *modules*, each of which you can include separately as you need functionality. You will work further with modules frequently from now on; you learn about consuming them and writing your own in Chapter 5, "Modules."

If you run this program as it is, it throws an error and terminates. How come? Because the `fs.open` function runs *asynchronously;* it returns immediately, before the file has been opened and the callback function invoked. The `file` variable is not set until the file has been opened and the handle to it has been passed to the callback specified as the third parameter to the `fs.open` function. Thus, you are trying to access an `undefined` variable when you try to call the `fs.read` function with it immediately afterward.

Fixing this program is easy:

```
var fs = require('fs');

fs.open('info.txt', 'r', (err, handle) => {
    var buf = new Buffer(100000);
    fs.read(handle, buf, 0, 100000, null, (err, length) => {
        console.log(buf.toString('utf8', 0, length));
        fs.close(handle, () => { /* Don't care */ });
    });
});
```

The key way to think of how these asynchronous functions work internally in Node is something along the following lines:

- Check and validate parameters.
- Tell the Node.js core to queue the call to the appropriate function for you (in the preceding example, the operating system `open` or `read` function) and to notify (call) the provided callback function when there is a result.
- Return to the caller.

You might be asking: if the `open` function returns right away, why doesn't the node process exit immediately after that function has returned? The answer is that Node operates with an *event queue;* if there are pending events for which you are awaiting a response, it does not exit until your code has finished executing *and* there are no events left on that queue. If you are waiting for a response (either to the `open` or the `read` function calls), it waits. See Figure 3.2 for an idea of how this scenario looks conceptually.

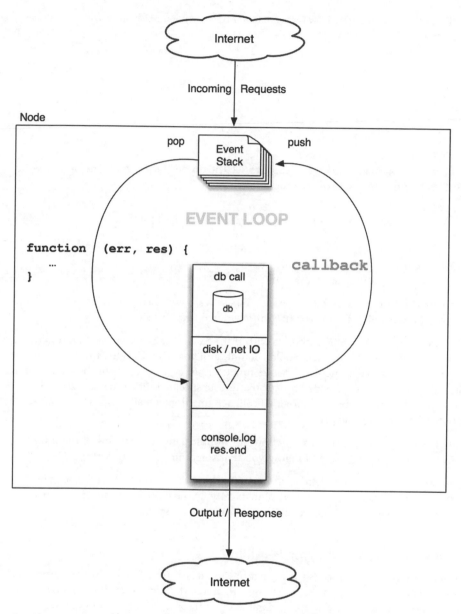

Figure 3.2   As long as there is code executing or somebody is waiting for something, Node runs

Error Handling and Asynchronous Functions

In the preceding chapter, I discussed error handling and events as well as the
try / catch block in JavaScript. The addition of nonblocking IO and asynchronous

function callbacks in this chapter, however, creates a new problem. Consider the following code:

```
try {
    setTimeout(() => {
        throw new Error("Uh oh!");
    }, 2000);
} catch (e) {
    console.log("I caught the error: " + e.message);
}
```

If you run this code, you might very well expect to see the output `"I caught the error: Uh oh!"`. But you do not. You actually see the following:

```
timers.js:103
            if (!process.listeners('uncaughtException').length) throw e;
                                                                 ^

Error: Uh oh, something bad!
    at Object._onTimeout errors_async.js:5:15)
    at Timer.list.ontimeout (timers.js:101:19)
```

What happened? Did I not say that `try` / `catch` blocks were supposed to catch errors for you? I did, but asynchronous callbacks throw a new little wrench into this situation.

In reality, the call to `setTimeout` *does* execute within the `try` / `catch` block. If that function were to throw an error, the `catch` block would catch it, and you would see the message that you had hoped to see. However, the `setTimeout` function just adds an event to the Node event queue (instructing it to call the provided function after the specified time interval—2000 ms in this example) and then returns. The provided callback function actually operates within its own entirely new context and scope!

As a result, when you call asynchronous functions for nonblocking IO, very few of them throw errors, but instead use a separate way of telling you that something has gone wrong.

In Node, you use a number of core *patterns* to help you standardize how you write code and avoid errors. These patterns are not enforced syntactically by the language or runtime, but you will see them used frequently and should absolutely use them yourself.

The callback Function and Error Handling

One of the first patterns you will see is the format of the *callback* function you pass to most asynchronous functions. It always has at least one parameter, the success or failure status of the last operation, and very commonly a second parameter with some sort of additional results or information from the last operation (such as a file handle, database connection, rows from a query, and so on); some callbacks are given even more than two:

```
do_something(param1, param2, ..., paramN, function (err, results) { ... });
```

The `err` parameter is either

- `null`, indicating the operation was a success, and (if there should be one) there will be a result.

- An instance of the `Error` object class. You will occasionally notice some inconsistency here, with some people always adding a `code` field to the `Error` object and then using the `message` field to hold a description of what happened, whereas others have chosen other patterns. For all the code you write in this book, you will follow the pattern of always including a `code` field and using the `message` field to provide as much information as you can. For all the modules you write, you will use a string value for the `code` because strings tend to be a bit easier to read. Some libraries provide extra data in the `Error` object with additional information, but at least the two members should always be there.

This standard prototype methodology enables you to always write predictable code when you are working with nonblocking functions. Throughout this book, I demonstrate two common coding styles for handling errors in callbacks. Here's the first:

```
fs.open('info.txt', 'r', (err, handle) => {
    if (err) {
        console.log("ERROR: " + err.code + " (" + err.message ")");
        return;
    }
    // success!! continue working here
});
```

In this style, you check for errors and return if you see one; otherwise, you continue to process the result. And now here's the other way:

```
fs.open('info.txt', 'r', (err, handle) => {
    if (err) {
        console.log("ERROR: " + err.code + " (" + err.message ")");
    } else {
        // success! continue working here
    }
});
```

In this method, you use an `if ... then ... else` statement to handle the error.

The difference between these two may seem like splitting hairs, but the former method is a little more prone to bugs and errors for those cases when you forget to use the `return` statement inside the `if` statement, whereas the latter results in code that indents itself much more quickly and you end up with lines of code that are quite long and less readable. We'll look at a solution to this second problem in the section titled "Managing Asynchronous Code" in Chapter 5.

A fully updated version of the file loading code with error handling is shown in Listing 3.1.

Listing 3.1 **File Loading with Full Error Handling**

```
var fs = require('fs');

fs.open('info.txt', 'r', (err, handle) => {
    if (err) {
        console.log("ERROR: " + err.code + " (" + err.message + ")");
        return;
    }
    var buf = new Buffer(100000);
    fs.read(handle, buf, 0, 100000, null, (err, length) => {
        if (err) {
            console.log("ERROR: " + err.code
                        + " (" + err.message + ")");
            return;
        }
        console.log(buf.toString('utf8', 0, length));
        fs.close(handle, () => { /* don't care */ });
    });
});
```

Who Am I? Maintaining a Sense of Identity

Now you're ready to write a little class to help you with some common file operations:

```
var fs = require('fs');

function FileObject () {
    this.filename = '';

    this.file_exists = function (callback) {
        console.log("About to open: " + this.filename);
        fs.open(this.filename, 'r', function (err, handle) {
            if (err) {
                console.log("Can't open: " + this.filename);
                callback(err);
                return;
            }
            fs.close(handle, function () { });
            callback(null, true);
        });
    };
}
```

You have currently added one property, `filename`, and a single method, `file_exists`. This method does the following:

- It tries to open the file specified in the `filename` property read-only.

- If the file doesn't exist, it prints a message and calls the callback function with the error info.

- If the file does exist, it calls the callback function indicating success.

Now, run this class with the following code:

```
var fo = new FileObject();
fo.filename = "file_that_does_not_exist";

fo.file_exists((err, results) => {
    if (err) {
        console.log("\nError opening file: " + JSON.stringify(err));
        return;
    }

    console.log("file exists!!!");
});
```

You might expect the following output:

```
About to open: file_that_does_not_exist
Can't open: file_that_does_not_exist
```

But, in fact, you see this:

```
About to open: file_that_does_not_exist
Can't open: undefined
```

What happened? Most of the time, when you have a function nested within another, it inherits the scope of its parent/host function and should have access to all the same variables. So why does the nested callback function not get the correct value for the `filename` property?

The problem lies with the `this` keyword and asynchronous callback functions. Don't forget that when you call a function like `fs.open`, it initializes itself, calls the underlying operating system function (in this case to open a file), and places the provided callback function on the event queue. Execution immediately returns to the `FileObject#file_exists` function, and then you exit. When the `fs.open` function completes its work and Node runs the callback, you no longer have the context of the `FileObject` class any more, and the callback function is given a new `this` pointer representing some other execution context!

The bad news is that you have, indeed, lost your `this` pointer referring to the `FileObject` class. The good news is that the callback function for `fs.open` does still have its function scope. A common solution to this problem is to "save" the disappearing `this` pointer in a variable called `self` or `me` or something similar. Now rewrite the `file_exists` function to take advantage of this:

```
    this.file_exists = function (callback) {
        var self = this;
```

```
        console.log("About to open: " + self.filename);
        fs.open(this.filename, 'r', function (err, handle) {
            if (err) {
                console.log("Can't open: " + self.filename);
                callback(err);
                return;
            }

            fs.close(handle, function () { });
            callback(null, true);
        });
    };
```

Because local function scope *is* preserved via closures, the new self variable is maintained for you even when your callback is executed asynchronously later by Node.js. You will make extensive use of this in all your applications. Some people like to use me instead of self because it is shorter; others still use completely different words. Pick whatever kind you like and stick with it for consistency.

The above scenario is another reason to use *arrow functions*, introduced in the previous chapter. Arrow functions capture the this value of the enclosing scope, so your code actually works as expected! Thus, as long as you are using =>, you can continue to use the this keyword, as follows:

```
var fs = require('fs');

function FileObject () {
    this.filename = '';

    // Always use "function" for member fns, not =>, see below for why
    this.file_exists = function (callback) {
        console.log("About to open: " + this.filename);
        fs.open(this.filename, 'r', (err, handle) => {
            if (err) {
                console.log("Can't open: " + this.filename);
                callback(err);
                return;
            }
            fs.close(handle, () => { });
            callback(null, true);
        });
    };
}
```

One other thing to note is that we *do not* use arrow functions for declaring member functions on objects or prototypes. This is because in those cases, we actually *do* want the this variable to update with the context of the currently executing object. Thus, you'll see us using => only when we're using anonymous functions in other contexts.

The key takeaway for this section should be: If you're using an anonymous function that's not a class or prototype method, you should stop and think before using this. There's a good chance it won't work the way you want. Use arrow functions as much as possible.

Being Polite—Learning to Give Up Control

Node runs in a single thread with a single event loop that makes calls to external functions and services. It places callback functions on the event queue to wait for the responses and otherwise tries to execute code as quickly as possible. So what happens if you have a function that tries to compute the intersection between two arrays:

```
function compute_intersection(arr1, arr2, callback) {
    var results = [];
    for (var i = 0 ; i < arr1.length; i++) {
        for (var j = 0; j < arr2.length; j++) {
            if (arr2[j] == arr1[i]) {
                results[results.length] = arr2[j];
                break;
            }
        }
    }
    callback(null, results);   // no error, pass in results!
}
```

For arrays of a few thousand elements, this function starts to consume significant amounts of time to do its work, on the order of a second or more. In a single-threaded model, where Node. js can do only one thing at a time, this amount of time can be a problem. Similar functions that compute hashes, digests, or otherwise perform expensive operations are going to cause your applications to temporarily "freeze" while they do their work? What can you do?

In the introduction to this book, I mentioned that there are certain things for which Node.js is not particularly well suited, and one of them is definitely acting as a *compute server*. Node is far better suited to more common network application tasks, such as those with heavy amounts of IO and requests to other services. If you want to write a server that does a lot of expensive computations and calculations, you might want to consider moving these operations to other services that your Node applications can then call remotely.

I am not saying, however, that you should completely shy away from computationally intensive tasks. If you're doing these only some of the time, you can still include them in Node.js and take advantage of a method on the process global object called nextTick. This method basically says "Give up control of execution, and then when you have a free moment, call the provided function." It tends to be significantly faster than just using the setTimeout function.

Listing 3.2 contains an updated version of the compute_intersection function that yields every once in a while to let Node process other tasks.

Listing 3.2   Using Process#nextTick to be Polite

```
function compute_intersection(arr1, arr2, callback) {
    // let's break up the bigger of the two arrays
    var bigger = arr1.length > arr2.length ? arr1 : arr2;
    var smaller = bigger == arr1 ? arr2 : arr1;
    var biglen = bigger.length;
    var smlen = smaller.length;

    var sidx = 0;           // starting index of any chunk
    var size = 10;          // chunk size, can adjust!
    var results = [];       // intermediate results

    // for each chunk of "size" elements in bigger, search through smaller
    function sub_compute_intersection() {
        for (var i = sidx; i < (sidx + size) && i < biglen; i++) {
            for (var j = 0; j < smlen; j++) {
                if (bigger[i] == smaller[j]) {
                    results.push(smaller[j]);
                    break;
                }
            }
        }

        if (i >= biglen) {
            callback(null, results);    // no error, send back results
        } else {
            sidx += size;
            process.nextTick(sub_compute_intersection);
        }
    }

    sub_compute_intersection();
}
```

In this new version of the function, you basically divide the bigger of the input arrays into chunks of 10 (you can choose whatever number you want), compute the intersection of that many items, and then call process#nextTick to allow other events or requests a chance to do their work. Only when there are no events in front of you any longer, will you continue to do the work. Don't forget that passing the callback function sub_compute_intersection to process#nextTick ensures that the current scope is preserved as a closure, so you can store the intermediate results in the variables in compute_intersection.

Listing 3.3 shows the code you use to test this new compute_intersection function.

Listing 3.3   **Testing the compute_intersection Function**

```
var a1 = [ 3476, 2457, 7547, 34523, 3, 6, 7,2, 77, 8, 2345,
          7623457, 2347, 23572457, 237457, 234869, 237,
          24572457524] ;
var a2 = [ 3476, 75347547, 2457634563, 56763472, 34574, 2347,
          7, 34652364 , 13461346, 572346, 23723457234, 237,
          234, 24352345, 537, 2345235, 2345675, 34534,
          7582768, 284835, 8553577, 2577257,545634, 457247247,
          2345 ];

compute_intersection(a1, a2, function (err, results) {
    if (err) {
        console.log(err);
    } else {
        console.log(results);
    }
});
```

Although this has made things a bit more complicated than the original version of the function to compute the intersections, the new version plays much better in the single-threaded world of Node event processing and callbacks, and you can use `process.nextTick` in any situation in which you are worried that a complex or slow computation is necessary.

Synchronous Function Calls

Now that I have spent nearly an entire chapter telling you how Node.js is very much asynchronous and about all the tricks and traps of programming nonblocking IO, I must mention that Node actually *does* have synchronous versions of some key APIs, most notably file APIs. You use them for writing command-line tools in Chapter 12, "Command-Line Programming."

To demonstrate briefly here, you can rewrite the first script of this chapter as follows:

```
var fs = require('fs');

var handle = fs.openSync('info.txt', 'r');
var buf = new Buffer(100000);
var read = fs.readSync(handle, buf, 0, 10000, null);
console.log(buf.toString('utf8', 0, read));
fs.closeSync(handle);
```

As you work your way through this book, I hope you are able to see quite quickly that Node.js isn't just for network or web applications. You can use it for everything from command-line utilities to prototyping to server management and more!

Summary

Switching from a model of programming where you execute a sequence of synchronous or blocking IO function calls and wait for each of them to complete before moving on to the next call, to a model where you do everything asynchronously and wait for Node to tell you when a given task is done requires a bit of mental gymnastics and experimentation. But I am convinced that when you get the hang of this, you'll never be able imagine going back to the other way of writing your web apps.

Next, you write your first simple JSON application server.

Part II

Learning to Run

Writing Simple Applications

Now that you have a better understanding of how the JavaScript language really works, it's time to start unleashing the power of Node.js to write web applications. As I mentioned in the introduction to this book, you will work on a small photo album website throughout this book. In this chapter you start by working on a JSON server to serve up the list of albums and pictures in each of those albums, and by the end, you add the capability to rename an album. In the process, you get a good understanding of the basics of running a JSON server, as well as how it interacts with a lot of the basic parts of HTTP such as GET and POST parameters, headers, requests, and responses. This first generation of the photo album application uses file APIs to do all its work; it's a great way to learn about them and lets you focus on the new concepts you want to learn.

Your First JSON Server

At the end of Chapter 1, "Getting Started," you wrote a little HTTP server that, for any incoming request, would return the plain text "Thanks for calling!\n". Now you can change this a little bit and have it do few things differently:

1. Indicate that the returned data is `application/json` instead of `text/plain`.

2. Print out the incoming request on `console.log`.

3. Return a JSON string.

Here is the trivial server, which is saved to simple_server.js:

```
var http = require('http');

function handle_incoming_request(req, res) {
    console.log("INCOMING REQUEST: " + req.method + " " + req.url);
    res.writeHead(200, { "Content-Type" : "application/json" });
    res.end(JSON.stringify( { error: null }) + "\n");
}
```

```
var s = http.createServer(handle_incoming_request);
s.listen(8080);
```

Run this program in one terminal window (Mac/Linux) or command prompt (Windows) by typing

```
node simple_server.js
```

It should just sit there doing nothing, waiting for a request. Now, in another terminal window or command prompt, type

```
curl -X GET http://localhost:8080
```

If you've done everything correctly, in the window running the server, you should see

```
INCOMING REQUEST: GET /
```

In the window where you ran the `curl` command, you should see

```
{"error":null}
```

Try running different variations on the `curl` command and see what happens. For example:

```
curl -X GET http://localhost:8080/gobbledygook
```

Starting with this first new program, you can standardize the output of your JSON responses to always have an `error` field in the output. This way, calling applications can quickly determine the success or failure of the request. In cases in which a failure does occur, you always include a `message` field with more information, and for cases in which the JSON response is supposed to return some data, you always include a `data` field:

```
// failure responses will look like this:
{ error: "missing_data",
  message: "You must include a last name for the user" }


// success responses will usually have a "data" object
{ error: null,
  data: {
     user: {
         first_name: "Horatio",
         last_name: "Gadsplatt III",
         email: "horatio@example.org"
     }
  }
}
```

Some applications prefer to use numeric codes for their error systems. Using such codes is entirely up to you, but I prefer to use text ones because they feel more descriptive and save the step of looking things up when I use command-line programs like `curl` to test programs—I think `no_such_user` is far more informative than −325.

Returning Some Data

When you start, your photo album application is quite simple: it is a collection of albums, each of which contains a collection of photos, as shown in Figure 4.1.

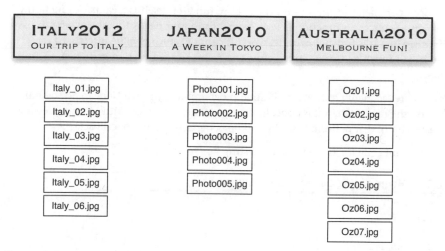

Figure 4.1   Albums and photos

For now, the albums are subfolders of the *albums/* subfolder of the location where you run your scripts:

```
scripts/
scripts/albums/
scripts/albums/italy2012
scripts/albums/australia2010
scripts/albums/japan2010
```

So, to get your list of albums, you just need to find the items inside the *albums/* subfolder. You do that using the `fs.readdir` function, which returns all items in the given folder except for "." and "..". The `load_album_list` function looks as follows:

```
function load_album_list(callback) {
    // we will just assume that any directory in our 'albums'
    // subfolder is an album.
    fs.readdir("albums", (err, files) => {
        if (err) {
            callback(err);
            return;
        }
        callback(null, files);
    });
}
```

Let's walk through this function carefully. To start, it calls the `fs.readdir` function and provides a function that should be called when all the items in the directory have been loaded. This callback function has the same prototype that most callbacks have: an *error* parameter and a *results* parameter; you are free to call these whatever we want.

Note that the only parameter to the `load_album_list` function itself is a callback function. Because the `load_album_list` function is itself asynchronous, it needs to know where to pass the list of albums when it is finished with its work. It cannot return a value directly to the caller, because it will finish executing long before the `fs.readdir` function calls back to give you the results.

Again, this is the core technique of Node application programming: you tell Node to do something and where to send the results when it is done. In the meantime, you go on with other processing. Many of the tasks you have it perform basically end up being a long series of callbacks.

Listing 4.1 has the full code for the new album-listing `server`.

Listing 4.1   **The Album-Listing Server (load_albums.js)**

```
var http = require('http'),
    fs = require('fs');

function load_album_list(callback) {
    // we will just assume that any directory in our 'albums'
    // subfolder is an album.
    fs.readdir("albums", (err, files) => {
        if (err) {
            callback(err);
            return;
        }
        callback(null, files);
    });
}

function handle_incoming_request(req, res) {
    console.log("INCOMING REQUEST: " + req.method + " " + req.url);
    load_album_list((err, albums) => {
        if (err) {
            res.writeHead(500, {"Content-Type": "application/json"});
            res.end(JSON.stringify(err) + "\n");
            return;
        }

        var out = { error: null, data: { albums: albums } };
        res.writeHead(200, {"Content-Type": "application/json"});
        res.end(JSON.stringify(out) + "\n");
    });
}

var s = http.createServer(handle_incoming_request);
s.listen(8080);
```

In Listing 4.1, after `fs.readdir` has finished, you check the results. If an error occurs, you invoke the callback (the anonymous function you passed to `load_album_list` in the `handle_incoming_request` function) with the error object; otherwise, you send the list of folders (albums) back to the caller along with `null` indicating no error.

This listing adds some new error handling code to the `handle_incoming_request` function: if the `fs.readdir` function tells you that something bad has happened, you would like the caller to be made aware of that fact, so you still return some JSON, and the HTTP response code `503` to indicate that something unexpected has happened. The JSON servers should always return as much information as possible to their clients to help them determine if a problem is something they did or something internally wrong on the server itself.

To test the program, make sure the folder from which you are running this script has the albums/ subfolder with some album folders in it. To run the server, you again run

```
node load_albums.js
```

And to get the results, you use

```
curl -X GET http://localhost:8080/
```

The results from the `curl` command should look something like this:

```
{"error":null,"data":{"albums":["australia2010","italy2012","japan2010"]}}
```

Node Pattern: Asynchronous Loops

What happens if you create a text file called info.txt in your *albums/* folder and rerun the album-listing server? You will probably see results like this:

```
{"error":null,"data":{"albums":["australia2010","info.txt","italy2012","japan2010"]}}
```

What you really want is for the program to check the results of `fs.readdir` and return only those entries that are folders, not regular files. To do this, you can use the `fs.stat` function, which passes an object you can use to test this.

So, rewrite the `load_album_list` function to loop through the results of `fs.readdir` and test whether they are folders:

```
function load_album_list(callback) {
    // we will just assume that any directory in our 'albums'
    // subfolder is an album.
    fs.readdir("albums", (err, files) => {
        if (err) {
            callback(err);
            return;
        }
```

```
       var only_dirs = [];

     for (var i = 0; files && i < files.length; i++) {
         fs.stat("albums/" + files[i], (err, stats) => {
             if (stats.isDirectory()) {
                 only_dirs.push(files[i]);
             }
         });
     }

     callback(null, only_dirs);
  });
}
```

Keep the rest of the program the same and then run the `curl` command. It should always return

`{"error":null,"data":{"albums":[]}}`

You broke the server! What happened?

The problem lies in the new `for` loop you added. *Most loops and asynchronous callbacks are not compatible.* Effectively, what you do in the preceding code is

- Create an array `only_dirs` to hold the response.

- For each item in the files array, call the nonblocking function `fs.stat` and pass it the provided function to test if the file is a directory.

- After all these nonblocking functions have been started, exit the `for` loop and call the `callback` parameter. Because Node.js is single-threaded, none of the `fs.stat` functions will have had a chance to execute and call the callbacks yet, so `only_dirs` is still `null`, and you pass that to the provided `callback`. Indeed, when the callbacks to `fs.stat` are finally called, nobody cares any more.

To get around this problem, you have to use recursion. You effectively create a new function with the following format and then immediately call it:

```
var loop_iterator = (i) => {
  if( i < array.length ) {
    async_work( function(){
      loop_iterator( i + 1 )
    })
  } else {
    callback(results);
  }
}
loop_iterator(0);
```

Thus, to rewrite the loop testing whether or not the files result from `fs.readdir` are folders, you can write the function as follows:

```
function load_album_list(callback) {
    // we will just assume that any directory in our 'albums'
    // subfolder is an album.
```

```
fs.readdir("albums", (err, files) => {
    if (err) {
        callback(err);
        return;
    }

    var only_dirs = [];

    var iterator = (index) => {
        if (index == files.length) {
            callback(null, only_dirs);
            return;
        }

        fs.stat("albums/" + files[index], (err, stats) => {
            if (err) {
                callback(err);
                return;
            }
            if (stats.isDirectory()) {
                only_dirs.push(files[index]);
            }
            iterator(index + 1)
        });
    }
    iterator(0);
});
}
```

Save this new version of the simple JSON server and then run the `curl` command, and you should now see the results with only album folders and no files included.

This recursive anonymous function works by not proceeding to the next item in the loop until the current item's callback returns. When we get a value from `fs.stat` (i.e., our anonymous function is invoked indicating it has completed its work), only then do we call `iterator(index + 1)` to move to the next item. When there are no more items left, we finally invoke the `callback` function with the results. If there is an error along the way, we immediately call the `callback` and stop all further processing.

Learning to Juggle: Handling More Requests

The photo-album JSON server currently responds to only one kind of request: a request for a list of albums. Indeed, it doesn't even really care how you call this request; it just returns the same thing all the time.

You can expand the functionality of the server a bit to allow you to request either of the following:

1. A list of albums available—you call this */albums.json*

2. A list of items in an album—you can call this */albums/album_name.json*

Adding the *.json* suffix to requests emphasizes that you are currently writing a JSON server that works only with that. There is no requirement for this; it is merely a convention I have adopted in all my servers.

A new version of the `handle_incoming_request` function with support for these two requests could be as follows:

```
function handle_incoming_request(req, res) {
    console.log("INCOMING REQUEST: " + req.method + " " + req.url);
    if (req.url == '/albums.json') {
        handle_list_albums(req, res);
    } else if (req.url.substr(0, 7) == '/albums'
               && req.url.substr(req.url.length - 5) == '.json') {
        handle_get_album(req, res);
    } else {
        send_failure(res, 404, invalid_resource());
    }
}
```

The two *if* statements in the preceding code are the bold ones; both look at the `url` property on the incoming *request* object. If the request is simply for */albums.json*, you can handle the request as before. If it's for */albums/something.json*, you can assume it's a request for the listing of an album's contents and process it appropriately.

The code to generate and return the albums list has been moved into a new function called `handle_list_albums`, and the code to get an individual album's contents is similarly organized into two functions called `handle_get_album` and `load_album`. Listing 4.2 contains the full listing for the server.

Starting with this new version of the code, we'll change the output of the JSON server slightly: everything returned will be objects, not just arrays of strings. This helps you later in the book when you start generating UI to match the JSON responses. I italicized the code in Listing 4.2 that makes this change.

Although I try to avoid long, tedious, multipage code dumps later in this book, this first version of the server here is worth browsing through fully because most things you do after this are based on the foundation built here.

Listing 4.2 **Handling Multiple Request Types**

```javascript
var http = require('http'),
    fs = require('fs');

function load_album_list(callback) {
    // we will just assume that any directory in our 'albums'
    // subfolder is an album.
    fs.readdir("albums", (err, files) => {
        if (err) {
            callback(make_error("file_error",  JSON.stringify(err)));
            return;
        }

        var only_dirs = [];

        var iterator = (index) => {
            if (index == files.length) {
                callback(null, only_dirs);
                return;
            }

            fs.stat("albums/" + files[index], (err, stats) => {
                if (err) {
                    callback(make_error("file_error",
                                        JSON.stringify(err)));
                    return;
                }
                if (stats.isDirectory()) {
                    var obj = { name: files[index] };
                    only_dirs.push(obj);
                }
                iterator(index + 1)
            });

        }
        iterator(0);
    });
}

function load_album(album_name, callback) {
    // we will assume that any directory in our 'albums'
    // subfolder is an album.
    fs.readdir("albums/" + album_name, (err, files) => {
        if (err) {
            if (err.code == "ENOENT") {
                callback(no_such_album());
```

```
            } else {
                callback(make_error("file_error",
                                    JSON.stringify(err)));
            }
            return;
        }

        var only_files = [];
        var path = `albums/${album_name}/`;

        var iterator = (index) => {
            if (index == files.length) {
                var obj = { short_name: album_name,
                            photos: only_files };
                callback(null, obj);
                return;
            }

            fs.stat(path + files[index], (err, stats) => {
                if (err) {
                    callback(make_error("file_error",
                                        JSON.stringify(err)));
                    return;
                }
                if (stats.isFile()) {
                    var obj = { filename: files[index],
                                desc: files[index] };
                    only_files.push(obj);
                }
                iterator(index + 1)
            });
        }
        iterator(0);
    });
}

function handle_incoming_request(req, res) {
    console.log("INCOMING REQUEST: " + req.method + " " + req.url);
    if (req.url == '/albums.json') {
        handle_list_albums(req, res);
    } else if (req.url.substr(0, 7) == '/albums'
               && req.url.substr(req.url.length - 5) == '.json') {
        handle_get_album(req, res);
    } else {
        send_failure(res, 404, invalid_resource());
    }
}
```

```javascript
function handle_list_albums(req, res) {
    load_album_list( (err, albums) => {
        if (err) {
            send_failure(res, 500, err);
            return;
        }

        send_success(res, { albums: albums });
    });
}

function handle_get_album(req, res) {
    // format of request is /albums/album_name.json
    var album_name = req.url.substr(7, req.url.length - 12);
    load_album(album_name, (err, album_contents) => {
        if (err && err.error == "no_such_album") {
            send_failure(res, 404, err);
        } else if (err) {
            send_failure(res, 500, err);
        } else {
            send_success(res, { album_data: album_contents });
        }
    });
}

function make_error(err, msg) {
    var e = new Error(msg);
    e.code = err;
    return e;
}

function send_success(res, data) {
    res.writeHead(200, {"Content-Type": "application/json"});
    var output = { error: null, data: data };
    res.end(JSON.stringify(output) + "\n");
}

function send_failure(res, server_code, err) {
    var code = (err.code) ? err.code : err.name;
    res.writeHead(server_code, { "Content-Type" : "application/json" });
    res.end(JSON.stringify({ error: code, message: err.message }) + "\n");
}


function invalid_resource() {
    return make_error("invalid_resource",
                      "the requested resource does not exist.");
}
```

```
function no_such_album() {
    return make_error("no_such_album",
                       "The specified album does not exist");
}


var s = http.createServer(handle_incoming_request);
s.listen(8080);
```

To avoid too much duplication of code, I also factored out a lot of the processing for sending the final success or response to the requesting client. This code is in the send_success and send_failure functions, both of which make sure to set the right HTTP response code and then return the correct JSON as appropriate.

You can see that the new function load_album is quite similar to the load_album_list function. It enumerates all the items in the album folder, then goes through each of them to make sure it is a regular file, and returns that final list. I also added a couple of extra lines of code to the error handling for fs.readdir in load_album:

```
if (err.code == "ENOENT") {
    callback(no_such_album());
} else {
    callback({ error: "file_error",
               message: JSON.stringify(err) });
}
```

Basically, if fs.readdir fails because it cannot find the album folder, that is a user error; the user specified an invalid album. You want to return an error indicating that fact, so you do that by using the helper function no_such_album. Most other failures, however, are likely to be server configuration problems, so you want to return the more generic "file_error" for those.

The output of getting the contents of /albums.json now looks as follows:

```
{"error":null,"data":{"albums":[{"name":"australia2010"},{"name":"italy2012"},{"name":
"japan2010"}]}}
```

After putting a few image files in each of the album folders, the output of getting the contents of an album (such as /albums/italy2012.json) now looks as follows (it's been cleaned up here):

```
{
  "error": null,
  "data": {
    "album_data": {
      "short_name": "/italy2012",
      "photos": [
        {
          "filename": "picture_01.jpg",
          "desc": "picture_01.jpg"
        },
```

```
                {
                  "filename": "picture_02.jpg",
                  "desc": "picture_02.jpg"
                },
                {
                  "filename": "picture_03.jpg",
                  "desc": "picture_03.jpg"
                },
                {
                  "filename": "picture_04.jpg",
                  "desc": "picture_04.jpg"
                },
                {
                  "filename": "picture_05.jpg",
                  "desc": "picture_05.jpg"
                }
            ]
        }
      }
}
```

More on the Request and Response Objects

Now enter and run the following program:

```
var http = require('http');

function handle_incoming_request(req, res) {
    console.log("--------------------------------------------------");
    console.log(req);
    console.log("--------------------------------------------------");
    console.log(res);
    console.log("--------------------------------------------------");
    res.writeHead(200, { "Content-Type" : "application/json" });
    res.end(JSON.stringify( { error: null }) + "\n");
}

var s = http.createServer(handle_incoming_request);
s.listen(8080);
```

Then, in another terminal window, run the `curl` command on something from this server:

```
curl -X GET http://localhost:8080
```

Your client window should just print `error: null`, but the server window prints an extremely large amount of text with information about the request and response objects passed to your HTTP server.

You've already used two properties on the request object: `method` and `url`. The former tells you if the incoming request is `GET`, `POST`, `PUT`, or `DELETE` (or something else such as `HEAD`), whereas the latter contains the URL requested on the server.

The request object is a `ServerRequest` object provided by the HTTP module included in Node.js, and you can learn all about it by consulting the Node documentation. You use these two properties and also see more in a little bit about handling POST data with the `ServerRequest`. You can also examine incoming headers by looking at the `headers` property.

If you look at the headers the `curl` program sends to you, you see

```
{ 'user-agent': 'curl/7.24.0 (x86_64-apple-darwin12.0) libcurl/7.24.0 OpenSSL/0.9.8r
zlib/1.2.5',
  host: 'localhost:8080',
  accept: '*/*' }
```

If you call the JSON server in the browser, you see something like

```
{ host: 'localhost:8080',
  'user-agent': 'Mozilla/5.0 (Macintosh; Intel Mac OS X 10.8; rv:16.0) Gecko/20100101
Firefox/16.0',
  accept: 'text/html,application/xhtml+xml,application/xml;q=0.9,*/*;q=0.8',
  'accept-language': 'en-US,en;q=0.5',
  'accept-encoding': 'gzip, deflate',
  connection: 'keep-alive' }
```

On the response side, you have already used two methods: `writeHead` and `end`. You must call `end` on the response object once and only once for each incoming request. Otherwise, the client never gets the response and continues to listen on the connection for more data.

When you are writing your responses, you should take care to make sure you think about your HTTP response codes (see the sidebar "HTTP Response Codes"). Part of writing your servers includes thinking logically about what you are trying to communicate to the calling clients and sending them as much information as possible to help them understand your response.

HTTP Response Codes

The HTTP specification contains a large number of response codes a server can return to calling clients. You can learn more about them on Wikipedia (http://en.wikipedia.org/wiki/List_of_ HTTP_status_codes).

Although a dizzying number of response codes is possible, you'll find yourself using a few of the more common responses in most of your applications:

- 200 OK—Everything went fine.
- 301 Moved Permanently—The requested URL has been moved, and the client should re-request it at the URL specified in the response.
- 302 Found—This used to be called "Moved Temporarily", and behaves much like the 301 above—if you see this, you should just re-request the page at the URL provided.
- 400 Bad Request—The format of the client's request is invalid and needs to be fixed.
- 401 Unauthorized—The client has asked for something it does not have permission to view. It should try again authenticating the request first.
- 403 Forbidden—For whatever reason, the server is refusing to process this request. This is not the same as 401, where the client *can* try again with authentication.
- 404 Not Found—The client has asked for something that does not exist.
- 500 Internal Server Error—Something happened resulting in the server being unable to process the request. You typically use this error for situations in which you know the code has entered some sort of inconsistent or buggy state and needs developer attention.
- 503 Service Unavailable—This indicates some sort of runtime failure, such as a server temporarily low on memory or having troubles with network resources. It's still a fatal error like 500, but it does suggest the client could try again in a while.

These are the codes you will use the most, but there are many others that you are encouraged to browse over. If you're unsure when to use one, look at code that others have written and see how they do it. The correct code for any given situation can be cause for great debate, but you can usually get the right ones without too much trouble.

Increased Flexibility: GET Params

When you start adding a lot of photos to your albums, you will have too many photos to display efficiently on one "page" of the application, so you should add paging functionality to it. Clients should be able to say how many photos they want and what page they want, like this:

```
curl -X GET 'http://localhost:8080/albums/italy2012.json?page=1&page_size=20'
```

If you're not familiar with the terminology, the bolded part of the preceding URL is the *query string*, commonly just referred to as the *GET params* for the request. If you run this curl command with the previous version of the program, you'll probably notice that it doesn't quite work anymore. If you add the following to the beginning of handle_incoming_request, you can see why:

```
console.log(req.url);
```

The URL now looks like this:

/albums/italy2012.json**?page=1&page_size=20**

The code is looking for the .json at the end of the string, not buried in the middle of it. To fix the code to handle paging, you have to do three things:

1. Modify the handle_incoming_request function to parse the URL properly.

2. Parse the query string and get the values for page and page_size.

3. Modify the load_album function to support these parameters.

You are fortunate in that you can do the first two in one fell swoop. If you add the *url* module that Node ships with, you can then use the url.parse function to extract both the core URL pathname and the query parameters. The url.parse function helps a little bit further in that you can add a second parameter, true, which instructs it to parse the query string and generate an object with the GET parameters in it. If you print out the results of url.parse on the preceding URL, you should see

```
{ search: '?page=1&page_size=20',
  query: { page: '1', page_size: '20' },
  pathname: '/albums/italy2012.json',
  path: '/albums/italy2012.json?page=1&page_size=20',
  href: '/albums/italy2012.json?page=1&page_size=20' }
```

Now you can modify the handle_incoming_request function to parse the URL and store it back on the request object in parsed_url. The function now looks like this:

```
var url = require('url');
function handle_incoming_request(req, res) {

    req.parsed_url = url.parse(req.url, true);
    var core_url = req.parsed_url.pathname;

    // test this fixed url to see what they're asking for
    if (core_url == '/albums.json') {
        handle_list_albums(req, res);
    } else if (core_url.substr(0, 7) == '/albums'
            && core_url.substr(core_url.length - 5) == '.json') {
        handle_get_album(req, res);
    } else {
        send_failure(res, 404, invalid_resource());
    }
}
```

For the last part, you modify the `handle_get_album` function to look for the page and `page_num` query parameters. You can set some reasonable default values for them when the incoming values are not provided or are not valid values (the servers should *always* assume that incoming values are dangerous or nonsensical and check them carefully).

```
function handle_get_album(req, res) {
    // get the GET params
    var getp = req.parsed_url.query;
    var page_num = getp.page ? parseInt(getp.page) : 0;
    var page_size = getp.page_size ? parseInt(getp.page_size) : 1000;

    if (isNaN(parseInt(page_num))) page_num = 0;
    if (isNaN(parseInt(page_size))) page_size = 1000;

    // format of request is /albums/album_name.json
    var core_url = req.parsed_url.pathname;

    var album_name = core_url.substr(7, core_url.length - 12);
    load_album(album_name, page_num, page_size, (err, album_contents) => {
        if (err && err.error == "no_such_album") {
            send_failure(res, 404, err);
        } else if (err) {
            send_failure(res, 500, err);
        } else {
            send_success(res, { album_data: album_contents });
        }
    });
}
```

Note that we call `parseInt` in the above function since the query parameters are all strings by default.

Finally, you modify the `load_album` function to extract the subarray of the `files_only` array when it's done with all its work:

```
function load_album(album_name, page, page_size, callback) {
    fs.readdir("albums/" + album_name, (err, files) => {
        if (err) {
            if (err.code == "ENOENT") {
                callback(no_such_album());
            } else {
                callback(make_error("file_error",
                                    JSON.stringify(err)));
            }
            return;
        }

        var only_files = [];
        var path = "albums/" + album_name + "/";
```

```
        var iterator = (index) => {
            if (index == files.length) {
                var ps;
                // slice fails gracefully if params are out of range
                var start = page * page_size
                ps = only_files.slice(start, start + page_size);
                var obj = { short_name: album_name,
                            photos: ps };
                callback(null, obj);
                return;
            }

            fs.stat(path + files[index], (err, stats) => {
                if (err) {
                    callback(make_error("file_error",
                                        JSON.stringify(err)));
                    return;
                }
                if (stats.isFile()) {
                    var obj = { filename: files[index], desc: files[index] };
                    only_files.push(obj);
                }
                iterator(index + 1)
            });
        }
        iterator(0);
    });
}
```

Modifying Things: POST Data

Now that I've largely covered how to get things *from* your JSON server, you might like to start being able to send data *to* it, either to create new things or modify existing ones. This is typically done with HTTP POST data, and you can send the data in many different formats. To send data using the `curl` client, you must do a few things:

1. Set the HTTP method parameter to *POST* (or *PUT*).

2. Set the `Content-Type` of the incoming data.

3. Send the data itself.

You can easily accomplish these tasks with `curl`. You do the first simply by changing the method name, the second by specifying HTTP headers with the -H flag to `curl`, and the last you can do in a few different ways, but here you can use the -d flag and just write the JSON as a string.

Now it's time add some new functionality to the server to allow you to rename albums. Make the URL format as follows and specify that it must be a POST request:

```
http://localhost:8080/albums/albumname/rename.json
```

So, the `curl` command to rename an album is now the following:

```
curl -s -X POST -H "Content-Type: application/json" \
    -d '{ "album_name" : "new album name" }' \
    http://localhost:8080/albums/old_album_name/rename.json
```

Modifying `handle_incoming_request` to accept the new request type is pretty easy:

```
var url = require('url');
function handle_incoming_request(req, res) {

    // parse the query params into an object and get the path
    // without them. (2nd param true = parse the params).
    req.parsed_url = url.parse(req.url, true);
    var core_url = req.parsed_url.pathname;

    // test this fixed url to see what they're asking for
    if (core_url == '/albums.json' && req.method.toLowerCase() == 'get') {
        handle_list_albums(req, res);
    } else if (core_url.substr(core_url.length - 12)  == '/rename.json'
            && req.method.toLowerCase() == 'post') {
        handle_rename_album(req, res);
    } else if (core_url.substr(0, 7) == '/albums'
            && core_url.substr(core_url.length   5) == '.json'
            && req.method.toLowerCase() == 'get') {
        handle_get_album(req, res);
    } else {
        send_failure(res, 404, invalid_resource());
    }
}
```

Note that you have to put the code to handle the rename request before the load-album request; otherwise, the code would have treated it as an album called *rename* and just executed `handle_get_album`.

Receiving JSON POST Data

To get the POST data in the program, you use a Node feature called *streams*. Streams are a powerful way to transfer large amounts of data in Node while maintaining the asynchronous, nonblocking nature of the system. I cover streams more fully in Chapter 6, "Expanding Your Web Server," but for now, you just need to know the key pattern for using streams:

```
.on(event_name, function (parm) { ... });
```

In particular, pay attention to two events for now: the `readable` and `end` events. The stream is actually just the `ServerRequest` object from the http module (which inherits from the class `Stream`; `ServerResponse` does too!), and you listen to these two events via the following pattern:

```
var json_body = '';
req.on('readable', () => {
    var d = req.read();
    if (d) {
        if (typeof d == 'string') {
            json_body += d;
        } else if (typeof d == 'object' && d instanceof Buffer) {
            json_body += d.toString('utf8');
        }
    }
});

req.on('end', () => {
    // did we get a valid body?
    if (json_body) {
        try {
            var body = JSON.parse(json_body);
            // use it and then call the callback!
            callback(null, ...);
        } catch (e) {
            callback({ error: "invalid_json",
                       message: "The body is not valid JSON" });
        }
    } else {
        callback({ error: "no_body",
                   message: "We did not receive any JSON" });
        }
    }
});
```

For each piece (chunk) of data forming the body of the incoming request, the function you pass to the `on('readable', ...)` handler is called. In the preceding code, you first read the data from the stream with the `read` method and append this incoming data to the end of the `json_body` variable; then when you get the end event, you take the resulting string and try to parse it. `JSON.parse` throws an error if the given string is not valid JSON, so you have to wrap it in a `try/catch` block.

The function to process the request for a rename is as follows:

```
function handle_rename_album(req, res) {

    // 1. Get the album name from the URL
    var core_url = req.parsed_url.pathname;
    var parts = core_url.split('/');
```

```
if (parts.length != 4) {
    send_failure(res, 404, invalid_resource());
    return;
}


var album_name = parts[2];

// 2. Get the POST data for the request. This will have the JSON
//    for the new name for the album.
var json_body = '';
req.on('readable', () => {
    var d = req.read();
    if (d) {
        if (typeof d == 'string') {
            json_body += d;
        } else if (typeof d == 'object' && d instanceof Buffer) {
            json_body += d.toString('utf8');
        }
    }
});

// 3. When we have all the post data, make sure we have valid
//    data and then try to do the rename.
req.on('end', () => {
    // did we get a valid body?
    if (json_body) {
        try {
            var album_data = JSON.parse(json_body);
            if (!album_data.album_name) {
                send_failure(res, 404, missing_data('album_name'));
                return;
            }
        } catch (e) {
            // got a body, but not valid json
            send_failure(res, 403, bad_json());
            return;
        }

        // we have a proposed new album name!
        do_rename(album_name, album_data.album_name, (err, results) => {
            if (err && err.code == "ENOENT") {
                send_failure(res, 403, no_such_album());
                return;
            } else if (err) {
                send_failure(res, 500, file_error(err));
                return;
            }
```

```
                    send_success(res, null);
                });
        } else {
            send_failure(res, 403, bad_json());
            res.end();
        }
    });
}
```

Notice that the `'readable'` event does not actually pass in the object from which to read—it merely specifies that the `req` object has some data to read, and we thus read from that.

The complete listing for the updated server that can now handle three requests is in the Chapter 4 GitHub source code as *post_data.js*.

Receiving Form POST Data

Although you won't use this as much in your application, a lot of data sent to servers from web applications is sent via `<form>` elements, for example:

```
<form name='simple' method='post' action='http://localhost:8080'>
  Name: <input name='name' type='text' size='10'/><br/>
  Age: <input name='age' type='text' size='5'/><br/>
  <input type='submit' value="Send"/>
</form>
```

If you write a little server program to fetch the POST data using the `readable` and `end` events as you did in the preceding section, printing out the data for the preceding form yields:

```
name=marky+mark&age=23
```

What you really need, however, is something similar to what you got previously with JSON: a JavaScript object that represents the data sent to you. To achieve this, you can use another module built into Node.js, *querystring*, and specifically, its parse function, as follows:

```
var POST_data = qs.parse(body);
```

The resulting object is as you expect it to be:

```
{ name: 'marky mark++', age: '23' }
```

The complete listing of the simple server to receive a form and print out its contents is as follows:

```
var http = require('http'), qs = require('querystring');

function handle_incoming_request(req, res) {
    var body = '';
    req.on('readable', () => {
        var d = req.read();
        if (d) {
            if (typeof d == 'string') {
```

```
            body += d;
        } else if (typeof d == 'object' && d instanceof Buffer) {
            body += d.toString('utf8');
        }
    }
});


// 3. when we have all the post data, make sure we have valid
//    data and then try to do the rename.
req.on('end', () => {
    if (req.method.toLowerCase() == 'post') {
        var POST_data = qs.parse(body);
        console.log(POST_data);
    }
    res.writeHead(200, { "Content-Type" : "application/json" });
    res.end(JSON.stringify( { error: null }) + "\n");
});
}


var s = http.createServer(handle_incoming_request);
s.listen(8080);
```

Starting in Chapter 6, however, when you learn how to use the *Express* web application framework for Node, you'll see that this functionality is typically all handled for you.

Summary

This chapter covered quite a lot of new material. You wrote your first web application by writing a simple JSON server. I like this approach for a few key reasons:

- It lets you focus on the server and the key concepts you need to get really comfortable with Node.js.

- You can make sure your server API is well organized and efficient.

- A nice, light application server should mean that the computer(s) running it will be able to handle the load without too much trouble. When you add in HTML UI and client-side features later, you can try to have the client do as much of the work as possible.

Now you not only have a basic working server but also have seen how to modify the output it sends you with different request URLs and query parameters. You have also seen how to send new data or modify existing data by submitting POST data along with the request. Although some of the programs look reasonably long and complicated already, you are working with just basic components right now to examine core Node principles. You start to replace these with more helpful and functional modules quite soon.

But first, take a break and learn more about *modules*—much more on how to consume them and also how to write your own.

5

Modules

In the Node.js servers and scripts you have written thus far, you have already consumed external functionality in the form of modules. In this chapter, I explain how this all works and how to write your own. In addition to all the powerful and functional modules that Node already provides for you, there is a huge community further developing modules that you can take advantage of in your programs, and indeed you can even write your own to give something back!

One of the cool things about Node is that you don't really distinguish between modules that you have produced and modules that you consume from external repositories, such as those you see later in this chapter via npm, the Node Package Manager. When you write separate classes and groups of functions in Node, you put them in basically the same format—perhaps with a bit less dressing and documentation—as modules you download from the Internet and use. In fact, it usually takes only an extra bit of JSON and maybe line or two of code to prepare your code for consumption by others!

Node ships with a large number of built-in modules, all of which are packaged in the node executable on your system. You can view their source if you download the Node source code from the nodejs.org website. They all live in the *lib/* subdirectory.

Writing Simple Modules

At a high level, modules are a way to group common functionality in Node.js. If you have a library of functions or classes for working with a particular database server, for example, it would make a lot of sense to put that code into a module and package it for consumption.

Every file in Node.js is a module, although modules do not necessarily have to be this simple. You can package complex modules with many files, unit tests, documentation, and other support files into folders and consume them in the same way you would a module with only a single JavaScript file (see "Writing Modules" later in this chapter).

To write your own module that exposes, or *exports*, a function called `hello_world`, you can write the following and save it to *mymodule.js*:

```
exports.hello_world = function () {
    console.log("Hello World");
}
```

The `exports` object is a special object created by the Node module system in every file you create and is returned as the value of the `require` function when you include that module. It lives off the `module` object that every module has and is used to expose functions, variables, or classes. In the simple example here, the module exposes a single function on the `exports` object, and to consume it, you could write the following and save it to modtest.js:

```
var mm = require ('./mymodule');
mm.hello_world();
```

Running `node modtest.js` causes Node to print out `"Hello World"` exactly as you would expect. You can expose as many functions and classes as you want off the `exports` object as you'd like. For example:

```
function Greeter (lang) {
    this.language = lang;
    this.greet = function () {
        switch (this.language) {
            case "en": return "Hello!";
            case "de": return "Hallo!";
            case "jp": return "こんにちは!";
            default: return "No speaka that language";
        }
    }
}

exports.hello_world = function () {
    console.log("Hello World");
}

exports.goodbye = function () {
    console.log("Bye bye!");
}

exports.create_greeter = function (lang) {
    return new Greeter(lang);
}
```

The `module` variable given to each module contains information such as the filename of the current module, its child modules, its parent modules, and more.

Modules and Objects

You frequently return objects from modules that you write. There are two key patterns through which you do this.

The Factory Model

The previous sample module contains a class called `Greeter`. To get an instance of a `Greeter` object, you call a creation function—or *factory function*—to create and return an instance of this class. The basic model is as follows:

```
function ABC (parms) {
    this.varA = ...;
    this.varB = ...;
    this.functionA = function () {
        ...
    }
}

exports.create_ABC = function (parms) {
    return new ABC(parms);
}
```

The advantage to this model is that the module can still expose other functions and classes via the `exports` object.

The Constructor Model

Another way to expose classes from a module you write would be to completely replace the `exports` object in the module with a class that you want people to use:

```
function ABC () {
    this.varA = 10;
    this.varB = 20;
    this.functionA = function (var1, var2) {
        console.log(var1 + " " + var2);
    }
}

module.exports = ABC;
```

To use this module, you would change your code to be the following:

```
var ABCClass = require('./conmod2');
var obj = new ABCClass();
obj.functionA(1, 2);
```

Thus, the only thing you are really exposing from the module is a constructor for the class. This approach feels nice and OOP-y, but has the disadvantage of not letting you expose much else from your module; it also tends to feel a bit awkward in the Node way of doing things. I showed it to you here so that you can recognize it for what it is when you see it, but you will almost never use it in this book or your projects—you will largely stick with the factory model.

npm: The Node Package Manager

Apart from writing your own modules and using those provided by Node.js, you will frequently use code written by other people in the Node community and published on the Internet. The most common way this is done today is by using npm, the *Node Package Manager*. npm is installed with your node installation (as you saw in Chapter 1, "Getting Started"), and you can go to the command line and type npm help to verify that it's still there and working.

To install modules via npm, you use the npm install command. This technique requires only the name of the module package you want to install. Many npm modules have their source code hosted on github.com, so they usually tell you the name required, for example:

```
host:ch5 marcw$ npm install mysql
Modules-Demo@0.0.1 /Users/marcwan/src/misc/LearningNodeJS/Chapter05
└─┬ mysql@2.11.1
  ├── bignumber.js@2.3.0
  ├─┬ readable-stream@1.1.14
  │ ├── core-util-is@1.0.2
  │ ├── inherits@2.0.1
  │ ├── isarray@0.0.1
  │ └── string_decoder@0.10.31
  └── sqlstring@2.0.1
```

If you're not sure of the name of the package you want to install, you can use the npm search command, as follows:

```
npm search sql
```

This command prints the name and description of all matching modules.

However, you're going to have a far richer and easier experience if you search by visiting *npmjs.org* and looking there.

npm installs module packages to the *node_modules/* subdirectory of your project. If a module package itself has any dependencies, they are installed to a *node_modules/* subdirectory of that module's folder.

```
+ project/
    + node_modules/
        module1
        module2
            + node_modules/
                dependency1
    main.js
```

To see a list of all modules that a project is currently using, you can use the `npm ls` command:

```
host:ch05 marcwan$ npm ls
Modules-Demo@0.0.1 /Users/marc/src/misc/LearningNodeJS/Chapter05
└─┬ async@2.0.1
  └── lodash@4.15.0
```

To update an installed package to a newer version, use the `npm update` command. If you specify a package name, it updates only that one. If you do not specify a package name, it updates all packages to their latest version. If there are no changes to the package, it will print out nothing:

```
host:ch5 marcw$ npm update mysql
host:ch5 marcw$
```

Consuming Modules

As you have already seen, to include a module in a Node file that you are writing, you use the `require` function. To be able to reference the functions and/or classes on that module, you assign the results (the `exports` object of the loaded module) to a variable:

```
var http = require('http');
```

Included modules are private to the module that includes them, so if *a.js* loads the *http* module, then *b.js* cannot reference it, unless it itself also loads *http*.

Searching for Modules

Node.js uses a pretty straightforward set of rules for finding modules requested with the `require` function:

1. If the requested module is a built-in one—such as *http* or *fs*—Node uses that.

2. If the module name in the `require` function begins with a path component (/, ../, or /). Node looks in the specified directory for that module and tries to load it there. If you don't specify a *.js* extension on your module name, Node first looks for a folder-based module of that name. If it does not find that, it then adds the extensions *.js*, *.json*, *.node* and tries to load modules of those types. (Modules with the extension *.node* are compiled add-on modules.)

3. If the module name does not have a path component at the beginning, Node looks in the *node_modules/* subfolder of the current folder for the module there. If it is found, that is loaded; otherwise, Node works its way up the path tree of the current location looking for *node_modules/* folders there. If those continue to fail, it looks in some standard default locations, such as */usr/lib*, */usr/local/lib*, or *C:\Program Files\User\App Data\location\npm* if you're running on Windows.

4. If the module isn't found in any of these locations, an error is thrown.

Module Caching

After a module has been loaded from a particular file or directory, Node.js caches it. Subsequent calls to `require` that would load the same module *from the same location* get the exact same code, with any initialization or other work that has taken place. Where this becomes interesting is in situations where we have a few different people asking for the same module. Consider the following project structure:

```
+ my_project/
    + node_modules/
        + special_widget/
            + node_modules/
                mail_widget (v2.0.1)
        mail_widget (v1.0.0)
    main.js
    utils.js
```

In this example, if either *main.js* or *utils.js* requires *mail_widget*, it gets v1.0.0 because Node's search rules find it in the *node_modules/* subdirectory of *my_project*. However, if they require *special_widget*, which in turn wishes to use *mail_widget*, *special_widget* gets its own privately included version of *mail_widget*, the v2.0.1 one in its own *node_modules/* folder.

This is one of the most powerful and awesome features of the Node.js module system! In so many other systems, modules, widgets, or dynamic libraries are all stored in a central location, which creates versioning nightmares when you require packages that themselves require different versions of some other module. In Node, they are free to include these different versions of the other modules, and Node's namespace and module rules mean that they do not interfere with each other at all! Individual modules and portions of a project are free to include, update, or modify included modules as they see fit without affecting the rest of the system.

In short, Node.js works intuitively, and for perhaps the first time in your life, you don't have to sit there endlessly cursing the package repository system you're using.

Cycles

Consider the following situation:

- *a.js* requires *b.js*.
- *b.js* requires *a.js*.
- *main.js* requires *a.js*.

You can see that you clearly have a cycle in the preceding modules. Node stops cycles from being a problem by simply returning uninitialized modules when it detects one. In the preceding case, the following happens:

- *main.js* is loaded, and code runs that requires *a.js*.
- *a.js* is loaded, and code runs that requires *b.js*.
- *b.js* is loaded, and code runs that requires *a.js*.

- Node detects the cycle and returns an object referring to *a.js*, but does not execute any more code—the loading and initialization of a.js are unfinished at this point!

- *b.js*, *a.js*, and main.js all finish initializing (in that order), and then the reference from *b.js* to *a.js* is valid and fully usable.

Writing Modules

Recall that every file in Node.js is itself a module, with a `module` and `exports` object. However, you also should know that modules can be a bit more complicated than that, with a directory to hold its contents and a file containing packaging information. For those cases in which you want to write a bunch of support files, break up the functionality of the module into separate JavaScript files, or even include unit tests, you can write modules in this format.

The basic format is as follows:

1. Create the folder to hold the module contents.

2. Put a file called *package.json* into this folder. This file should contain at least a name for the module and main JavaScript file that Node should load initially for that module.

3. If Node cannot find the *package.json* file or no main JavaScript file is specified, it looks for *index.js* (or *index.node* for compiled add-on modules).

Creating Your Module

Now take the code you wrote for managing photos and albums in the preceding chapter and put it into a module. Doing so lets you share it with other projects that you write later and isolate the code so you can write unit tests, and so on.

First, create the following directory structure in the source scratch directory (that is, *~/src/scratch* or wherever you're playing around with Node):

```
+ album_mgr/
    + lib/
    + test/
```

In the album_mgr folder, create a file called *package.json* and put the following in it:

```
{ "name": "album-manager",
  "version": "1.0.0",
  "main": "./lib/albums.js" }
```

This is the most basic of *package.json* files; it tells npm that the package should have the friendly name *album-manager* and that the "main" or starting JavaScript file for the package is the *albums.js* file in the *lib/* subdirectory. *Package.json* files can contain many other fields, including descriptions, author information, licensing, etc. The npm documentation covers this in detail.

The preceding directory structure is by no means mandatory or written in stone; it is simply one of the common layouts for packages that I have found to be useful and have thus latched on to. You are under no obligation to follow it. I do, however, recommend that you start doing things this way and start experimenting with different layouts only after you're comfortable with the whole system.

Sites such as github.com that are frequently used to host Node module source automatically display Readme documentation if they find it. Thus, it is pretty common for people to include a *Readme.md* (the "md" stands for *markdown* and refers to the standard documentation format that github.com uses). You are highly encouraged to write documentation for your modules to help people get started using it. For the *album-manager* module, I wrote the following Readme file:

```
# Album-Manager

This is our module for managing photo albums based on a directory. We
assume that, given a path, there is an albums sub-folder, and each of
its individual sub-folders are themselves the albums. Files in those
sub-folders are photos.

## Album Manager

The album manager exposes a single function, `albums`, which returns
an array of `Album` objects for each album it contains.

## Album Object

The album object has the following two properties and one method:

* `name` -- The name of the album
* `path` -- The path to the album
* `photos()` -- Calling this method will return all the album's photos
```

Now you can write your actual module files. First, start with the promised *lib/albums.js*, which is just some of the album-loading code from Chapter 4, "Writing Applications," repackaged into a module-like JavaScript file:

```
var fs = require('fs'),
    album = require('./album.js');


exports.version = "1.0.0";


exports.albums = function (root, callback) {
    // we will just assume that any directory in our 'albums'
    // subfolder is an album.
    fs.readdir(root + "/albums", (err, files) => {
        if (err) {
            callback(err);
            return;
        }
```

```
        var album_list = [];

        (function iterator(index) {
            if (index == files.length) {
                callback(null, album_list);
                return;
            }

            fs.stat(root + "albums/" + files[index], (err, stats) => {
                if (err) {
                    callback(make_error("file_error",
                                        JSON.stringify(err)));
                    return;
                }
                if (stats.isDirectory()) {
                    var p = root + "albums/" + files[index];
                    album_list.push(album.create_album(p));
                }
                iterator(index + 1)
            });
        })(0);
    });
};

function make_error(err, msg) {
    var e = new Error(msg);
    e.code = err;
    return e;
}
```

One of the standard things to provide in the exported functionality of modules is a `version` member field. Although I don't always use it, it can be a helpful way for calling modules to check your version and execute different code depending on what it has.

You can see that the album functionality is split into a new file called *lib/album.js*, and there is a new class called `Album`. This class looks as follows:

```
function Album (album_path) {
    this.name = path.basename(album_path);
    this.path = album_path;
}


Album.prototype.name = null;
Album.prototype.path = null;
Album.prototype._photos = null;
```

```
Album.prototype.photos = function (callback) {
    if (this._photos != null) {
        callback(null, this._photos);
        return;
    }

    fs.readdir(this.path, (err, files) => {
        if (err) {
            if (err.code == "ENOENT") {
                callback(no_such_album());
            } else {
                callback(make_error("file_error", JSON.stringify(err)));
            }
            return;
        }

        var only_files = [];

        var iterator = (index) => {
            if (index == files.length) {
                callback(null, only_files);
                return;
            }

            fs.stat(this.path + "/" + files[index], (err, stats) => {
                if (err) {
                    callback(make_error("file_error",
                                        JSON.stringify(err)));
                    return;
                }
                if (stats.isFile()) {
                    only_files.push(files[index]);
                }
                iterator(index + 1)
            });
        };
        iterator(0);
    });
};
```

If you're confused by the `prototype` keyword used a few times in the preceding source
code, perhaps now is a good time to jump back to Chapter 2 and review the section on writing
classes in JavaScript. The `prototype` keyword here is simply a way to set properties on all
instances of our Album class.

Again, this is pretty much what you saw in Chapter 4 with the basic JSON server. The only real
difference is that it is packaged into a class with a prototype object and method called `photos`.

I hope you also noted the following two things:

1. You now use a new built-in module called *path*, and you use the `basename` function on it to extract the album's name from the path.

2. By using arrow functions for anonymous callbacks within this class, we avoid the problems with the `this` pointer mentioned in "Who Am I? Maintaining a Sense of Identity" in Chapter 3, "Asynchronous Programming." If you're not sure what we're talking about here, please take a moment to refer back to that section.

The rest of the *album.js* file is simply as follows:

```
var path = require('path'),
    fs = require('fs');

// Album class code goes here

exports.create_album = function (path) {
    return new Album(path);
};
function make_error(err, msg) {
    var e = new Error(msg);
    e.code = err;
    return e;
}
function no_such_album() {
    return { error: "no_such_album",
             message: "The specified album does not exist." };
}
```

And that is all you need for your *album-manager* module! To test it, go back to the scratch directory and enter the following test program as *atest.js*:

```
var amgr = require('./album_mgr');  // Our module is in the album_mgr dir as per above

amgr.albums('./', function (err, albums) {
    if (err) {
        console.log("Unexpected error: " + JSON.stringify(err));
        return;
    }

    var iterator = (index) => {
        if (index == albums.length) {
            console.log("Done");
            return;
        }
```

```
        albums[index].photos(function (err, photos) {
            if· (err) {
                console.log("Err loading album: " + JSON.stringify(err));
                return;
            }

            console.log(albums[index].name);
            console.log(photos);
            console.log("");
            iterator(index + 1);
        });
    }
    iterator(0);
});
```

Now, all you have to do is ensure you have an *albums/* subfolder in the current directory, and you should be able to run atest.js and see something like the following:

```
hostname:Chapter05 marcw$ node atest
australia2010
[ 'aus_01.jpg',
  'aus_02.jpg',
  'aus_03.jpg',
  'aus_04.jpg',
  'aus_05.jpg',
  'aus_06.jpg',
  'aus_07.jpg',
  'aus_08.jpg',
  'aus_09.jpg' ]

italy2012
[ 'picture_01.jpg',
  'picture_02.jpg',
  'picture_03.jpg',
  'picture_04.jpg',
  'picture_05.jpg' ]

japan2010
[ 'picture_001.jpg',
  'picture_002.jpg',
  'picture_003.jpg',
  'picture_004.jpg',
  'picture_005.jpg',
  'picture_006.jpg',
  'picture_007.jpg' ]

Done
```

Developing with Your Module

You now have a module for working with albums. If you would like to use it in multiple projects, you could copy it to the *node_modules/* folder of your other projects, but then you would have a problem: What happens when you want to make a change to your albums module? Do you have to copy the source code over to all the locations it is being used each and every time you change it? Ideally, we'd like to be able to use npm even for our own private modules but not risk having them get uploaded to the actual npm repository on the Internet.

Fortunately, npm solves both of these problems for us. You can modify the *package.json* file to add the following:

```
{ "name": "album-manager",
  "version": "1.0.0",
  "main": "./lib/albums.js",
  "private": true }
```

This code tells npm to never accidentally publish this to the live npm repository, which you don't want for this module now.

Then, you can use the npm link command, which tells npm to put a link to the *album-manager* package in the local machine's default public package repository (such as */usr/local/lib/node_modules* on Linux and Mac machines, or *C:\Users\username\AppData\location\npm* on Windows).

```
host:Chapter05 marcw$ cd album_mgr
host:album_mgr marcw$ sudo npm link
/usr/local/lib/node_modules/album-manager ->
/Users/marcw/src/scratch/Chapter05/album_mgr
```

Note that depending on how the permissions and such are set up on your local machine, you might need to run this command as super-user with sudo (Windows users will certainly not need to).

Now, to consume this module, you need to do two things:

1. Refer to 'album-manager' instead of 'album_mgr' in the code (because npm uses the name field in *package.json*).

2. Create a reference to the album-manager module with npm for each project that wants to use it. You can just type npm link album-manager:

```
host:Chapter05 marcw$ mkdir test_project
host:Chapter05 marcw$ cd test_project/
host:test_project marcw$ npm link album-manager
/Users/marcw/src/scratch/Chapter05/test_project/node_modules/album-manager ->
   /usr/local/lib/node_modules/album-manager ->
   /Users/marcw/src/scratch/Chapter05/album_mgr
host:test_project marcw$ dir
drwxr-xr-x  3 marcw  staff  102 11 20 18:38 node_modules/
host:test_project marcw$ dir node_modules/
lrwxr-xr-x  1 marcw  staff   41 11 20 18:38 album-manager@ ->
   /usr/local/lib/node_modules/album-manager
```

Now, you are free to make changes to your original album manager source, and all referencing projects will see changes right away.

Publishing Your Modules

If you have written a module that you would like to share with other users, you can publish it to the official npm registry using npm publish. This requires you to do the following:

- Remove the "private": true line from the *package.json* file.

- Create an account on the npm registry servers with npm adduser.

- Optionally, choose to fill in more fields in *package.json* (run npm help json to get more information on which fields you might want to add) with things such as a description, author contact information, and host website.

- Finally, run npm publish from the module directory to push it to npm. That's it!

```
host:album_mgr marcw$ npm adduser
Username: learningnode_test
Password:
Email: (this IS public) learningnodetest@example.org
Logged in as learningnode_test on https://registry.npmjs.org/.
host:album_mgr marcw$ npm publish
+ album-manager@1.0.0
```

If you accidentally publish something you didn't mean to or otherwise want to remove from the npm registry, you can use npm unpublish:

```
host:album_mgr marcw$ npm unpublish
npm ERR! Refusing to delete entire project.
npm ERR! Run with --force to do this.
npm ERR! npm unpublish <project>[@<version>]
host:album_mgr marcw$ npm unpublish --force
npm WARN using --force I sure hope you know what you are doing.
- album-manager@1.0.0
```

If you see the following when trying to publish a module:

```
npm ERR! publish Failed PUT 403
npm ERR! Darwin 15.6.0
npm ERR! argv "/usr/local/bin/node" "/usr/local/bin/npm" "publish"
npm ERR! node v6.3.1
npm ERR! npm  v3.10.3
npm ERR! code E403

npm ERR! you do not have permission to publish "album-manager". Are you logged in as
the correct user? : album-manager
```

It most likely means that somebody else has registered a module with this name. Your best bet is to choose another name.

Managing Asynchronous Code

You have already used a few of the Node.js built-in modules in code written thus far (*http*, *fs*, *path*, *querystring*, and *url*), and you will use many more throughout the rest of the book. However, there are one or two modules you will find yourself using for nearly every single project to manage a problem every Node.js programmer runs into: *managing asynchronous code*. We show two solutions here.

The Problem

Consider the case in which you want to write some asynchronous code to

- Open a handle to a path.

- Determine whether or not the path points to a file.

- Load in the contents of the file if the path does point to a file.

- Close the file handle and return the contents to the caller.

You've seen almost all this code before, and the function to do this looks something like the following, where functions you call are bold and the callback arrow functions you write are bold and italic:

```
var fs = require('fs');

function load_file_contents(path, callback) {
    fs.open(path, 'r', (err, f) => {
        if (err) {
            callback(err);
            return;
        } else if (!f) {
            callback({ error: "invalid_handle",
                    message: "bad file handle from fs.open"});
            return;
        }
        fs.fstat(f, (err, stats) => {
            if (err) {
                callback(err);
                return;
            }
            if (stats.isFile()) {
                var b = new Buffer(stats.size);
                fs.read(f, b, 0, stats.size, null, (err, br, buf) => {
                    if (err) {
```

```
                    callback(err);
                    return;
                }

                fs.close(f, (err) => {
                    if (err) {
                        callback(err);
                        return;
                    }
                    callback(null, b.toString('utf8', 0, br));
                });
            });
        } else {
            callback({ error: "not_file",
                    message: "Can't load directory" });
            return;
        }
    });
});
}
```

As you can, even for a short, contrived example such as this, the code is starting to nest pretty seriously and deeply. Nest more than a few levels deep, and you'll find that you cannot fit your code in an 80-column terminal or one page of printed paper any more. It can also be quite difficult to read the code, figure out what variables are being used where, and determine the flow of the functions being called and returned.

Our Preferred Solution—*async*

To solve this problem, you can use an npm module called *async*. The *async* module provides an intuitive way to structure and organize asynchronous calls, and removes many, if not all, of the tricky parts of asynchronous programming you encounter in Node.js.

Executing Code in Serial

You can execute code serially in async in two ways: through the `waterfall` function or the `series` function (see Figure 5.1)

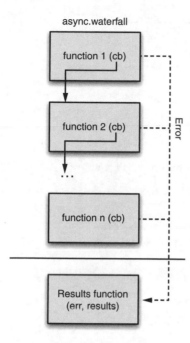

async.waterfall

function 1 (cb)

function 2 (cb)

...

function n (cb)

Error

Results function
(err, results)

Figure 5.1   Serial execution with async.waterfall

The `waterfall` function takes an array of functions and executes them one at a time, passing the results from each function to the next. At the end, a resulting function is called with the results from the final function in the array. If an error is signaled at any step of the way, execution is halted, and the resulting function is called with that error instead.

For example, you could easily rewrite the previous code cleanly (it's in the GitHub source tree) using `async.waterfall`:

```
var fs = require('fs');
var async = require('async');

function load_file_contents(path, callback) {
    async.waterfall([
        function (callback) {
            fs.open(path, 'r', callback);
        },
        // the f (file handle) was passed to the callback at the end of
        // the fs.open function call. async passes all params to us.
        function (f, callback) {
            fs.fstat(f, function (err, stats) {
                if (err)
```

```
                    // abort and go straight to resulting function
                    callback(err);
                else
                    // f and stats are passed to next in waterfall
                    callback(null, f, stats);
            });
        },
        function (f, stats, callback) {
            if (stats.isFile()) {
                var b = new Buffer(stats.size);
                fs.read(f, b, 0, stats.size, null, function (err, br, buf) {
                    if (err)
                        callback(err);
                    else
                        // f and string are passed to next in waterfall
                        callback(null, f, b.toString('utf8', 0, br));
                });
            } else {
                callback({ error: "not_file",
                           message: "Can't load directory" });
            }
        },
        function (f, contents, callback) {
            fs.close(f, function (err) {
                if (err)
                    callback(err);
                else
                    callback(null, contents);
            });
        }
    ]
    // this is called after all have executed in success
    // case, or as soon as there is an error.
    , function (err, file_contents) {
        callback(err, file_contents);
    });
}
```

Although the code has grown a little bit in length, when you organize the functions serially in an array like this, the code is significantly cleaner looking and easier to read.

The `async.series` function differs from `async.waterfall` in two keys ways:

- Results from one function are not passed to the next; instead, they are collected in an array, which becomes the "results" (the second) parameter to the final resulting function. Each step of the serial call gets one slot in this results array.

- You can pass an object to `async.series`, and it enumerates the keys and executes the functions assigned to them. In this case, the results are not passed as an array, but an object with the same keys as the functions called.

Consider this example:

```
var async = require("async");

async.series({
    numbers: (callback) => {
        setTimeout(function () {
            callback(null, [ 1, 2, 3 ]);
        }, 1500);
    },
    strings: (callback) => {
        setTimeout(function () {
            callback(null, [ "a", "b", "c" ]);
        }, 2000);
    }
},
(err, results) => {
    console.log(results);
});
```

This function generates the following output:

```
{ numbers: [ 1, 2, 3 ], strings: [ 'a', 'b', 'c' ] }
```

Executing in Parallel

In the previous `async.series` example, there was no reason to use a serial execution sequence for the functions; the second function did not depend on the results of the first, so they could have executed in parallel (see Figure 5.2). For this, async provides `async.parallel`, as follows:

```
var async = require("async");

async.parallel({

    numbers: function (callback) {
        setTimeout(function () {
            callback(null, [ 1, 2, 3 ]);
        }, 1500);
    },
    strings: function (callback) {
        setTimeout(function () {
            callback(null, [ "a", "b", "c" ]);
        }, 2000);
    }
},
function (err, results) {
    console.log(results);
});
```

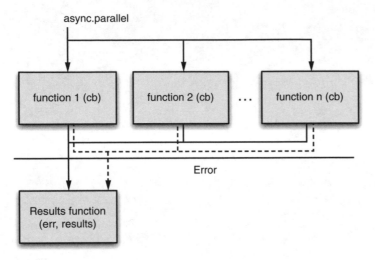

Figure 5.2   Parallel execution with async.parallel

This function generates the exact same output as before.

Mixing It Up

The most powerful function of them all is the `async.auto` function, which lets you mix ordered and unordered functions together into one powerful sequence of functions. In this, you pass an object where keys contain either

- A function to execute or
- An array of dependencies and then a function to execute. These dependencies are strings and are the names of properties in the object provided to `async.auto`. The `auto` function waits for these dependencies to finish executing before calling the provided function.

The `async.auto` function figures out the required order to execute all the functions, including which can be executed in parallel and which need to wait for others (see Figure 5.3). As with the `async.waterfall` function, you can pass results from one function to the next via the `callback` parameter:

```
var async = require("async");

async.auto({
    numbers: (callback) => {
        setTimeout(() => {
            callback(null, [ 1, 2, 3 ]);
        }, 1500);
    },
```

```
    strings: (callback) => {
        setTimeout(() => {
            callback(null, [ "a", "b", "c" ]);
        }, 2000);
    },
    // do not execute this function until numbers and strings are done
    // thus_far is an object with numbers and strings as arrays.
    assemble: [ 'numbers', 'strings', (thus_far, callback) => {
        callback(null, {
            numbers: thus_far.numbers.join(",  "),
            strings: "'" + thus_far.strings.join("',  '") + "'"
        });
    }]
},
// this is called at the end when all other functions have executed. Optional
(err, results) => {
    if (err)
        console.log(err);
    else
        console.log(results);
});
```

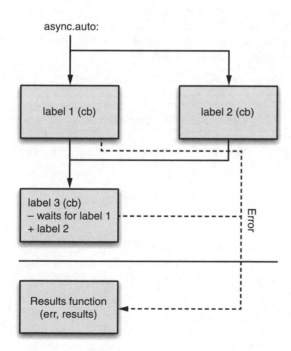

Figure 5.3   Mixing execution models with async.auto

The `results` parameter passed to the final resulting function is an object in which the properties hold the results of each of the functions executed on the object:

```
{ numbers: [ 1, 2, 3 ],
  strings: [ 'a', 'b', 'c' ],
  assemble: { numbers: '1,  2,  3', strings: '\'a\',  \'b\',  \'c\'' } }
```

Looping Asynchronously

In Chapter 3, I showed you how you can use the following pattern to iterate over the items in an array with asynchronous function calls:

```
var iterator = (i) => {
  if( i < array.length ) {
    async_work( function(){
      iterator( i + 1 )
    })
  } else {
    callback(results);
  }
}
iterator(0);
```

Although this technique works great and is indeed gloriously geeky, it's a bit more complicated than I'd like. The async module comes to the rescue again with `async.forEachSeries`. It iterates over every element in the provided array, calling the given function for each. However, it waits for each to finish executing before calling the next in the series:

```
async.forEachSeries(
    arr,
    // called for each element in arr
    (element, callback) => {
        // use element
        callback(null);  // YOU MUST CALL ME FOR EACH ELEMENT!
    },
    // called at the end
    function (err) {
        // was there an error?  err will be non-null then
    }
);
```

To simply loop over every element in a loop and then have async wait for all of them to finish, you can use `async.forEach`, which is called in the exact same way and differs in that it doesn't execute the functions serially.

The async module contains a ton of other functionality and is truly one of the indispensable modules of Node.js programming today. I highly encourage you to browse the documentation at *https://github.com/caolan/async* and play around with it. It truly takes the already-enjoyable Node.js programming environment and makes it even better.

Making Promises and Keeping Them

While the methods we have looked at thus far for managing asynchronous programming—patterns and the *async* module—are the primary ways you'll work with Node.js throughout this book, another popular pattern for managing asynchronous programming is *promises*.

Promises come in various implementations and flavors. The one we will be discussing here will come via the use of the *bluebird* module in Node, which can be installed by running npm install bluebird. There are a number of other modules for doing promises in Node, most notably *promises*, and *Q*, but we'll use *bluebird* for now, for it has the ability to "promisify" entire modules in Node, which we'll find quite useful—working with promises requires APIs to be written differently, and better promises packages will be able to take a regular module and wrap it in promise-ready versions.

Just like *async*, promises seek to make writing asynchronous code easier for you by automatically passing parameters from callbacks to the next function invocation. Similarly, they aim to centralize all error processing in one place at the end.

Looking back to the above example of opening a file, seeing if it's actually a file, reading its contents, and then closing it, we can rewrite this using promises in the following manner:

```
var Promise = require("bluebird");
var fs = Promise.promisifyAll(require("fs"));

function load_file_contents2(filename, callback) {
    var errorHandler = (err) => {
        console.log("SO SAD: " + err);
        callback(err, null);
    }

    fs.openAsync(filename, 'r', 0)
    .then(function (fd) {                            // 1
        fs.fstatAsync(fd)
        .then(function (stats) {
            if (stats.isFile()) {                   // 2
                var b = new Buffer(stats.size);
                return fs.readAsync(fd, b, 0, stats.size, null)
                    .then(fs.closeAsync(fd))
                    .then(function () {
                        callback(null, b.toString('utf8'))
                    })
                    .catch(errorHandler);
            }
        })
    })
    .catch(errorHandler);
}
```

Using APIs with the promise pattern requires modification and conversion to promise-compatible versions. For example, we want to use the File System (fs) APIs with promises in the above example, so we import *bluebird* and convert the module as follows:

```
var Promise = require("bluebird");
var fs = Promise.promisifyAll(require("fs"));
```

The *bluebird* module leaves all the original functions and adds new *promisified* versions for all functions that have an error as the first parameter to the callback in the module. These modified function versions have async appended to the function name.

Effectively, when calling the then function:

- The provided function is executed.

- If the callback has a non-null error, all further promises are skipped until the catch method is reached, and it is passed the error.

- If the callback has a value, this is passed to the next then function in the chain.

In the above promises code, we have to deal with a couple of interesting problems. For the part marked with // 1, we originally wanted to write the code like this:

```
fs.openAsync("promises.js", 'r')
    .then(fs.fstatAsync)           // fd passed from openAsync to us by promises
    .then(function (stats) {
        if (stats.isFile() {
            fs.readAsync(fd, ...); // etc
```

This, however presents a problem. Once you've verified the path is a file, we want to read from it, which requires the fd (file descriptor) parameter that openAsync passes to its callback. Because you just consumed this quietly in the promise chain above, you don't have it anywhere to pass to readAsync. Thus, you can see in the code that you've actually created a new function with fd as one of the parameters so that code anywhere in that scope can refer to the file descriptor.

Our second problem is then how to deal with the branching in // 2. You want to execute different code depending on whether the given path is a file or not. Looking at the above code, you can see that the way to do this is to just start another promise chain within the first promise chain—there is no limit to how deeply you nest them!

So, while our code is still nests a bit dealing with all the possible paths, we've managed to make it significantly more compact, and also factor out all the error handling code into one place, which is still a big improvement to our original function. Much like *async*, the promises model of asynchronous programming comes with solutions to asynchronous looping and parallel execution constructs that you would expect from the asynchronous world of Node.

How We'll Manage Asynchronous Code

While promises can be an effective and common solution to managing asynchronous code, we'll continue using mostly *async* and regular callbacks in this book as I find promises to have two shortcomings that don't really work for me:

1. Using promises requires either rewriting your APIs to be promise-enabled or using promise modules such as bluebird that provide *promisify* functionality. The former adds complexity and differs between the various promises systems, while the latter is limited and can't always provide promisified versions of things (e.g., the old `fs.exists` function, which never returned an `(err)` in its callback).

2. I find the code you write in promises not particularly readable. To my eyes, it looks complicated and introduces too many new concepts and functions you have to get used to in order to solve all the different problems. In this regard, I find async produces far cleaner code.

As always, you are encouraged to play around with all the different paradigms out there (there are other approaches to solving the asynchronous programming problem!) and choose which one works best for you.

Summary

In this chapter you were more formally introduced to modules in Node.js. Although you have seen them before, now you finally know how they're written, how Node finds them for inclusion, and how to use npm to find and install them. You can write your own complex modules now with *package.json* files and link them across your projects or even publish them for others to use via npm.

Finally, you are now armed with knowledge of various approaches to cleaning up asynchronous programming, in particular async, one of the modules that you will use in nearly every single Node project you write from now on.

Next up: Putting the "web" back in web servers. You look at some cool ways to use JSON and Node in your web apps and how to handle some other core Node technologies such as events and streams.

6

Expanding Your Web Server

In this last chapter of Part II, "Learning to Run," you expand the web server a little bit with some key new functionality; you learn how to serve up static content such as HTML pages, JavaScript files, cascading style sheets, and even image files. Armed with this knowledge, you turn your focus away from the server and look at programming the client.

In the new Node.js world of programming websites, you're going to migrate from the traditional model of generating HTML on the server before sending it down to clients and instead have your server serve up only static files or JSON. The web browser can then use AJAX calls along with template libraries to generate pages on the fly as the user navigates around the site. Finally, you look at uploading files to your servers and see some of the tools you can use to help make that task easier.

You begin by taking another look at Node.js *streams*.

Serving Static Content with Streams

In the asynchronous, nonblocking IO world of Node.js, you previously saw that you can use `fs.open` and `fs.read` in a loop to read the contents of a file. However, Node.js provides another, far more elegant mechanism for reading (and even writing) files called *streams*. They act an awful lot like UNIX pipes—even on Windows—and you briefly saw them in use in the section "Receiving JSON POST Data" in Chapter 4, "Writing Simple Applications," when you needed to load in the data users sent along with requests.

In the basic usage, you use the `on` method to add *listeners* to *events*. The provided functions are called whenever one of those events is triggered. The `readable` event is sent whenever a read stream has read something in for you to process. The `end` event is sent whenever a stream has nothing more to read, and `error` events are sent whenever something has gone wrong.

Reading a File

As a simple example, write the following code and save it to simple_stream.js:

```
var fs = require('fs');
var contents;

var rs = fs.createReadStream("simple_stream.js");

rs.on('readable', () => {
    var str;
    var d = rs.read();
    if (d) {
        if (typeof d == 'string') {
            str = d;
        } else if (typeof d == 'object' && d instanceof Buffer) {
            str = d.toString('utf8');
        }
        if (str) {
            if (!contents)
                contents = d;
            else
                contents += str;
        }
    }
});

rs.on('end', () => {
    console.log("read in the file contents: ");
    console.log(contents.toString('utf8'));
});
```

If you're looking at the preceding code (it creates an object, adds two listeners, and then does... seemingly nothing) and wondering why it doesn't just exit before the loading is done, recall in Chapter 3, "Asynchronous Programming," I said that Node runs in an event loop waiting for things to happen and executing code when something finally does happen.

Well, part of this is knowing when events are *pending* or going to happen, such as the case in which you have a read stream open and it actually has calls to the file system waiting to finish reading in content. As long as there is something that is expected to happen, Node does not exit until all those events are finished and user code (if there is any) is executed.

The preceding example creates a new read stream given a path with the `fs.createReadStream` function. It then simply reads itself and prints the contents to the output stream. When it gets a `readable` event, it calls the `read` method on the stream and gets back whatever data is currently available. If no data is returned, it just waits until another `readable` event comes in or an `end` event is received.

Manipulating Binary Data with Buffers

Thus far in your Node.js experience, you have been using strings, typically UTF-8 strings, to do your work. However, when working with streams and files, you actually work mostly with the `Buffer` class.

Buffers work more or less as you'd expect them to: they hold binary data that can be converted into other formats, used in operations to file writes, or broken apart and reassembled.

One critical point to remember about buffers is that the `length` property on the object does not return the size of the content, but that of the buffer itself! For example:

```
var b = new Buffer(10000);
var str = "我叫王马克";
b.write(str); // default is utf8, which is what we want
console.log( b.length ); // will print 10000 still!
```

Node.js does not keep track of what you have written to which place in the buffer, so you must keep track of these things yourself.

Sometimes a string does not have the same byte length as the number of characters—for example, the preceding string "我叫王马克". `Buffer.byteLength` returns the former:

```
console.log( str.length );              // prints 5
console.log( Buffer.byteLength(str) );  // prints 15
```

To convert a buffer to a string, you should use the `toString` method. You will almost always have it convert to UTF-8 strings:

```
console.log(buf.toString('utf8'));
```

To append one buffer to the end of another, you can use the `concat` method, as follows:

```
var b1 = new Buffer("My name is ");
var b2 = new Buffer("Marc");
var b3 = Buffer.concat([ b1, b2 ]);
console.log(b3.toString('utf8'));
```

Finally, you can "zero out" or otherwise fill in all the values in the buffer by using the `fill` method, such as `buf.fill("\0")`.

Serving Static Files in a Web Server with Buffers

For this next exercise, write a little web server that serves up static content (an HTML file) using Node buffers. You start with the `handle_incoming_request` function:

```
function handle_incoming_request(req, res) {
    if (req.method.toLowerCase() == 'get'
        && req.url.substring(0, 9) == '/content/') {
        serve_static_file(req.url.substring(1), res);
```

```
    } else {
        res.writeHead(404, { "Content-Type" : "application/json" });

        var out = { error: "not_found",
                    message: "'" + req.url + "' not found" };
        res.end(JSON.stringify(out) + "\n");
    }
}
```

If an incoming request requests */content/something.html*, you try to serve that up by calling the serve_static_file function. The design of the *http* module in Node.js is sufficiently clever that the ServerResponse object you get to each request on your server is itself actually a stream to which you can write your output! You do this writing by calling the write method on the Stream class:

```
function serve_static_file(file, res) {
    var rs = fs.createReadStream(file);
    var ct = content_type_for_path(file);
    res.writeHead(200, { "Content-Type" : ct });

    rs.on('readable', () => {
        var d = rs.read();
        if (d) {
            if (typeof d == 'string')
                res.write(d);
            else if (typeof d == 'object' && d instanceof Buffer)
                res.write(d.toString('utf8'));
        }
    });

    rs.on('end', () => {
        res.end();  // we're done!!!
    });
}


function content_type_for_path(file) {
    return "text/html";
}
```

The rest of the server's code is as you have seen before:

```
var http = require('http'),
    fs = require('fs');


var s = http.createServer(handle_incoming_request);
s.listen(8080);
```

Create a file called *test.html* in the *content/* folder with some simple HTML content in it; then run the server (assuming we saved the code we just wrote into *server.js*) with

```
node server.js
```

And then ask for that test.html file using `curl`:

```
curl -i -X GET http://localhost:8080/content/test.html
```

You should see output similar to the following (depending on what exactly you put in test.html):

```
HTTP/1.1 200 OK
Date: Mon, 26 Nov 2012 03:13:50 GMT
Connection: keep-alive
Transfer-Encoding: chunked

<html>
<head>
  <title> WooO! </title>
</head>
<body>
  <h1> Hello World! </h1>
</body>
</html>
```

You are now able to serve up static content!

There is a small problem you might have to deal with: what happens if the write stream cannot accept data as fast as you're sending it—perhaps the disk can't write that fast or the network is particularly slow? In these cases, the write method on the streaming object will return false. When you get this, you will need to pause your reading stream and listen for the drain event on the writing stream. Once you get this drain event, then you can resume on the read stream, as follows:

```
function serve_static_file(file, res) {
    var rs = fs.createReadStream(file);

    var ct = content_type_for_path(file);
    res.writeHead(200, { "Content-Type" : ct });

    rs.on('error', (e) => {
        res.writeHead(404, { "Content-Type" : "application/json" });
        var out = { error: "not_found",
                    message: "'" + file + "' not found" };
        res.end(JSON.stringify(out) + "\n");
    });

    rs.on('readable', () => {
        var data = rs.read();
        if (!res.write(data)) {
            rs.pause();
        }
    });
```

```
        res.on('drain', () => {
            rs.resume();
        });

        rs.on('end', () => {
            res.end();  // we're done!!!
        });
    }
```

With that fixed, we still have two rather serious problems. First, what happens if you ask for */content/blargle.html*? In its current form, the script throws an error and terminates, which isn't what you want. In this case, you want to return a *404* HTTP response code and perhaps even an error message.

To do this, you can listen to the error event on read streams. Add the following few lines to the serve_static_file function:

```
rs.on('error', (e) => {
        res.writeHead(404, { "Content-Type" : "application/json" });
        var out = { error: "not_found",
                    message: "'" + file + "' not found" };
        res.end(JSON.stringify(out) + "\n");
        return;
    }
);
```

Now, when you get an error (after which no data or end events are called), you update the response header code to 404, set a new Content-Type, and return JSON with the error information that the client can use to report to the user what has happened.

Serving Up More Than Just HTML

The second problem is that you can currently serve up only HTML static content. The content_type_for_path function only ever returns "text/html". We want to be more flexible and serve up other types, which you can accomplish as follows:

```
function content_type_for_file (file) {
    var ext = path.extname(file);
    switch (ext.toLowerCase()) {
        case '.html': return "text/html";
        case ".js": return "text/javascript";
        case ".css": return 'text/css';
        case '.jpg': case '.jpeg': return 'image/jpeg';
        default: return 'text/plain';
    }
}
```

Now you can call the curl command with a number of different file types and should get the expected results. For binary files such as JPEG images, you can use the -o flag to curl to tell it to write the output to the specified filename. First, copy a JPEG to your *content/* folder, run the server with `node server.js`, and then add the following:

```
curl -o abc.jpg http://localhost:8080/content/test.jpg
```

Chances are, you now have a file called *abc.jpg* that is exactly what you expect it to be.

Shuffling data from stream (`rs` in the preceding example) to stream (`res`) is such a common scenario that the `Stream` class in Node.js has a convenience method to take care of all this for you: `pipe`. The `serve_static_file` function then becomes much simpler:

```
function serve_static_file(file, res) {
    var rs = fs.createReadStream(file);
    var ct = content_type_for_path(file);
    res.writeHead(200, { "Content-Type" : ct });

    rs.on('error', (e) => {
        res.writeHead(404, { "Content-Type" : "application/json" });
        var out = { error: "not_found",
                    message: "'" + file + "' not found" };
        res.end(JSON.stringify(out) + "\n");
        return;
    });

    rs.pipe(res);
}
```

Events

Streams are actually a subclass of the Node.js `Event` class, which provides all the functionality for connecting and emitting events in your JavaScript files. You can inherit from this class to create your own event-firing classes. For this example, create a dummy downloader class that simulates a remote download via a two-second `setTimeout` call:

```
var events = require('events');


function Downloader () {
}
Downloader.prototype = new events.EventEmitter();
Downloader.prototype.__proto__ = events.EventEmitter.prototype;
Downloader.prototype.url = null;
Downloader.prototype.download_url = function (path) {
    var self = this;
    self.url = path;
    self.emit('start', path);
```

```
        setTimeout(function () {
            self.emit('end', path);
        }, 2000);
    }


var d = new Downloader();
d.on("start", function (path) {
    console.log("started downloading: " + path);
});
d.on("end", function (path) {
    console.log("finished downloading: " + path);
});
d.download_url("http://marcwan.com");
```

You signal that an event has happened by using the emit method with the name of the event and any arguments you would like passed to the listening function. You should make sure that all possible code paths (including errors) signal an event; otherwise, your Node program might hang.

Assembling Content on the Client: Templates

In more traditional web application models, the client sends an HTTP request to the server, the server gathers all the data and generates the HTML response, and it sends that down as text. While this way of doing things is very reasonable, it has a few key disadvantages:

- It doesn't take advantage of any of the computing power available on the average client computer these days. Even the average mobile phone or tablet is many times more powerful than PCs of 10 years ago.

- It makes your life more difficult when you have multiple types of clients. Some people might access you through a web browser, others through mobile apps, even others through desktop applications or third-party apps.

- It's frustrating to have to perform so many different types of things on the server. It would be great if you could have your server focus just on processing, storing, and generating data, letting the client decide how to present the data.

An increasingly common way of doing things, and something I've found particularly compelling and fun with Node, is to convert the server back end to serve only JSON, or as absolutely little of anything else as possible. The client app can then choose how to present the returned data to the user. Scripts, style sheets, and even most HTML can be served from file servers or content delivery networks (CDNs).

For web browser applications, you can use *client-side templates* (see Figure 6.1). In this way of doing things,

1. The client downloads a skeleton HTML page with pointers to JavaScript files, CSS files, and an empty `body` element from the Node server.

2. One of the referenced JavaScript files is a *bootstrapper* that does all the work of gathering everything and putting the page together. It is given the name of an HTML template and a server JSON API to call. It downloads the template and then applies the returned JSON data to that template file using a *template engine*. You will use a template engine called "Mustache" (see the sidebar "Template Engines").

3. The resulting HTML code is inserted into the body of the page, and all the server has to do is serve up a little bit of JSON.

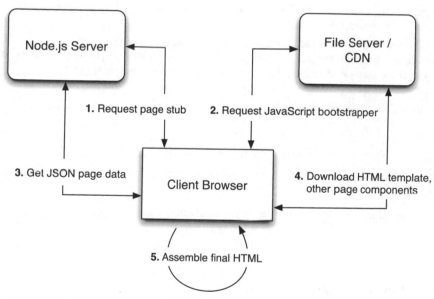

Figure 6.1   Client-side page generation with templates

It has been in preparation for this that you have been developing the photo album application as a JSON-only server thus far. Although you will add the capability now for it to serve up static files, this is largely for convenience and educational purposes; in a production environment, you would probably move these files to a CDN and update the URLs to point to them as appropriate.

Template Engines

A large number of client-side (and even server-side) template engines or libraries are available. For the jQuery JavaScript library that you're using most often in this book, there are a few, such as JSRender or jQote, both of which are just fine. There are others that don't necessarily have to fit in with your chosen JavaScript helper library as well.

For your purposes here, *they're all about the same.* The feature sets all tend to be roughly equal, with similar ways of doing things and reasonably similar performance. When you are choosing a library, I recommend just picking one that is actively being developed and/or maintained and that seems to have a reasonable syntax that you find comfortable.

For this book and many of my recent projects, I am using a template engine called *Mustache*. As I just said, this decision is semi-arbitrary but was helped by mustache.js:

- Being a reasonably small and fast JavaScript library.
- Being a feature-complete templating solution.
- Having a pretty cool name. Tags in Mustache are delimited by {{ and }}, which many feel look like mustaches.

This solution is by no means perfect, but I suspect you'll find Mustache has the right trade-offs between features and speed for you, too. You are always encouraged to explore other solutions and read one of the dozens of blog posts and tutorials for all the other packages.

To convert your photo album to this new world of templates, you need to do the following:

1. Generate the HTML skeleton for your pages.
2. Add support to the app for serving static file content.
3. Modify the list of supported URLs to add /pages/ and /templates/ for HTML pages and templates, respectively.
4. Write the templates and JavaScript files that load them.

Let's go!

The HTML Skeleton Page

Although you might attempt to do all HTML generation on the client, you cannot completely avoid the server doing any at all; you still need the server to send down the initial page skeleton that the client can use to perform the rest of the generation.

For this example, you use a reasonably simple HTML page, which is saved as *basic.html*, shown in Listing 6.1.

Listing 6.1   **The Simple App Page Bootstrapper (basic.html)**

```html
<!DOCTYPE html>
<html>
<head>
  <title>Photo Album</title>

  <!-- Meta -->
  <meta http-equiv="content-type" content="text/html; charset=utf-8" />

  <!-- Stylesheets -->
  <link rel="stylesheet" href="http://localhost:8080/content/style.css"
        type="text/css" />

  <!-- javascripts -->
  <script src="http://localhost:8080/content/jquery-1.8.3.min.js"
          type="text/javascript"></script>
  <script src="http://localhost:8080/content/mustache.js"
          type="text/javascript"></script>
  <script src="http://localhost:8080/content/{{PAGE_NAME}}.js"
          type="text/javascript"></script>
</head>
<body></body>

</html>
```

This file is straightforward; it has a style sheet, and then you include jQuery and Mustache. The last `script` tag is the most interesting: this file is the page *bootstrapper* that holds the code that will download the template, get the JSON data from the server for the page, and generate the HTML for the page based on these two things. You can see that it is set up with a parameter `{{PAGE_NAME}}` to replace with the actual page you will be loading at any given time. (Note that the {{ and }} mustache characters here indicate a variable that will be replaced on the server, not via *mustache.js* on the client—we just chose them since they're familiar).)

Serving Static Content

Now you are going to modify the application server's folder layout a little bit as follows:

```
+ project_root/
    + contents/     # JS, CSS, and HTML files
    + templates/    # client-side HTML templates
    + albums/       # the albums we've seen already
```

You've seen the *albums/* folder before, but now you are going to add the *contents/* and *templates/* folders to handle additional content you're going to add.

The updated `handle_incoming_request` function looks something like the following. The `serve_static_file` function is identical to the one you just wrote in the preceding section.

```
function handle_incoming_request(req, res) {
    // parse the query params into an object and get the path
    // without them. (true for 2nd param means parse the params).
    req.parsed_url = url.parse(req.url, true);
    var core_url = req.parsed_url.pathname;

    // test this updated url to see what they're asking for
    if (core_url.substring(0, 9) == '/content/') {
        serve_static_file(core_url.substring(1), res);
    } else if (core_url == '/albums.json') {
        handle_list_albums(req, res);
    } else if (core_url.substr(0, 7) == '/albums'
              && core_url.substr(core_url.length - 5) == '.json') {
        handle_get_album(req, res);
    } else {
        send_failure(res, 404, invalid_resource());
    }
}
```

For example, in the *content/* folder, you start with three files:

- **jquery-1.8.3.min.js**—You can download this file directly from jquery.com. Most versions of jQuery from the past couple of years should work just fine.

- **mustache.js**—You can download this file from a number of places. In this case, simply use the generic mustache.js from github.com/janl/mustache.js. There are also some server-side versions of mustache as well, which are not what we want for this chapter.

- **style.css**—You can just create this as an empty file or start to fill in CSS to modify the pages that you'll generate for the album app.

Modifying Your URL Scheme

The app server thus far supports only */albums.json* and */albums/*album_name.*json*. You can now add support for static content, pages and template files as follows:

```
/content/some_file.ext
/pages/some_page_name[/optional/junk]
/templates/some_file.html
```

For content and template files, there are actually real files to download directly from the hard disk. For page requests, however, you always return some variation on the *basic.html* you saw in the previous section. It has the {{PAGE_NAME}} macro replaced with the name of the page passed in through the URL; for example, /page/*home*.

The updated `handle_incoming_request` now looks as follows:

```
function handle_incoming_request(req, res) {
    // parse the query params into an object and get the path
    // without them. (true for 2nd param means parse the params).
    req.parsed_url = url.parse(req.url, true);
    var core_url = req.parsed_url.pathname;

    // test this fixed url to see what they're asking for
    if (core_url.substring(0, 7) == '/pages/') {
        serve_page(req, res);
    } else if (core_url.substring(0, 11) == '/templates/') {
        serve_static_file("templates/" + core_url.substring(11), res);
    } else if (core_url.substring(0, 9) == '/content/') {
        serve_static_file("content/" + core_url.substring(9), res);
    } else if (core_url == '/albums.json') {
        handle_list_albums(req, res);
    } else if (core_url.substr(0, 7) == '/albums'
                && core_url.substr(core_url.length - 5) == '.json') {
        handle_get_album(req, res);
    } else {
        send_failure(res, 404, invalid_resource());
    }
}
```

The `serve_page` function actually determines what page the client has asked for, fixes up the basic.html template file, and sends the resulting HTML skeleton down to the browser:

```
/**
 * All pages come from the same one skeleton HTML file that
 * just changes the name of the JavaScript loader that needs to be
 * downloaded.
 */
function serve_page(req, res) {
    var page = get_page_name(req);

    fs.readFile('basic.html', (err, contents) => {
        if (err) {
            send_failure(res, 500, err);
            return;
        }

        contents = contents.toString('utf8');

        // replace page name, and then dump to output.
        contents = contents.replace('{{PAGE_NAME}}', page);
        res.writeHead(200, { "Content-Type": "text/html" });
        res.end(contents);
    });
}
```

```
function get_page_name(req) {
    var core_url = req.parsed_url.pathname;
    var parts = core_url.split("/");
    return parts[2];
}
```

Instead of using `fs.createReadStream`, you use `fs.readFile`, which reads in the entire contents of a file to a `Buffer`. You have to convert this `Buffer` to a string, and then you can fix up the contents so the right JavaScript bootstrapper is indicated. This approach is not recommended for large files because it wastes a lot of memory, but for something as short as this *basic.html* file, it's perfectly fine and convenient!

The JavaScript Loader/Bootstrapper

The HTML pages are going to be quite simple, so you can start with a reasonably trivial JavaScript bootstrapper. As you add more functionality later in the book, you make it a bit more complicated, but Listing 6.2 shows the one you can start with now, which you save as home.js.

Listing 6.2   **The JavaScript Page Loader (home.js)**

```
$(function(){

    var tmpl,    // Main template HTML
    tdata = {};  // JSON data object that feeds the template

    // Initialize page
    var initPage = function() {

        // Load the HTML template
        $.get("/templates/home.html", function(d){          // 1
            tmpl = d;
        });

        // Retrieve the server data and then initialize the page
        $.getJSON("/albums.json", function (d) {            // 2
            $.extend(tdata, d.data);
        });

        // When AJAX calls are complete parse the template
        // replacing mustache tags with vars
        $(document).ajaxStop(function () {
            var renderedPage = Mustache.to_html(tmpl, tdata);  // 3
            $("body").html(renderedPage);
        })
    }();
});
```

The `$(function () { ...` syntax is basically the same as `$(document).ready(function ()` `...` in jQuery, just a bit shorter. So, this function is called after all the other resources (most notably jQuery and Mustache) are loaded. It then does the following three things:

1. It requests the template file, home.html, from the server by calling the URL */templates / home.html*.

2. It asks for the JSON data representing albums in the application, */albums.json*.

3. Finally, it gives these two things to Mustache to do its templating magic.

Templating with Mustache

The template engine I chose for the photo album app, Mustache, is easy to use, fast, and small. Most interestingly, it has only tags, wrapped in { { and } }, known as *mustaches*. It does not have any *if* statements or looping constructs. Tags act as a set of rules that play out depending on the data you provide.

The basic usage of Mustache, which you saw in the preceding sections, is

```
var html_text = Mustache.to_html(template, data);
$("body").html(html text);
```

To print properties from an object, you use the following:

Mustache template:

```
The album "{{name}}" has {{photos.length}} photos.
```

JSON:

```
{
  "name": "Italy2012",
  "photos" : [ "italy01.jpg", "italy02.jpg" ]
}
```

Output:

```
The album "Italy2012" has 2 photos.
```

To apply a template over every item in a collection or array, you use the # character. For example:

Mustache:

```
{#albums}}
   * {{name}}
{{/albums}}
```

JSON:

```
{
  "albums" : [ { "name" : "italy2012" },
               { "name" : "australia2010" },
               { "name" : "japan2010" }]
}
```

Output:

```
* italy2012
* australia2010
* japan2010
```

If you do not have any matching results, nothing is printed. You can capture this case by adding the ^ character:

Mustache:

```
{{#albums}}
    * {{name}}
{{/albums}}
{{^albums}}
    Sorry, there are no albums yet.
{{/albums}}
```

JSON:

```
{ "albums" : [ ]  }
```

Output:

```
Sorry, there are no albums yet.
```

If the object after the # character isn't a collection or array but just an object, the values from it are used without iterating:

Mustache:

```
{{#album}}
  The album "{{name}}" has {{photos.length}} photos.
{{/album}}
```

JSON:

```
{
  "album": {  "name": "Italy2012",
              "photos" : [ "italy01.jpg", "italy02.jpg" ] }
}
```

Output:

```
The album "Italy2012" has 2 photos.
```

By default, all values are HTML escaped; that is, < and > are replaced with < and > respectively, and so on. To tell Mustache not to do this, use the extra hairy Mustache triple brackets, {{{ and }}}:

Mustache:

```
{{#users}}
    * {{name}} says {{{ saying }}}
      * raw saying: {{ saying }}
{{/users}}
```

JSON:

```
{
  "users" : [ { "name" : "Marc", "saying" : "I like <em>cats</em>!" },
              { "name" : "Bob", "saying" : "I <b>hate</b> cats" },
}
```

Output:

```
  * Marc says I like <em>cats</em>!
    * raw saying: I like &lt;em&gt;cats&lt;/em&gt;!
  * Bob says I <b>hate</b> cats
    * raw saying: I  &lt;b&gt;hate&lt;/b&gt; cats
```

Your Home Page Mustache Template

Now, it's time to write your first template for your home page, which you can save in *home. html*, shown in Listing 6.3.

Listing 6.3   **The Home Page Template File (home.html)**

```
<div id="album_list">
  <p> There are {{ albums.length }} albums</p>
  <ul id="albums">
    {{#albums}}
      <li class="album">
        <a href='http://localhost:8080/pages/album/{{name}}'>{{name}}</a>
      </li>
    {{/albums}}
    {{^albums}}
      <li> Sorry, there are currently no albums </li>
    {{/albums}}
  </ul>
</div>
```

If you have any albums, this code iterates over each of them and provides an `<li>` element with the name of the album and a link to the album page, accessed via the URL */page/album/* album_name. When there are no albums, a simple message is printed instead.

Putting It All Together

I threw a lot of new stuff at you in the preceding sections, so stop now and make this all run. You should now have the following file layout for your web application:

```
+ project_root/
    package.json                   // We need async 2.x
    server.js                      // GitHub source
    basic.html                     // Listing 6.1
```

```
+ content/
    home.js                                // Listing 6.2
    album.js                               // Listing 6.5
    jquery-1.8.3.min.js
    mustache.js
    style.css
  + templates/
    home.html                              // Listing 6.3
    album.html                             // Listing 6.4
+ albums/
      + whatever albums you want
```

The code for *home.html* and *album.html*, which we have not previously seen, can be found in Listings 6.4 and 6.5.

To run this project, you should be able to type

```
node server.js
```

You can then switch to a web browser and browse to *http://localhost:8080/page/home*. If you want to see what happens on the command line, try using `curl` as follows:

```
curl -i -X GET http://localhost:8080/page/home
```

Because `curl` executes no client-side JavaScript for you, the template and JSON date are not loaded via Ajax, and you get only the basic HTML skeleton from basic.html.

Listing 6.4 **Another Mustache Template Page (album.html)**

```
<div id="album_page">
  {{#photos}}
  <p> There are {{ photos.length }} photos in this album</p>
  <div id="photos">
      <div class="photo">
        <div class='photo_holder'>
          <img style='width: 250px; height: 250px; background-color: #fbb'
              src="{{url}}" border="0"/></div>
          <div class='photo_desc'><p>{{ desc }}</p></div>
      </div>
  </div> <!-- #photos -->
  <div style="clear: left"></div>
  {{/photos}}
  {{^photos}}
      <p> This album doesn't have any photos in it, sorry.<p>
  {{/photos}}
</div> <!-- #album_page -->
```

Listing 6.5 Our Album Page Bootstrapper JavaScript File (album.js)

```javascript
$(function(){

    var tmpl,    // Main template HTML
    tdata = {};  // JSON data object that feeds the template

    // Initialize page
    var initPage = function() {

        // get our album name.
        parts = window.location.href.split("/");
        var album_name = parts[5];

        // Load the HTML template
        $.get("/templates/album.html", function(d){
            tmpl = d;
        });

        // Retrieve the server data and then initialize the page
        $.getJSON("/albums/" + album_name + ".json", function (d) {
            var photo_d = massage_album(d);
            $.extend(tdata, photo_d);
        });

        // When AJAX calls are complete parse the template
        // replacing mustache tags with vars
        $(document).ajaxStop(function () {
            var renderedPage = Mustache.to_html( tmpl, tdata );
            $("body").html( renderedPage );
        })
    }();
});

function massage_album(d) {
    if (d.error != null) return d;
    var obj = { photos: [] };

    var af = d.data.album_data;

    for (var i = 0; i < af.photos.length; i++) {
        var url = "/albums/" + af.short_name + "/" + af.photos[i].filename;
        obj.photos.push({ url: url, desc: af.photos[i].filename });
    }
    return obj;
}
```

If you've done everything correctly, you should see output something similar to that shown in Figure 6.2. It's not pretty, but now you can start to play around with the template file and the style.css file to really make the application yours!

Figure 6.2   The template-enabled JSON application running in the browser

Summary

This chapter introduced two key Node.js features, streams and events, that you used to serve up static content from your web application. Equally importantly, this chapter introduced client-side template engines, and you used Mustache to put together a simple start to a front end for your photo album application.

You might have noticed, however, that some of the things you have been doing thus far seem unnecessarily complicated, tedious, or possibly even worryingly bug-prone (the handle_ incoming_request function in particular). It would be nice if there were some further modules to help you keep track of things more easily.

It is thus that you are not going to develop the photo album much further in its current form but continue to look at some modules that will clean up your code significantly and allow you to add features quickly and with little code. You will do so using the *Express Application Framework for Node*.

Part III

Writing Web Applications

7

Building Web Applications with Express

Thus far, you have been learning the fundamentals and core concepts of Node.js; armed with these ideas, you have built some simple applications, although you've had to write a lot of code to do some reasonably basic things. It's time to change gears a bit and start building more interesting web applications, using one of the biggest strengths of Node: the huge collection of libraries and modules available to you through npm. Now that you understand the core workings of Node and modules, it's time to start finding ways to make your life significantly easier and your development much faster.

In this chapter, you start working with *express*, a web application framework for Node. It takes care of many of the basic tasks you learned about in previous chapters and even exposes some powerful new functionality that you can take advantage of in your apps. I show you how to build apps with express and update your photo album app to use it. Then you look a bit more at application design, learn how to expose the API from your JSON server, and explore some new functionality you haven't seen before.

Installing Express

In this chapter, you are going to slowly change the way you install applications via npm. You might expect that, to install express, you'd just type

```
npm install express
```

and this would work just fine. However, it always installs the latest version of the express node module, which you might not want when you're deploying your application to live production servers. When you develop and test against a particular version, it's good to have that same version run on the live servers. Only after you update to a newer version and fully test against that version do you want to use it on the live servers.

So, the basic methodology for building Node applications is now as follows:

1. Create an application folder.

2. Write a *package.json* file describing the package and stating which npm modules are needed.

3. Run npm install to make sure these modules are installed properly.

So, create a new folder called *trivial_express/* for your express test application and then put the following into *package.json* in that folder:

```
{
  "name": "Express-Demo",
  "description": "Demonstrates Using Express and Connect",
  "version": "0.0.1",
  "private": true,
  "dependencies": {
    "express": "4.x"
  }
}
```

The name and description fields are reasonably self-explanatory, and the app is just a toy right now, so it has an appropriate version number. As you saw in Chapter 5, "Modules," you can set private to true, which tells npm never to try installing it in the live npm registry because it is just a test project for your own use.

After creating the file, you can run the following to read in the dependencies section and install all the appropriate modules:

```
npm install
```

Because express itself depends on many different modules, you see a decent amount of output before it exits, but then your *node_modules/* folder should be ready to go. If you ever make a change to your *package.json*, you can just run npm update to make sure all the modules are correctly installed.

Hello World in Express

Recall from Chapter 1, "Getting Started," that your first web server in Node.js was roughly like the following:

```
var http = require("http");

function process_request(req, res) {
    res.end("Hello World");
}

var s = http.createServer(process_request);
s.listen(8080);
```

Well, in express, it looks quite similar:

```
var express = require('express');
var app = express();

app.get('/', function(req, res){
  res.end('hello world');
});


app.listen(8080);
```

Save that, run it, and then either run `curl localhost:8080` or enter *localhost:8080* in the web browser, and you should get the `hello world` output you expect. One of the great things about express is that it *is built on top of everything you have seen so far*, so the HTTP request and response objects have the same methods and properties they had before. To be certain, they have many new things added that make them more interesting and powerful, but you are not operating in a completely new world here—just an extended version of the one with which you are already familiar and comfortable!

Routing and Layers in Express

Express implements a system known as *middleware* that provides a collection of common functions that network applications might need. While previous versions of Express used a Node module called *connect* to implement this, versions starting with 4.0 no longer do so—it is now built in to Express.

At the heart of this middleware model is the concept of a flow of functions, or what some people like to describe as a *layered* set of functions.

Middleware: What's in a Name?

When you run into the term *middleware* for the first time, you can be forgiven for being worried that you've missed out on some key new concept or technology shift. Fortunately, it's nothing so complicated.

Effectively, middleware originally was used to describe software components (typically on the server side of things) that connected two things together, such as a business logic layer and a database server, or storage services with application modules, and so on.

Over time, however, the term seems to have become more generic and broad and now seems to cover any piece of software that connects two things together in some way, shape, or form.

For the purposes of this book, the middleware exposed by *connect* that you see in *express* is basically just a collection of modules that allow your web apps to seamlessly integrate functionality from either the server or browser.

You set up your application by creating a sequence of functions (layers) through which express navigates. When one decides that it wants to take over, it can complete the processing and stop the sequence. Express then walks back up through the sequence to the end (some layers do their process "on the way in"; others "on the way out").

So, in the preceding express application, there is only one layer in the sequence:

```
app.get('/', function(req, res){ });
```

This function, which is a helper provided by express, processes the incoming request (by calling the provided function) if the following are both true:

- The HTTP request method is GET.

- The requested URL is /.

If the incoming request does not match these criteria, the function is not called. If no function matches the requested URL—for example, browse or curl to /some/other/url—express just gives a default response:

```
Cannot GET /some/other/url
```

Routing Basics

The general format of the URL routing functions is as follows:

```
app.method(url_pattern, optional_functions, request_handler_function);
```

The preceding route handler is for handling GET requests for the URL /. To support handling a POST request on a particular URL, you can use the post method on the express application object:

```
app.post("/forms/update_user_info.json", function (req, res) { ... });
```

Similarly, express supports DELETE and PUT methods, both of which you use in the photo-sharing application, via the delete and put methods, respectively. Alternately, you can use the all method to indicate that the routing function should accept the given URL with any given HTTP method.

```
app.all("/users/marcwan.json", function (req, res) { ... });
```

The first parameter to the routing function is a regular expression to match an incoming request URL. It can be simple as follows:

```
/path/to/resources
```

Or it can contain regular expression features, such as

```
/user(s)?/list
```

which matches both /users/list and /user/list, while

```
/users/*
```

matches anything starting with /users/.

One of the most powerful features of routing is the ability to use *placeholders* to extract named values from the requested route, marked by the colon (:) character. When the route is parsed, express puts the matched placeholders on the `req.params` object for you. For example:

```
app.get("/albums/:album_name.json", function (req, res) {
    res.end("Requested " + req.params.album_name);
});
```

If you call the preceding app requesting */albums/italy2012.json*, you get the following output:

```
Requested italy2012.
```

You can put multiple parameters in the same URL as well:

```
app.get("/albums/:album_name/photos/:photo_id.json", function (req, res) { ... );
```

If your function is called, `req.params` has both `album_name` and `photo_id` set with the appropriate incoming values. Placeholders match any sequence of characters except for forward slashes.

The function you provide to the routing method is given the request and response object, as you have seen. However, it is also given a third parameter, which you are free to use or ignore. It is usually labeled `next` (the flow of the layered functions is always continued through functions called `next`), and gives you the opportunity to do some additional examinations on the incoming URL and still choose to ignore it, as follows:

```
app.get("/users/:userid.json", function (req, res, next) {
    var uid = parseInt(req.params.userid);
    if (uid < 2000000000) {
        next();                  // don't want it. Let somebody else process it.
    } else {
        res.end(get_user_info(uid));
    }
});
```

Updating Your Photo Album App for Routing

The photo album app is quite easy to adapt to express. You have to do only a few things to get it working:

- Create a *package.json* and install *express*.
- Replace the http module's server with that of *express*.
- Replace the `handle_incoming_request` function with routing handlers.
- Update the way you get query parameters in *express* (they are placed on `req.query` for your convenience).

Now copy the last version of the photo app you created at the end of Chapter 6, "Expanding Your Web Server," to a new folder (you can call it basic_routing/) and place the following *package.json* inside:

```json
{
  "name": "Photo-Sharing",
  "description": "Our Photo Sharing Application",
  "version": "0.0.2",
  "private": true,
  "dependencies": {
    "async": "2.x",
    "express": "4.x"
  }
}
```

You can run `npm install` to make sure express and async are installed to *node_modules/*. You can then change the top of the *server.js* file to use express instead of the http module:

```js
var express = require('express');
var app = express();

var path = require("path"),
    async = require('async');
    fs = require('fs');
```

And you change

```js
http.listen(8080);
```

to

```js
app.listen(8080);
```

Next, you have to replace the `handle_incoming_request` function, which looks as follows:

```js
function handle_incoming_request(req, res) {
    req.parsed_url = url.parse(req.url, true);
    var core_url = req.parsed_url.pathname;

    // test this fixed url to see what they're asking for
    if (core_url.substring(0, 7) == '/pages/') {
        serve_page(req, res);
    } else if (core_url.substring(0, 11) == '/templates/') {
        serve_static_file("templates/" + core_url.substring(11), res);
    } else if (core_url.substring(0, 9) == '/content/') {
        serve_static_file("content/" + core_url.substring(9), res);
    } else if (core_url == '/albums.json') {
        handle_list_albums(req, res);
    } else if (core_url.substr(0, 7) == '/albums'
            && core_url.substr(core_url.length - 5) == '.json') {
        handle_get_album(req, res);
```

```
    } else {
        send_failure(res, 404, invalid_resource());
    }
}
```

You replace it with these routing functions:

```
app.get('/albums.json', handle_list_albums);
app.get('/albums/:album_name.json', handle_get_album);
app.get('/content/:filename', function (req, res) {
    serve_static_file('content/' + req.params.filename, res);
});
app.get('/templates/:template_name', function (req, res) {
    serve_static_file("templates/" + req.params.template_name, res);
});
app.get('/pages/:page_name', serve_page);
app.get('*', four_oh_four);

function four_oh_four(req, res) {
    send_failure(res, 404, invalid_resource());
}
```

Not only do the routing functions seem much cleaner and simpler than the previous function you had, but it is much easier to see the URLs that will be matched and how the app will function. You added a new route matching "*" so that all other requests will be given a 404 response.

There is one problem with the routing functions right now, however. What happens if the user asks for */pages/album/italy2012*? Currently, the app will fail: the regular expression matching for parameters never includes forward slash (/) characters, so the route /pages/:page_name does not match. To solve this problem, you must add the extra route:

```
app.get('/pages/:page_name/:sub_page', serve_page);
```

Now all the pages will route to the correct function, and you have also set yourself up to quickly identify the subpage being requested.

One of the nice things about the app now is that you no longer need to parse the incoming requests or parameters; express does all this for you. So, whereas before you had to include the *url* module to parse the incoming URL, it's now ready for you right when you get to the routing functions. Similarly, you never need to parse GET query parameters because they are also prepared for you in advance. So you can update the small helper functions as follows:

```
function get_album_name(req) {
    return req.params.album_name;
}
function get_template_name(req) {
    return req.params.template_name;
}
```

```
function get_query_params(req) {
    return req.query;
}
function get_page_name(req) {
    return req.params.page_name;
}
```

With those changes, the photo-sharing app should be updated and ready to go with express. It should behave exactly like the old one.

REST API Design and Modules

When you are designing JSON servers such as the one you are writing, it is important to spend some time thinking about the API and how clients will use it. Spending some time up front to design a good API helps you to think about how people will use the application and also helps you organize and refactor the code to reflect this conceptual understanding.

API Design

For the photo-sharing JSON server, you are developing what's called a RESTful JSON server. The word REST comes from *Representational State Transfer*, and basically implies that you can request an accurate representation of an object from the server. REST APIs focus on four core operations (which, coincidentally, map to four HTTP request methods):

- Creation (PUT)
- Retrieval (GET)
- Updating (POST)
- Destruction (DELETE)

Some people refer to these operations as *CRUD*, and pretty much everything you do in your API centers around doing one of these things to objects, whether they are albums, photos, comments, or users. Although it is not possible to design the perfect API, I will do my absolute best to help you design one that is at least extremely intuitive and doesn't leave the client authors scratching their heads as to what you intended. Here are some principles to follow when designing RESTful interfaces:

- There are two basic kinds of URLs. Most URLs you design will be a variation on these two:
    1. Collections—for example, /albums.
    2. Specific items within these collections—for example, /albums/italy2012.
- Collections should be nouns, specifically plural nouns, such as *albums*, *users*, or *photos*.
    - PUT /albums.json—The HTTP request body contains the JSON with the data for the new album.

- You fetch or update an object by specifying the specific instance on the collection with GET or POST, respectively:

    - GET /albums/italy2012.json—The request returns this album.

    - POST /albums/italy2012.json—The HTTP request body contains the JSON with the new data for this album.

- You destroy objects with DELETE.

    - DELETE /albums/italy2012.json–Destroys this album.

- If you have collections off collections, for example, photos associated with albums, you just continue the pattern:

    - GET /albums/italy2012/photos.json—Returns all the photos in this album.

    - PUT /albums/italy2012/photos.json–Adds a new photo to this collection.

    - GET /albums/italy2012/photos/23482938424.json—Fetches the photo with the given ID.

- Slight changes to the way in which you get data from these collections, such as pagination or filtering, should all be done via GET query parameters:

    - GET /albums.json?located_in=Europe—Fetches only those albums in Europe.

    - GET /albums/japan2010/photos.json?page=1&page_size=25—Fetches the given page of 25 photos for the japan2010 album.

- You assign a version number to the API so that if you want to make major changes to it in future versions that would not be compatible, you can simply update the version number. You prefix the API URLs with */v1/* for this first version.

- Finally, you suffix all your URLs that return JSON with *.json* so that clients know what data will be in the responses. In the future, you could also add support for *.xml* or whatever other formats you want.

With this in mind, the new API for the photo-sharing application centers around albums. It looks as follows:

```
/v1/albums.json
/v1/albums/:album_name.json

/pages/:page_name
/templates/:template_name
/content/:filename
```

Why don't you put version numbers on the static content URLs? Because they're not part of the JSON server interface, but more helpers to provide the contents for the web browser client. Users always get the latest version of this and thus get code that knows how to use the correct version of the API.

It should be trivial for you to update the server.js file with this API design change. Don't forget to also update the bootstrapping JavaScript files in /content/ with the new URLs as well! Give that a try before continuing onward.

Modules

With the APIs updated around the new REST interface, you can take advantage of some of the clarity you have given to the application. You now have clear functionality boundaries around albums and pages, so you can put those areas of functionality into their own modules.

Create a subfolder of the application folder called *handlers/* and put the new modules in there. For albums, create a file in that folder called albums.js and move the four album manipulation functions into that file. You can view the source for this project on GitHub under the folder named *handlers_as_modules/*. Effectively, all you are doing is taking the code for the functions `handle_get_album` and `handle_list_albums` and putting them, along with their accompanying helper functions `load_album` and `load_album_list`, into the new module. Take a look at this for a minute and see how easy it is to reorganize the code quickly.

Recall that the *server.js* file has a few functions to help you extract album names and query parameters and the like. You can get rid of them and just put the appropriate member references for `req.params` and `req.query` in the right place.

There are also a few functions to help you simplify sending success and error codes, such as `send_success`, `send_failure`, and `invalid_resource`. You can put them into their own module called helpers.js in the *handlers/* directory. You refer to this at the top of the albums.js file, and the contents are shown in Listing 7.1.

Listing 7.1 **Helper Functions (helpers.js)**

```
exports.version = '0.1.0';

exports.make_error = function(err, msg) {
    var e = new Error(msg);
    e.code = err;
    return e;
}

exports.send_success = function(res, data) {
    res.writeHead(200, {"Content-Type": "application/json"});
    var output = { error: null, data: data };
    res.end(JSON.stringify(output) + "\n");
}

exports.send_failure = function(res, server_code, err) {
    var code = (err.code) ? err.code : err.name;
    res.writeHead(server_code, { "Content-Type" : "application/json" });
    res.end(JSON.stringify({ error: code, message: err.message }) + "\n");
}
```

```
exports.invalid_resource = function() {
    return make_error("invalid_resource",
                      "the requested resource does not exist.");
}

exports.no_such_album = function() {
    return make_error("no_such_album",
                      "The specified album does not exist");
}
```

Now, when you want to refer to the album functions, you add the following `require` to the top of *server.js*:

```
var album_hdlr = require('./handlers/albums.js');
```

And then you can update the routing handlers for the album functions to be as follows:

```
app.get('/v1/albums.json', album_hdlr.list_all);
app.get('/v1/albums/:album_name.json', album_hdlr.album_by_name);
```

Similarly, you can move the functionality to build pages into the *handlers/* directory in a file called *pages.js*, as in Listing 7.2. This task really only involves moving the `serve_page` function.

Listing 7.2   **Building Pages (pages.js)**

```
var helpers = require('./helpers.js'),
    fs = require('fs');

exports.version = "0.1.0";

exports.generate = function (req, res) {
    var page = req.params.page_name;

    fs.readFile(
        'basic.html',
        function (err, contents) {
            if (err) {
                send_failure(res, 500, err);
                return;
            }

            contents = contents.toString('utf8');

            // replace page name, and then dump to output.
            contents = contents.replace('{{PAGE_NAME}}', page);
            res.writeHead(200, { "Content-Type": "text/html" });
            res.end(contents);
        }
    );
};
```

You can then update the routing handler for pages, as follows:

```
var page_hdlr = require('./handlers/pages.js');
app.get('/v1/pages/:page_name', page_hdlr.generate);
```

After all is said and done, the server.js file has left only the functions for serving static content, which you can view in the GitHub source for Chapter 7 in the *handlers_as_modules/* project folder.

The application should have the same functionality as before but is now much more modularized and is easier to read and follow along. You now also have an idea of how you can add functionality to it as you proceed.

Additional Middleware Functionality

I've mentioned before that express implements what is called a middleware library. These components chain together and are given every incoming request one at a time until one of them decides to process it and ceases calling the provided next function. The routing handlers form part of this chain. Express used to come with quite a large number of other useful components built in, but most have been split out into separate npm modules now. Let's spend a while reviewing some of the more interesting ones that we'll make use of.

Usage

You use middleware components in express with the use method. For example, there is a great middleware package called *morgan* that will log all requests to your app in various configurable ways. To use it, you would write the following:

```
var express = require('express'),
    morgan = require('morgan');
var app = express();


app.use(morgan('dev'));
/* etc. ... */
```

To use this, we'd need to add

```
    "morgan": "1.x",
```

to the dependencies section of our *package.json* file. The morgan function that you call returns a function that will form part of the filter layering in your application.

Express comes with a few of components built in, but you are allowed to use any compatible middleware component. You can use any of those in the following manner, provided you've added it to the dependencies section of your *package.json* file:

```
var express = require('express');
var compression = require('compression');
var app = express();


app.use(compression());
/* etc. ... */
```

Or you can download third-party components from npm or somewhere else and install them directly:

```
var express = require('express');
var middle_something = require('middle_something');
var app = express();

app.use(middle_something());
/* etc. ... */
```

Configurations

Using some middleware only in certain configurations can be helpful. Some might modify your output for speed or size so that it can be difficult or annoying to use curl to test your server. To do this, you call the configure method on the express app, providing it with the name of the configuration you want to target and a function that will be called when that configuration is needed. If you don't provide a name, that function is called always, and you can provide multiple configuration names separated by a comma before you provide the function, as shown here:

```
app.configure(function () {
  app.use(bodyParser());
});

app.configure('dev', function () {
  app.use(morgan('dev'));
});
app.configure('production', 'staging', function () {
  app.use(morgan());
});
```

Middleware or routes that are set up outside configure function calls are considered applicable for all configurations.

To run your app with a particular configuration, set the NODE_ENV environment variable to the one you want. On most shells on your Mac or UNIX computer, you can run node as follows:

```
NODE_ENV=production node program.js
```

On Windows, you can, in the command prompt, just set the NODE_ENV and then run node:

```
set NODE_ENV=production
node program.js
```

Ordering of Middleware

The layering and order of these middleware components is important. As I mentioned, express and connect work through them one at a time until it finds one that decides it can handle the request. To see how this is relevant, consider the following simple app:

```
var express = require('express'),
    morgan = require('morgan');
var app = express();

app.use(express.logger('dev'))
    // move this to AFTER the next use() and see what happens!
    .use(express.responseTime())
    .use(function(req, res){
        res.end('hello world\n');
    })
    .listen(8080);
```

Call this app by using

```
curl -i localhost:8080/blargh
```

You should see the following:

```
HTTP/1.1 200 OK
X-Powered-By: Express
X-Response-Time: 0ms
Date: Wed, 05 Dec 2012 04:11:43 GMT
Connection: keep-alive
Transfer-Encoding: chunked
```

```
hello world
```

Now, watch what happens if you move the `responseTime` middleware component to the end, as follows:

```
var express = require('express');
var app = express();

app.use(express.logger('dev'))
    // move this to AFTER the next use() and see what happens!
    .use(function(req, res){
        res.end('hello world\n');
    })
    .use(express.responseTime())
    .listen(8080);
```

Notice that the `X-Response-Time` header is gone!

```
HTTP/1.1 200 OK
X-Powered-By: Express
Date: Wed, 05 Dec 2012 04:14:05 GMT
```

```
Connection: keep-alive
Transfer-Encoding: chunked
```

```
hello world
```

The function that prints "Hello World!" took the request and handled it fully by not calling `next` and by using `res.end` to close down the response, so the `responseTime` middleware never got a chance to inspect the request. As you're adding middleware components, think about how they're going to fit together for the various routes your app will be using.

Static File Handling

You have written a little bit of Node code to serve static files in your application, but it turns out that doing so is largely unnecessary. Express provides a static middleware component that can do all this work for you!

To use it, you just pass the name of the base folder whose contents you want to serve statically to the middleware creation function, as follows:

```
app.use(express.static("/secure/static_site_files"));
```

You put this before the URL routers, and when a request comes in, this static layer takes the URL, appends it to its base folder name, and looks to see whether that file exists. For example, if you request /content/style.css, this middleware looks to see whether */secure/static_site_files/ content/style.css* exists and is readable. If it is, the middleware serves that file and stops calling further layers. If not, it calls the `next` function.

If you want to serve static content from multiple locations, add multiple components:

```
app.use(express.static("/secure/core_site_content"));
app.use(express.static("/secure/templates_and_html"));
```

Note that while you technically can serve content from your application's folder by using the `__dirname` predefined variable in Node (it gives you the path to the currently executing Node script), *this is a terrible idea and you should never do it.*

The static middleware provides no security at all, so say you take the photo-sharing application from before and just add

```
app.use(express.static(__dirname));
```

You could then—as expected—browse for */content/style.css* and */templates/home.html* without any problems. The problem is that if the user asks for */server.js* or */handlers/albums.js*, the static middleware happily serves that as well because they both lie off the `__dirname` base folder.

You might ask why security has not been added to the *static* middleware component, but this is the wrong question—it's an unnecessary complication. If you want to use this component, put your static content outside your application source tree. Indeed, as I've hinted before, you might even choose to have your application avoid serving static content altogether and opt to put the static content on CDNs instead. So get used to separating those components out from your source tree right from the start.

If you rewrite the *server.js* file to use the static middleware, it looks something like the following. It does, require, however, that you move the *content/*, *templates/*, and *album/* folders to another location so that you can avoid the security problem I just mentioned. The updated app structure looks as follows:

```
+ root_folder/
  + static/
    + albums/
    + content/
    + templates/
  + app/
    + handlers/
    + node_modules/
```

Then the *server.js* file can look like that shown in Listing 7.3. One nice thing about this new version of the server is that you've managed to remove two routing functions—those for content and templates.

Listing 7.3   **Using the Static Middleware (server.js)**

```
var express = require('express');
var app = express();

var fs = require('fs'),
    album_hdlr = require('./handlers/albums.js'),
    page_hdlr = require('./handlers/pages.js'),
    helpers = require('./handlers/helpers.js');

app.use(express.static(__dirname + "/../static"));

app.get('/v1/albums.json', album_hdlr.list_all);
app.get('/v1/albums/:album_name.json', album_hdlr.album_by_name);
app.get('/pages/:page_name', page_hdlr.generate);
app.get('/pages/:page_name/:sub_page', page_hdlr.generate);

app.get("/", function (req, res) {
    res.redirect("/pages/home");
    res.end();
});

app.get('*', four_oh_four);

function four_oh_four(req, res) {
    res.writeHead(404, { "Content-Type" : "application/json" });
    res.end(JSON.stringify(helpers.invalid_resource()) + "\n");
}

app.listen(8080);
```

If you're paying attention, you might have noticed the new route added for / that reroutes you to */pages/home* using the `ServerResponse.redirect` method to save some typing in the web browser!

POST Data, Cookies, and Sessions

Express already provides you with some help with the query parameters by parsing them and placing them in `req.query`. Although you saw back in Chapter 4, "Writing Applications," that it's possible to load and parse form POST data yourself using streams, the good news is that you don't have to do this—middleware can do all this work for you. And you can even have it set up cookies and sessions for you. The middleware component modules to do this are *body-parser (1.x)*, *cookie-parser (1.x)*, and *express-session (1.x)*, respectively:

```
var bodyParser = require('body-parser'),
    cookieParser = require('cookie-parser');

// parse application/x-www-form-urlencoded
app.use(bodyParser.urlencoded({ extended: false }))
// parse application/json
app.use(bodyParser.json())
app.use(cookieParser());
```

For the `bodyParser`, you specify which formats you want to support, and then they are parsed and placed in `req.body` as an object. `cookieParser` does something similar, except it places the values in `req.cookies` instead and needs no configuration at all.

To set a cookie on the *outgoing* response, use the `cookie` function on the response object, with the name and value (and optional timeout values):

```
var express = require('express'),
    morgan = require('morgan');
    cookieParser = require('cookie-parser');

var app = express()
    .use(morgan('dev'))
    .use(cookieParser())
    .use(function(req, res){
        res.cookie("pet", "Zimbu the Monkey",
                    { expires: new Date(Date.now() + 86400000) });
        res.end(JSON.stringify(req.query) + "\n");
    })
    .listen(8080);
```

To clear a cookie you've set, just use the `clearCookie` method on the response object with the name of the cookie you'd like removed.

Setting up sessions is a bit more involved, requiring that you first provide a few variables to configure everything:

```
.use(session({ secret: "blargleipoajsdfoiajf",
               resave: false,
               saveUninitialized: true,
               cookie: { maxAge: 1800000 } }))
```

In this example, you set a secret key, and then tell the session middleware it's not necessary to force a resave if nothing has changed during a request. We also tell it to save the session data at the end of a request even if nothing has been set. Finally, we set an age for the session cookie (about three weeks here). If you want to expire them, provide the number of milliseconds of validity. Here, the code indicates you will not accept session cookies older than 30 minutes.

When you have the sessions ready to go, `req.session` is populated with the session data. To add new session data, you simply set a new value on this object. It is persisted and sent with the response:

```
var express = require('express'),
    morgan = require('morgan'),
    cookieParser = require('cookie-parser'),
    session = require('express-session');

var app = express()
    .use(morgan('dev'))
    .use(cookieParser())
    .use(session({ secret: "blargleipoajsdfoiajf",
                   resave: false,
                   saveUninitialized: true,
                   cookie: { maxAge: 1800000 } }))
    .use(function (req, res){
        var x = req.session.last_access;
        req.session.last_access = new Date();
        res.end("You last asked for this page at: " + x);
    })
    .listen(8080);
```

File Uploads

The *body-parser* middleware component lets you parse data sent along with POST requests. Combined with the *multer* middleware component (add version *1.x* to your *package.json*), you can additionally accept multipart bodies that include uploaded files and similar things. If you upload a file to your app using the *multipart/form-data* enctype, you see `req.file` or `req.files` contain any files sent with the request, depending on whether you told *multer* to expect a single file or multiple files (it can handle both!):

```
var express = require('express'),
    morgan = require('morgan'),
    multer = require('multer');                    // includes body-parser
```

```
var upload = multer({ dest: "ul/" });                              // 1

var app = express()
    .use(morgan('dev'));

app.post('/uptest', upload.single("album_cover"), function (req, res) {  // 2
    console.log("BODY: " + JSON.stringify(req.body, 0, 2));
    console.log("FILE: " + JSON.stringify(req.file, 0, 2));

    if (!req.file || req.file.fieldname != 'album_cover') {
        res.end("Hunh. Did you send a file?\n");
    } else {
        res.end("You have asked to set the album cover for "
                + req.body.albumid
                + " to '" + req.file.originalname + "'\n");
    }
});


app.listen(8080);
```

To test this, you can still use `curl`! It can upload files along with the request by combining the `--form` (`-F`)option (for form data) and the `@` operator with a filename, which tells it to send that file:

```
curl -i -H "Expect:" --form 'album_cover=@oranges.jpg' \
 --form albumid=italy2012 http://localhost:8080/uptest
```

There is one trick, however, and that is that `curl` sometimes expects the server to send the response `100 Continue` and then hang waiting. To get around this, you pass `-H "Expect:"` to `curl`, which lets you test file uploads normally.

In the example above, after we've initialized the *multer* module, we have to configure it, which you see in `// 1`. We create an object called `upload`, and indicate that we want all uploaded files to go in a folder called *ul/*. Of course, you should choose a path that is isolate and doesn't leave you open to a DoS attack (imagine if somebody just kept uploading files until your hard disk was full!).

Next we tell *multer* that we want to allow a single file upload with the field name `album_cover` with the POST request */uptest*. This will be placed in `req.file`. We could instead tell *multer* we wanted to accept multiple files by using `upload.array("field_name")` (expect an array of files all with the field `field_name`), or `upload.fields("field1", "field2", etc.)` (expect multiple files with the specified field names). For these, we would have `req.files` with a list of all files that were parsed from the incoming request.

Whenever you're using *multer* or just the *body-parser* middleware modules on its own, you'll have `req.body` parsed and ready for you to use in your code.

Better Browser Support for PUT and DELETE

PUT (object creation) and DELETE (object destruction) are critical parts of the REST APIs that you are using, and the client web pages send data to the server via these methods. For example, to say you want to delete a comment in jQuery, you use

```
$.ajax({
    url: 'http://server/v1/comments/234932598235.json',
    type: 'DELETE'
}
```

In most modern web browsers, this technique works just fine. However, in some older browsers (and in any Internet Explorer version before 10), it fails. The reason is that their implementation of XmlHttpRequest, the object via which AJAX requests are done, does not support PUT or DELETE as a method.

A common and elegant solution is to add a new header called X-HTTP-Method-Override to your output, with the method you really want to use, and then just use POST to post the request to the server. The jQuery code would then become

```
 $.ajax({
    beforeSend: function(xhr) {
        xhr.setRequestHeader('X-HTTP-Method-Override', 'DELETE');
    },
    url: 'http://server/v1/comments/234932598235.json',
    type: 'POST'
}
```

To support this solution on your server, you use the *method-override* middleware, as follows:

```
var methodOverride = require('method-override');    // add v2.x to package.json!
app.use(methodOverride());
```

It looks for this header and converts POST requests to DELETE or PUT as necessary. Thus, the app.delete and app.put routes work exactly as expected.

Compressing Output

To save on bandwidth costs and speed, many web servers compress output using gzip or some similar algorithm before sending it down to the client. This requires that the client first indicate that it is able to accept compressed output with the Accept-Encoding HTTP header. If this is provided and the server knows how, it adds the Content-Encoding header on output with the appropriate algorithm specified and then sends down the compressed data.

To use this feature in your app, you can use the *compression* middleware. It is truly a hassle-free component; it checks whether the client accepts compressed output via headers, sets the response headers, and compresses the output, as shown here:

```
var express = require('express'),
    compression = require('compression');
var app = express();
```

```
app.use(express.logger('dev'));
app.use(compression());

app.get('/', function(req, res){
    res.end('hello world this should be compressed\n');
});


app.listen(8080);
```

The only downside to this module is that it might interfere with some of your development testing (curl just prints the compressed binary data to the screen, which can be annoying), so it is common for you to use this only in a production configuration, as follows:

```
var express = require('express'),
    morgan = require('morgan'),
    compression = require('compression');
var app = express();

app.use(morgan('dev'));
app.configure('production', function () {
    app.use(compression());
});

app.get('/', function(req, res){
    res.end('hello world this may or may not be compressed\n');
});

app.listen(8080);
```

Adding Authentication to our Application

Pretty much every interesting application being written today requires authentication of some sort. Doing this from scratch on your own can be a hassle—not only do you have to write a lot of code, but it's also error prone and can lead to serious security holes.

Fortunately, there exists a module for Node.js that can handle a vast majority of this for us, called *passportjs.* or just *passport*.

In this section, we're going to create a simple application that supports authentication and shows off all the key parts of passport that we'll want to add to our applications.

Passport supports a huge variety of authentication schemes, ranging from storing usernames and passwords in your local application to authentication schemes used by Facebook, Twitter, and Google, as well as supporting generic OAuth 2.0 authentication.

Getting Started

Let's build an application that authenticates requests with passport by using local storage for usernames and passwords (we might put these in a database, for example). For the purposes of this sample, we'll just hardcode the acceptable combinations directly in our app.

To start, we'll need to include a number of modules in our package json as follows:

```
{
    "name": "authtest",
    "description": "Testing passport",
    "version": "0.0.1",
    "private": true,
    "dependencies": {
        "body-parser": "1.x",
        "cookie-parser": "1.x",
        "express": "4.x",
        "express-flash": "0.x",
        "express-session": "1.x",
        "passport" : "0.3.x",
        "passport-local": "1.x"
    }
}
```

We'll then include these in our *server.js* file:

```
var express = require('express'),
    cookieParser = require('cookie-parser'),
    session = require('express-session'),
    passport = require("passport"),
    LocalStrategy = require('passport-local').Strategy,
    bodyParser = require('body-parser'),
    flash = require('express-flash');
```

Passport itself is highly configurable, and the way you add support for additional authentication schemes is by adding modules! So, we'll include both *passport* and *passport-local* to give us all the functionality we need.

Let's enable all these modules in our *express* application:

```
var app = express();

var session_configuration = {
    secret: 'whoopity whoopity whoop whoop',
    resave: false,
    saveUninitialized: true,
    cookie: { secure: true }
};

session_configuration.cookie.secure = false;
```

```
app.use(flash());
app.use(session(session_configuration));
app.use(cookieParser('whoopity whoopity whoop whoop'));
app.use(passport.initialize());
app.use(passport.session());

// parse application/x-www-form-urlencoded
app.use(bodyParser.urlencoded({ extended: false }))

// parse application/json
app.use(bodyParser.json())
```

In the above example, we turn off secure cookies because they require us to use HTTPS, which is inconvenient for development. In a production environment, we would use `app.configure` to ensure the right options were set for production vs development.

Finally, we make sure we support the upload of forms using both the *urlencoded* form format (from FORM elements on HTTP pages) as well as JSON POST data from other sources.

Laying Down the Plumbing

Next, we need to set up our app to:

- Store usernames and passwords.
- Configure *passport-local* to validate an incoming username and password against our list of users.
- Serialize a user.
- Deserialize a user.

Most of these are intuitive, except for perhaps the last two: *passport* does not serialize our entire user object to the session storage—this is potentially insecure. Instead it asks us what value it should use to store a user to session data by calling `serializeUser`. Then, when a new page is loaded, it will pass that value to `deserializeUser`, where we can pass back the full user object.

The code for the above plumbing is as follows:

```
var users = {
    "id123456" :  { id: 123456, username: "marcwan", password: "boo" },
    "id1" : { id: 1, username: "admin", password: "admin" }
};


passport.use(new LocalStrategy(
    function (username, password, done) {
        for (userid in users) {
            var user = users[userid];
            if (user.username.toLowerCase() == username.toLowerCase()) {
```

```
                    if (user.password == password) {
                        return done(null, user);
                    }
                }
            }
            return done(null, false, { message: 'Incorrect credentials.' });
        }
));

passport.serializeUser(function (user, done) {
    if (users["id" + user.id]) {
        done(null, "id" + user.id);
    } else {
        done(new Error("CANT_SERIALIZE_INVALID_USER"));
    }
});

passport.deserializeUser(function (userid, done) {
    if (users[userid]) {
        done(null, users[userid]);
    } else {
        done(new Error("CANT_FIND_USER_TO_DESERIALIZE"));
    }
});
```

There should be no surprises in this code: our "storage" for users is just an array. We configure passport with `passport.use` and pass in the strategy we want to use. We're going to use a `LocalStrategy` object, to which we pass our authentication function, which simply authenticates a given username/password combination against our known array. Finally, when passport wants to serialize users, we tell it to save the `id#user.id` string, and then we can use that to deserialize a user later in an efficient manner.

Creating a Login Form

We can make our app show a login form by adding a route to the GET */login*, as follows:

```
app.get('/', function (req, res) {
    console.log(req.flash());
    res.end('<a href="/login">Login Here</a>');
});

app.get("/login", function (req, res) {
    var error = req.flash("error");
    var form = '<form action="/login" method="post">' +
        '    <div>' +
        '        <label>Username:</label>' +
```

```
'            <input type="text" name="username"/>' +
'        </div>' +
'        <div>' +
'            <label>Password:</label>' +
'            <input type="password" name="password"/>' +
'        </div>' +
'        <div>' +
'            <input type="submit" value="Log In"/>' +
'        </div>' +
'</form>';

    if (error && error.length) {
        form = "<b> " + error[0] + "</b><br/>" + form;
    }

    res.end(form);
});
```

You should be able to see that submitting this form will go to POST *login*. We'll talk about what exactly `req.flash` is for in a bit.

Logging the User In

Next, we'll implement the POST *login* method. This is where we get passport to do all the work for us, as follows:

```
app.post("/login",
        passport.authenticate('local', { successRedirect: '/members',
                                          failureRedirect: '/login',
                                          successFlash: { message: "welcome back" },
                                          failureFlash: true })
        );
```

Whenever we get a POST request to *login*, we'll tell passport to do the work. It'll use the local strategy, and we'll give it some instructions:

- If the authentication succeeds, send the user to the /members page.

- If the authentication fails, send the user back to the GET /login page.

- We'll set up flash messages (again, we'll talk about this in a bit).

Under the hood, passport will use all the functions we've provided thus far to validate the user form. (It assumes you're sending it `username` and `password` fields but can be configured to look for others.) It'll then send redirects back to the browser, telling it where to go when it's finished.

Restricting Access to a Page

Certain pages should not be accessible unless the user has logged in. To do this, we take advantage of middleware to add a function to first make sure the user can view the page, as follows:

```
app.get("/members", authenticatedOrNot, function (req, res) {
    res.end("secret members only area!");
});
```

Here, we add the `authenticateOrNot` function:

```
function authenticatedOrNot(req, res, next){
    if(req.isAuthenticated()){
        next();
    }else{
        res.redirect("/login");
    }
}
```

By calling `req.isAuthenticated`, we can ask passport if our session has gone through successful authentication or not. If so, we allow access to the page (by calling `next` and allowing the request to continue). If not, we stop processing and immediately redirect the user back to the GET */login* page.

And those are the basics of how to use passport authentication in our applications. It's extremely powerful and doesn't require too much plumbing to be useful.

Flash Messages

Sometimes, when you're writing an application, you want to show a message, but only once. Of course, we could write code to save the message somewhere to our session data, and then once we've accessed it, we delete it from said session data storage. It turns out that this is a sufficiently common thing, however, that it's been put into its own package and called a *flash* message. To use these, you add *express-flash* to your *package.json* (we're using version 0.x) and tell *express* to use a *flash* instance.

In our authentication function that we pass to the passport `LocalStrategy` object, you'll see that when the request fails authentication, we call:

```
    return done(null, false, { message: 'Incorrect credentials.' });
```

This `message` is a flash message! The next time a page request comes in, this message will be available in req.flash, which you see when we construct the login form:

```
    var error = req.flash("error");
    ...
    if (error && error.length) {
        form = "<b> " + error[0] + "</b><br/>" + form;
    }
```

Finally, when we have passport validate our login information in POST */login*, we can set flash messages for both the success and failure cases there:

```
passport.authenticate('local', { successRedirect: '/members',
                                  failureRedirect: '/login',
                                  successFlash: { message: "welcome back" },
                                  failureFlash: true })
```

Running the Sample

You can run this sample by going to the *authentication/* folder in Chapter07 on GitHub. Basically, run the server and then visit *localhost:8080* in the browser. Without too much code, we've added pretty robust authentication to our application. You'll see this integrated into our photo-sharing application and databases in upcoming chapters.

Error Handling

Although you can handle errors individually for each request, sometimes you might like to have a global error handler for common situations. To do this, you provide a function that takes four parameters to the app.use method:

```
app.use(function (err, req, res, next) {
    res.status(500);
    res.end(JSON.stringify(err) + "\n");
});
```

This method is placed after all the other middleware setup and routing functions so that it's the last function that express calls in the app. You can examine the exact error in this function and decide what to return to the user. As an example, here is a version that converts any given err object or thrown Error object to appropriate JSON and returns it to the client as a server error:

```
var express = require('express');
var app = express();

app.get('/', function(req, res){
    throw new Error("Something bad happened");
    res.end('Probably will never get to this message.\n');
});

app.use(function (err, req, res, next) {
    res.status(500);
    res.end(err + "\n");
});

app.listen(8080);
```

Finally, Node.js allows you to specify a global application-wide error handler via the `process` object:

```
process.on('uncaughtException', function (err) {
    console.log('Caught exception: ' + err);
});
```

It is, however, a *terrible* idea to use this for anything other than logging or diagnostic purposes. If this function is called, you should assume that node is in a very unhappy or unstable state and should be restarted. For those situations when you use this function, it should merely log the error and then terminate the node process:

```
process.on('uncaughtException', function (err) {
    console.log('Caught exception: ' + err);
    process.exit(-1);
});
```

You should use `try/catch blocks` around situations in which errors are possible, and for those extremely catastrophic or completely unexpected scenarios, let the process die and restart it—automatically if possible.

Summary

This is another big chapter with tons of fun new stuff. I introduced the express application framework, talked about middleware, described how to use cookies and sessions, and helped you convert some of the code in your photo-sharing application into modules. You also managed to get rid of a lot of code by using static file-serving middleware and can now add compression, authentication, and better error handling to your applications.

The photo-sharing application is shaping up quite nicely, but it still feels a bit rudimentary; you have only pictures in the albums and no great place to store any additional information you might like to add to albums or photos. With this issue in mind, in the following chapters you start looking at databases—first NoSQL (CouchDB) and then MySQL—and see how you can use them in Node. You also look at some caching solutions and continue to grow out the little app into something more useful.

8

Databases I: NoSQL (MongoDB)

Now that you have a solid foundation for your web application and are fully set up with the express web application framework and Mustache templating, you are ready to spend a couple of chapters adding a back end to it. In these next two chapters, you look at two common ways this is done. You start in this chapter by looking at a popular NoSQL database called MongoDB, which provides a quick and easy way to serialize JSON data directly to a database. This chapter covers the basics of using it, and then you update your album handler to let you store album and photo data to the database.

I chose to work with MongoDB instead of other popular NoSQL databases—in particular CouchDB—because it's particularly easy to use and has some wonderful querying functionality that others don't provide so readily. Because the goal of this book is to teach you about working with Node.js, I wanted to choose the database server that was easiest to work with and would let you focus on your primary mission.

If you're more comfortable working with MySQL or other relational databases, this chapter is still very much worth reading because you see how you move the album and photo handlers from file-based to database-backed modules. In the next chapter, where I discuss relational database systems, I provide a version of the code for MySQL as well.

Setting Up MongoDB

To use MongoDB in your Node.js applications, you need to do two things: install the database server itself and make it work with Node.

Installing MongoDB

To get started with MongoDB, you can just download the binaries from *http://mongodb.com*. Distributions for most platforms are in *zip* or *.tar.gz* file format, and you extract them to some location from which you'd like to run MongoDB.

In the *bin/* subfolder, you should find a file called *mongod*, which is the base database server *daemon*. To run the server in a development environment, you typically just use

```
./mongod --dbpath /path/to/db/dir               # unix
mongod --dbpath \path\to\db\dir                 # windows
```

You can create a folder like *~/src/mongodbs* or something similar to hold your databases. To quickly delete them and restart your database server, just press Ctrl+C to kill the current server and then run one of the following:

```
rm /path/to/db/dir/* && ./mongod --dbpath /path/to/db/dir     # unix
del \path\to\db\dir\*                                         # windows 1
mongod --dbpath \path\to\db\dir                              # windows 2
```

To test your installation, open another terminal window or command prompt, and run the mongo program, which runs a simple interpreter that looks a lot like the Node REPL:

```
Kimidori:bin marcw$ ./mongo
MongoDB shell version: 3.2.9
connecting to: test
> show dbs
local (empty)
>
```

For deployment to a live production environment, you should read the MongoDB documentation a bit further and learn about best practices and configuration options, including setting up replication and backups, for example.

Using Mongo DB in Node.js

After verifying the MongoDB installation, you need to hook it up to Node.js. The most popular driver being used currently is the official *mongodb* for Node written by the company that produces MongoDB. There is a relational-object mapping (ROM) layer called *mongoose* for MongoDB and Node.js that is quite popular, but you can stick with the simple driver for this book because it provides everything you want (your data needs are not terribly complicated) and lets you structure your code to be more database agnostic (as we'll see in the next chapter).

To install the mongodb module, add the following to your *package.json* file:

```
{
  "name": "MongodB-Demo",
  "description": "Demonstrates Using MongoDB in Node.js",
  "version": "0.0.1",
  "private": true,
  "dependencies": {
    "async": "2.x",
    "mongodb": "2.x"
  }
}
```

You can then run `npm update` to get the latest version of all the drivers. If you look in the *node_modules/* folder, you should see the *mongodb/* subfolder there.

Structuring Your Data for MongoDB

MongoDB is quite suitable for use in your applications because it uses JSON for storage itself. Whenever you create or add things to your database, you pass around JavaScript objects— which is extremely convenient for you in Node!

If you've used relational databases before, you're likely familiar with the terminology of databases, tables, and rows. In MongoDB, these elements are called *databases*, *collections*, and *documents*, respectively. Databases can be partitioned into collections of like objects, all of which are represented by JSON documents.

All objects in MongoDB have a unique identifier, represented by `_id`. It can basically be any type as long as it's a unique value. If you do not provide one, MongoDB creates one for you: it is an instance of the class `ObjectID`. When printed, it returns a 24-character hexadecimal string, such as `50da80c04d403ebda7000012`.

It's All JavaScript

For the photo album application, you need to create two document types: one for albums and one for photos within albums. You do not need to use MongoDB's autogenerated `_id` values because you always have unique identifying information for your documents: for albums, the `album_name` is always unique, and for photos, the combination of `album_name` and photo `filename` is unique.

Thus, you store your albums as follows:

```
{ _id: "italy2012",
  name:"italy2012",
  title:"Spring Festival in Italy",
  date:"2012/02/15",
  description:"I went to Italy for Spring Festival." }
```

And your photo documents look similar to the following:

```
{ _id: "italy2012_picture_01.jpg",
  filename: "picture_01.jpg",
  albumid: "italy2012",
  description: "ZOMGZ it's Rome!",
  date: "2012/02/15 16:20:40" }
```

Attempting to insert values into a collection with duplicate `_id` values causes MongoDB to signal an error. You use this capability to ensure that albums are unique and that image files within an album are also unique.

Data Types

For the most part, working with MongoDB in JavaScript feels entirely natural and straightforward. There are, however, a couple of scenarios in which you might run into some trouble, so it's worth covering theme now.

As you saw back in Chapter 2, "A Closer Look at JavaScript," JavaScript represents all numbers as 64-bit double-precision floating-point numbers. This gives you 53 bits of integer precision. But there is frequently a legitimate need for fully 64-bit integer values. When the reduced precision and approximations are unacceptable, you can use the `Long` class that the *mongodb* driver for Node has provided. It takes a string value in its constructor and lets you perform operations on 64-bit integer values. It has a number of methods, such as `toString`, `compare`, and `add`/`subtract`/`multiply`, to mimic all common operations you'd expect for integer values.

JavaScript also has a `Binary` class that, as you might expect, lets you store binary data in your documents. You can pass the constructor either a string or a `Buffer` object instance, and the data is stored as binary data. When you reload the document later, the value is returned to you again with some extra metadata describing how Mongo is storing it in the collection.

Finally, I want to mention the `Timestamp` class, which saves times to the database document but does so when you actually write the record! So you can just set a value as follows:

```
{ _id: "unique_idnetifier1234",
  when: new TimeStamp(),
  what: "Good News Everyone!" };
```

For a complete list of the data type helpers that the *mongodb* module provides, check out the documentation at *github.com/mongodb/node-mongodb-native* and also look at the source code in *github.com/mongodb/js-bson* in the directory *lib/bson/*.

Understanding the Basic Operations

Now it's time to make some things happen with MongoDB and Node.js. At the top of every file that uses the *mongodb* module, include the following:

```
var MongoClient = require('mongodb').MongoClient;
```

For those situations in which you use extra types, such as `Long` or `Binary`, you can refer to them through the mongodb module as follows:

```
var mongodb = require('mongodb');
var b = new mongodb.Binary(binary_data);
var l = new mongodb.Long(number_string);
```

Connecting and Creating a Database

To connect to a MongoDB server, you simply refer to it with a URL pointing to the server and database you plan to use. The code to get a handle to the database (which we'll store in db) is as follows:

```
var url = 'mongodb://HOSTNAME:27017/MY_DATABASE_NAME';
var db;
MongoClient.connect(url, (err, dbase) => {
    if (err) return cb(err);
    console.log("Connected correctly to server");
    db = dbase;
});
```

For most of our test projects, our URL will be *mongodb://localhost:27017/photosharingapp*. The name of the database you want to create, or use if it already exists, is passed via the URL. It is created if it does not exist.

You do not need to create a new Db object for each incoming request to your application server, nor do you need to worry about multiple people trying to work with the database server at the same time: the *mongodb* module handles connection pooling and manages multiple requests at the same time for you. You can configure your *mongodb* connections by sending an additional object to MongoClient.connect, as follows:

```
MongoClient.connect(url, { w: 1, poolSize : 200 }, (err, dbase) => { ... });
```

MongoDB and the *mongodb* module you use are quite flexible with the way they handle writes and data integrity. The { w: 1 } flag you pass to the constructor (called the *write concern*) tells them to wait until at least *one confirmed write* has succeeded before calling any callbacks you provide to database operations. You can specify higher numbers for environments with replication or 0 for those cases in which you don't care to know when the writes are finished (such as high-volume logging). Finally, "majority" may be passed instead of a number for the write concern in cases where you just want to be sure that a large enough number of your servers have confirmed the write.

You configure how many connections to maintain to the MongoDB server by adjusting the value of the poolSize option, as shown in the preceding code. For a full list of configurable options for your connection refer to the documentation on the GitHub pages for the *mongodb* module.

Creating Collections

As mentioned previously, collections are the MongoDB equivalent of tables from relational database systems, and you create them with a call to the collection method on the Db object. By specifying the { safe: true } option as a second parameter, you can control exactly how they work with regards to existing or nonexistent collections (see Table 8.1).

Table 8.1 **Creating Collections**

Function	{ safe: true }	Effect
collection	Yes	Opens a collection if it exists; returns an error if not
collection	No	Opens a collection if it exists; creates the collection on first insertion if not

To use the { safe: true } option, you write your code as follows:

```
db.collection("albums", { safe: true }, (err, albums) => {
    if (err) {
        // album already exists or other network error.
    }
    // etc. ...
});
```

The code you will use most commonly to create or open a collection, however, is simply:

```
db.collection("albums", (err, albums) => {
    if (err) {
        console.error(err);
        return;
    }

    // albums can now be used to do stuff ...
});
```

Inserting Documents into Collections

To insert a document (i.e., an object) into a collection, you use the insertOne method as follows:

```
var album = { _id: "italy2012",
              name: "italy2012",
              title: "Spring Festival in Italy",
              date: "2012/02/15",
              description: "I went to Italy for Spring Festival." };

albums.insertOne(album, (err, inserted_doc) => {
    if (err) {
        console.log("Something bad happened.");
        return;
    }
    // continue as normal
});
```

You see that you are specifying your own _id field for the document. If you did not, MongoDB would provide one for you. If a document with that _id exists already, the callback is called with an error.

You can insert multiple documents at the same time by passing an array to the `insertMany` function:

```
var docs = [{ _id: "italy2012",
              name: "italy2012",
              title: "Spring Festival in Italy",
              date: "2012/02/15",
              description: "I went to Italy for Spring Festival." },
            { _id: "australia2010",
              name: "australia2010",
              title: "Vacation Down Under",
              date: "2010/10/20",
              description: "Visiting some friends in Oz!" },
            { _id: "japan2010",
              name: "japan2010",
              title: "Programming in Tokyo",
              date: "2010/06/10",
              description: "I worked in Tokyo for a while."
            }];
albums.insertMany(docs, callback);
```

Updating Document Values

To update a document, you can call the `updateOne` method on a collection. The first parameter identifies a document (if multiple documents match, only the first is updated), and the second is an *object description* of how to modify the matching document(s). The object description comes in the form of a command and a field or fields to accompany it:

```
photos.updateOne({ filename: "photo_03.jpg", albumid: "japan2010" },
                 { $set: { description: "NO SHINJUKU! BAD DOG!" } },
                 callback);
```

In this description, you use the command `$set`, which tells MongoDB to update the value of the provided field with the provided new value; here, you tell it to update the *description* field with a new value. There are a many different commands you can use, some of the more interesting of which are listed in Table 8.2.

Table 8.2   **Update Commands**

Command	Effect
$set	Sets the value of the given field to the given value.
$inc	Increments the value of the specified field.
$rename	Renames the specified field to the given new name.
$push	If the field is an array, this pushes a new value to the end of it.

Command	Effect
$pushAll	If the field is an array, this pushes the given new multiple values to the end of it.
$pop	Removes the last element of the array field.
$pull	Removes the given value(s) from an array field.

As with insertOne and it's insertMany complement, you can update multiple documents
with the updateMany method, where the update applies to all documents matching the first
parameter:

```
// Change album name of all photos in japan2010.
photos.updateOne({ albumid: "japan2010" },
                 { $set: { albumid: "japan2010mkii" } },
                 callback);
```

Deleting Documents from Collections

To delete a document from a collection, you use the deleteOne method on the collection
object. You can specify any set of fields to identify a document or set of documents:

```
photos.deleteOne({ filename: "photo_04.jpg", albumid: "japan2010" },
                 callback);
```

As with updateOne, if multiple documents match, only the first is deleted. You can skip the
safe: true option and the callback if you don't care to confirm that the delete completed:

```
photos.deleteOne({ filename: "photo_04.jpg", albumid: "japan2010" });
```

To delete more than one, you use deleteMany:

```
photos.deleteOne({ albumid: "japan2010" });    // delete all in this album
```

You can also remove all documents in a collection by simply calling deleteMany with no
arguments:

```
photos.deleteMany();     // DANGER ZONE!!
```

Querying Collections

By far, the biggest reason that MongoDB is the most popular of the NoSQL database engines
is that its ability to find documents in collections most closely matches the behavior of
traditional SQL database queries and feels incredibly natural. All your work here is done with
the find function on collections.

Find Basics

Before starting, note that the find method itself does not actually do any work; it sets up a
results cursor (which is an object that can iterate over the set of rows returned from executing
a query). The query is not executed and the contents of the cursor are not actually generated
until you call one of the functions on it: nextObject, each, toArray, or streamRecords.

The first three operate as you'd expect: `nextObject` can be called to get one document, `each` calls a function with each resulting document, and `toArray` fetches all the documents and passes them as a parameter to a callback:

```
var cursor = albums.find();

cursor.nextObject(function(err, first_match) {});
cursor.each(function(err, document) {});
cursor.toArray(function(err, all_documents) {});
```

If you call the `find` method with no arguments, it matches all documents in the collection.

You can use the `streamRecords` method on the cursor to create a `Stream` object, which you can then use as you use other streams:

```
var stream = collection.find).streamRecords();
stream.on("data", function(document) {});      // why data and not readable? See text!
stream.on("end", function() {});
```

This is the preferred way to fetch large numbers of records because it has a lower memory footprint than methods such as `toArray`, which return all the documents in a single chunk. At the time of the writing of this book, the `mongodb` module still had not been updated to the new `"readable"` event model that streams in Node.js use now (since 2012 or so); it is entirely possible that this will have changed by the time you start using it. So, double-check, just to be sure. (The best place would be at the official site for the driver, *mongodb.github.com/node-mongodb-native/*.)

To find specific documents in your collection, you can specify the fields to match as the first parameter to the `find` function:

```
photos.find({ albumid: "italy2012" }).toArray(function (err, results));
```

You can use operators in `find` queries quite similar to those you saw previously for the `update` function. For example, if you had documents for people, you could find all people older than age 20 with

```
users.find({ age: { $gt: 20 } }).toArray(callback);
```

You can combine these operators using logical operations such as `$and` `$or` to give more powerful queries. For example, to return all users between the ages of 20 and 40 (inclusive), you could use

```
users.find({ $and: [ { age: { $gte: 20 } }, { age: { $lte: 40 } } ] });
```

Some more operators are shown in Table 8.3. For a full listing of them, consult the MongoDB query documentation.

Table 8.3 **Find Operators**

Operator	Meaning
$ne	Not equal
$lt	Less than

Operator	Meaning
`$lte`	Less than or equal
`$gt`	Greater than
`$gte`	Greater than or equal
`$in`	Matches if the field value is one of the values in the given array of values
`$nin`	Matches if the field value is *not* one of the values in the given array of values
`$all`	Matches if the given field is an array and contains all the values in the given array of values

Searching for Mongo DB Generated IDs

I mentioned previously that if you do not provide an `_id` field in documents you insert, Mongo DB provides one for you. These autogenerated `_id` fields are of type `ObjectID` and are represented as 24-character hexadecimal strings.

The problem is that if you use these fields, you cannot search for them simply by specifying the string value of the ID. You need to wrap them back in an `ObjectID` class constructor, as follows:

```
var ObjectID = require('mongodb').ObjectID;

var idString = '50da9d8d138cbc5da9000012';

collection.find({_id: new ObjectID(idString)}, callback);
```

If you try to execute the following, you don't get any matches:

```
collection.find({ _id: idString }, callback);
```

You won't encounter this problem in the apps you're developing in this book because you are going to always generate your own _id fields.

Further Refining Your Finds

To implement paging and sorting on your pages, you need to be able to manipulate or otherwise modify the results of the `find` operations. The *mongodb* module lets you do this by chaining additional function calls with these effects to the `find` operation, before you call one of the functions to generate a cursor.

The methods you'll use the most are `skip`, `limit`, and `sort`. The first indicates how many documents in the result set should be ignored before you start returning any, the second controls how many should be returned after you've done any skipping, and the last controls ordering and sorting—you are welcome to sort on more than one field.

So, to fetch all the photos in an album sorted ascending by date, you would write

```
photos.find({ albumid: "italy2012" })
    .sort({ date: 1})       // 1 is asc, -1 is desc
    .toArray(function (err, results));
```

To return the third page of these photos, assuming pages are 20 photos each, you would use

```
photos.find({ albumid: "italy2012" })
    .sort({ date: 1})        // 1 is asc, -1 is desc
    .skip(40)
    .limit(20)
    .toArray(function (err, results) { });
```

Again, anything called before the `toArray` function at the end is just setting up the results cursor, and the query is not executed until that last function call.

You can pass multiple fields to the `sort` function for sorting on multiple values:

```
collection.find()
    .sort({ field1: -1, field2: 1 })
    .toArray(callback);
```

Seeing it all in Action

On the GitHub page for this book, you can look in the *Chapter08* folder and look for the *mongo_basics/* folder there. A script called *mongo_basics.js* in there runs through much of what we have covered so far in this chapter. Start up a `mongod` server, run this script, and see what happens. You can look through the code to see how we've applied everything we've talked about so far.

Updating Your Photo Albums App

With this understanding of the basics of using MongoDB in Node.js, you can update your photo-sharing application to use a database instead of just the simple file system functions to store album and photo information. You still keep the actual image files on your hard disk, but in a real production environment, you would put them on some sort of storage server or content delivery network (CDN).

Writing the Low-Level Operations

You begin by adding a new folder named *data/* to your application. You put low-level operations to the back end in this folder. You also create a file called *backend_helpers.js* that will contain some functions to help you work with and generate errors, validate parameters, and do some other common back-end operations. These tasks are all pretty simple, and you can view the source code on GitHub.

Creating a Configuration File

In the application root folder, create a new file called *local.config.json*, which contains the following JavaScript:

```
{
    "config" : {
        "db_config": {
```

```
        "host_url": "mongodb://localhost:27017/photosharingapp"
    },

        "static_content": "../static/"
    }
}
```

Including this file means that all of the configuration options are handily located in one place, and you can change it trivially without having to rummage through code looking for things.

Getting Your Databases and Collections

Next, create a file called *db.js* in *data/*. In this file, you create the database connection and collections you use for your photo application. In this file, you also create the connection to the *PhotoSharingApp* database using the information in the *local.config.json* file:

```
var MongoClient = require('mongodb').MongoClient,
    async = require('async'),
    local = require("../local.config.json");

// We'll keep this private and not share it with anybody.
var db;

// Before the app can start, call this method. If it fails, don't start!
exports.init = function (callback) {
    async.waterfall([
        // 1. open database connection
        function (cb) {
            console.log("\n** 1. open db");
            var url = local.config.db_config.host_url;
            MongoClient.connect(url, (err, dbase) => {
                if (err) return cb(err);
                console.log("**    Connected to server");
                db = dbase;
                cb(null);
            });
        },
```

Next we'll get the collections for albums and photos within those albums using the `collection` method. You do this by adding the following code to the `async.waterfall` we started above in the `init` function:

```
        // 2. create collections for our albums and photos. if
        //    they already exist, then we're good.
        function (cb) {
            console.log("** 2. create albums and photos collections.");
            db.collection("albums", cb);
        },
```

```
        function (albums_coll, cb) {
            exports.albums = albums_coll;
            db.collection("photos", cb);
        },

        function (photos_coll, cb) {
            exports.photos = photos_coll;
            cb(null);
        }
    ], callback);
};

exports.albums = null;
exports.photos = null;
```

You can see that `albums` and `photos` are now exported objects in *db.js*, so people can fetch them whenever they need them by writing

```
var db = require('./db.js');
var albums = db.albums;
```

Finally, you need to make sure your `db.init` function is called before the application starts, so replace the call in *server.js*:

```
app.listen(8080);
```

with

```
db.init( (err, results) => {
    if (err) {
        console.error("** FATAL ERROR ON STARTUP: ");
        console.error(err);
        process.exit(-1);
    }

    console.log("** Database initialized, listening on port 8080");
    app.listen(8080);
});
```

Creating an Album

We'll now create a file called *album.js* in *data/*. This file will contain all the backend primitive operations you can perform on an album using *mongodb*.

The code to create a new album is thus:

```
exports.create_album = function (data, callback) {
    var final_album;
    var write_succeeded = false;
    async.waterfall([
        function (cb) {
```

```
            try {
                backhelp.verify(data,
                                [ "name", "title", "date", "description" ]);
                if (!backhelp.valid_filename(data.name))
                    throw invalid_album_name();
            } catch (e) {
                cb(e);
            }
            cb(null, data);
        },

        // create the album in mongo.
        function (album_data, cb) {
            var write = JSON.parse(JSON.stringify(album_data));
            write._id = album_data.name;
            db.albums.insert(write, { w: 1, safe: true }, cb);
        },

        // make sure the folder exists in our static folder.
        function (new_album, cb) {
            write_succeeded = true;   // inserted the album.
            final_album = new_album[0];
            fs.mkdir(local.config.static_content
                    + "albums/" + data.name, cb);
        }
    ],
    function (err, results) {
        if (err) {
            if (write_succeeded)
                db.albums.remove({ _id: data.name }, function () {});
            if (err instanceof Error && err.code == 11000)
                callback(backhelp.album_already_exists());
            else if (err instanceof Error && err.errno != undefined)
                callback(backhelp.file_error(err));
            else
                callback(err);
        } else {
            callback(err, err ? null : final_album);
        }
    });
};
```

Although the async module makes the code a bit "longer" and spread out, I hope you can already see how much it cleans things up. All the asynchronous operations are expressed as a sequence of things that need to be done; async takes care of all the messy details for you!

You do one trick here in the code to clone an object:

```
var write = JSON.parse(JSON.stringify(album_data));
```

It turns out that quickly serializing and deserializing an object is one of the quickest ways to clone it in JavaScript. We clone the object in the code above so that we do not modify an object that "isn't ours" per se. It can be considered rude (or downright buggy) to modify objects passed in to our function, so we have just quickly cloned it before adding the _id field. Note that *backhelp* is simply the backend (in the data/ folder) version of the helper functions we've seen before in *helpers.js*.

Finding Albums

Loading an album given its name is quite an easy operation:

```
exports.album_by_name = function (name, callback) {
    db.albums.find({ _id: name }).toArray((err, results) => {
        if (err) {
            callback(err);
            return;
        }

        if (results.length == 0) {
            callback(null, null);
        } else if (results.length == 1) {
            callback(null, results[0]);
        } else {
            console.error("More than one album named: " + name);
            console.error(results);
            callback(backutils.db_error());
        }
    });
};
```

You spend more time on error handling and validation than you do actually finding the album!

Listing All Albums

Similarly, listing all the albums is quite easy:

```
exports.all_albums = function (sort_field, sort_desc, skip, count, callback) {
    var sort = {};
    sort[sort_field] = sort_desc ? -1 : 1;
    db.albums.find()
        .sort(sort)
        .limit(count)
        .skip(skip)
        .toArray(callback);
};
```

Getting the Photos in an Album

Finding all photos in a given album is also simple:

```
exports.photos_for_album = function (album_name, pn, ps, callback) {
    var sort = { date: -1 };
    db.photos.find({ albumid: album_name })
        .skip(pn)
        .limit(ps)
        .sort("date")
        .toArray(callback);
};
```

Adding a Photo to an Album

Indeed, the only other semicomplicated operation you need to perform is adding a photo to an album, and that is a bit more work because you have to add the step to copy the uploaded temporary file to its final place in the *static/albums/* folder:

```
exports.add_photo = function (photo_data, path_to_photo, callback) {
    var final_photo;
    var base_fn = path.basename(path_to_photo).toLowerCase();
    async.waterfall([
        function (cb) {
            try {
                backhelp.verify(photo_data,
                                [ "albumid", "description", "date" ]);
                photo_data.filename = base_fn;
                if (!backhelp.valid_filename(photo_data.albumid))
                    throw invalid_album_name();
            } catch (e) {
                cb(e);
            }
            cb(null, photo_data);
        },

        // add the photo to the collection
        function (pd, cb) {
            pd._id = pd.albumid + "_" + pd.filename;
            db.photos.insert(pd, { w: 1, safe: true }, cb);
        },

        // now copy the temp file to static content
        function (new_photo, cb) {
            final_photo = new_photo[0];
            var save_path = local.config.static_content + "albums/"
                + photo_data.albumid + "/" + base_fn;
            backhelp.file_copy(path_to_photo, save_path, true, cb);
        }
    ],
```

```
    function (err, results) {
        if (err && err instanceof Error && err.errno != undefined)
            callback(backhelp.file_error(err));
        else
            callback(err, err ? null : final_photo);
    });
};
```

Modifying the API for the JSON Server

Next, you add the following two new API functions to the JSON server to facilitate creating albums and adding photos to them:

```
app.put('/v1/albums.json', album_hdlr.create_album);
app.put('/v1/albums/:album_name/photos.json', album_hdlr.add_photo_to_album);
```

The nice thing about *express* is that it makes this process that simple. When you add these two lines, the API is expanded with new functionality, and now you just need to update the album handler to support these new features.

Because the API now supports putting data, including files and POST bodies, you need to add some more middleware to support this capability, and we need to be sure we're including all the correct files. So, the top of our *server.js* file will now look as follows:

```
var express = require('express'),
    bodyParser = require('body-parser'),
    morgan = require('morgan'),
    multer = require('multer');

var db = require('./data/db.js'),
    album_hdlr = require('./handlers/albums.js'),
    page_hdlr = require('./handlers/pages.js'),
    helpers = require('./handlers/helpers.js');

var app = express();
app.use(express.static(__dirname + "/../static"));
app.use(morgan('dev'));

// Parse application/x-www-form-urlencoded & JSON and set up file uploads.
app.use(bodyParser.urlencoded({ extended: false }))
app.use(bodyParser.json())
var upload = multer({ dest: "uploads/" });
```

We are going to use *multer* again to handle our file uploads and *body-parser* to handle POST data, and we'll set up *morgan* for logging and make sure to include *express static* file handling.

We'll also be sure to include all the modules that we've written that we'll need to coordinate things. Although *db.js* contains mostly backend functions we shouldn't be calling from *server.js*, we *do* need to initialize the database, so we include it here.

Updating Your Handlers

Now that you have the database primitives for your album and photo operations, you need to modify the album handler to use them instead of file system operations.

Some Helpful Classes

Begin by creating a couple of helpful little classes. The one for photos is as follows:

```
function Photo (photo_data) {
    this.filename = photo_data.filename;
    this.date = photo_data.date;
    this.albumid = photo_data.albumid;
    this.description = photo_data.description;
    this._id = photo_data._id;
}
Photo.prototype._id = null;
Photo.prototype.filename = null;
Photo.prototype.date = null;
Photo.prototype.albumid = null;
Photo.prototype.description = null;
Photo.prototype.response_obj = function() {
    return {
        filename: this.filename,
        date: this.date,
        albumid: this.albumid,
        description: this.description
    };
};
```

The only really interesting function here is `response_obj`. You use it because the `Photo` class theoretically holds everything you could want to know about a photo, but when you pass it back in JSON to the caller of an API, there might be some data you don't want to include in that response object. Consider a `User` object; you would certainly want to scrub out passwords and other sensitive data.

A basic version of an `Album` object would also look as follows:

```
function Album (album_data) {
    this.name = album_data.name;
    this.date = album_data.date;
    this.title = album_data.title;
    this.description = album_data.description;
    this._id = album_data._id;
}

Album.prototype._id = null;
Album.prototype.name = null;
Album.prototype.date = null;
```

```
Album.prototype.title = null;
Album.prototype.description = null;

Album.prototype.response_obj = function () {
    return { name: this.name,
             date: this.date,
             title: this.title,
             description: this.description };
};
```

Now, look at how the handler class is reorganized to use the low-level album operations you wrote in the previous section.

Creating an Album

Again, you almost write more code checking for errors than you do performing the operation. This is the nature of good coding. Too many books and tutorials skip over these things, and it's one of the reasons there's so much bad code in the world today!

```
var album_data = require('../data/album.js');
// ... etc. ...
exports.create_album = function (req, res) {
    async.waterfall([
        // make sure the albumid is valid
        function (cb) {
            if (!req.body || !req.body.name) {
                cb(helpers.no_such_album());
                return;
            }

            // TODO: we should add some code to make sure the album
            // doesn't already exist!
            cb(null);
        },

        function (cb) {
            album_data.create_album(req.body, cb);
        }
    ],
    function (err, results) {
        if (err) {
            helpers.send_failure(res, helpers.http_code_for_error(err), err);
        } else {
            var a = new Album(results);
            helpers.send_success(res, {album: a.response_obj() });
        }
    });
};
```

Loading an Album by Name

Once again, error checking and handling make up 90 percent of your work. I highlighted the
call here to the back end that actually fetch the album:

```
exports.album_by_name = function (req, res) {
    async.waterfall([
        // get the album
        function (cb) {
            if (!req.params || !req.params.album_name)
                cb(helpers.no_such_album());
            else
                album_data.album_by_name(req.params.album_name, cb);
        }
    ],
    function (err, results) {
        if (err) {
            helpers.send_failure(res, helpers.http_code_for_error(err), err);
        } else if (!results) {
            helpers.send_failure(res,
                                 helpers.http_code_for_error(err),
                                 helpers.no_such_album());
        } else {
            var a = new Album(album_data);
            helpers.send_success(res, { album: a.response_obj() });
        }
    });
};
```

Listing All Albums

Here, you fetch only 25 albums at a time so you will not have overly complicated pages. You
could make these configurable via query parameters if you wanted.

```
exports.list_all = function (req, res) {
    album_data.all_albums("date", true, 0, 25, function (err, results) {
        if (err) {
            helpers.send_failure(res, err);
        } else {
            var out = [];
            if (results) {
                for (var i = 0; i < results.length; i++) {
                    out.push(new Album(results[i]).response_obj());
                }
            }
            helpers.send_success(res, { albums: out });
        }
    });
};
```

This model of separating the handlers and database code seems as though it creates a bit more work (and it does a little bit), but it has the huge advantage of giving you a very flexible back end. In the next chapter you see that you can switch the data storage for albums and photos to another database system without touching the album handler at all! You only need to modify the classes in the data/ folder.

Getting All Photos for an Album

The code to view photos in an album is shown in Listing 8.1. It involves two new methods, `exports.photos_for_album` and a new function to the `Album` object, `photos`. Most of the complexity of these functions comes from handling paging and slicing up the output array of photos.

Listing 8.1   **Getting all the Photos in an Album**

```
Album.prototype.photos = function (pn, ps, callback) {
    if (this.album_photos != undefined) {
        callback(null, this.album_photos);
        return;
    }
    album_data.photos_for_album(
        this.name,
        pn, ps,
        function (err, results) {
            if (err) {
                callback(err);
                return;
            }
            var out = [];
            for (var i = 0; i < results.length; i++) {
                out.push(new Photo(results[i]));
            }
            this.album_photos = out;
            callback(null, this.album_photos);
        }
    );
};


exports.photos_for_album = function(req, res) {
    var page_num = req.query.page ? req.query.page : 0;
    var page_size = req.query.page_size ? req.query.page_size : 1000;

    page_num = parseInt(page_num);
    page_size = parseInt(page_size);
    if (isNaN(page_num)) page_num = 0;
    if (isNaN(page_size)) page_size = 1000;
```

```
    var album;
    async.waterfall([
        function (cb) {
            // first get the album.
            if (!req.params || !req.params.album_name)
                cb(helpers.no_such_album());
            else
                album_data.album_by_name(req.params.album_name, cb);
        },

        function (album_data, cb) {
            if (!album_data) {
                cb(helpers.no_such_album());
                return;
            }
            album = new Album(album_data);
            album.photos(page_num, page_size, cb);
        },
        function (photos, cb) {
            var out = [];
            for (var i = 0; i < photos.length; i++) {
                out.push(photos[i].response_obj());
            }
            cb(null, out);
        }
    ],
    function (err, results) {
        if (err) {
            helpers.send_failure(res, err);
            return;
        }
        if (!results) results = [];
        var out = { photos: results,
                    album_data: album.response_obj() };
        helpers.send_success(res, out);
    });
};
```

Adding a Photo

Finally, you can write the API to add photos; it is shown in Listing 8.2. This API also involves adding a new method to the Album object. I've highlighted the code that handles the incoming file upload, as it's how *multer* tells us what the user sent.

Listing 8.2 **Adding Photos Using the API**

```
Album.prototype.add_photo = function (data, path, callback) {
    album_data.add_photo(data, path, function (err, photo_data) {
        if (err)
            callback(err);
        else {
            var p = new Photo(photo_data);
            if (this.all_photos)
                this.all_photos.push(p);
            else
                this.app_photos = [ p ];
            callback(null, p);
        }
    });
};


exports.add_photo_to_album = function (req, res) {
    var album;
    async.waterfall([
        // make sure we have everything we need.
        function (cb) {
            if (!req.body)
                cb(helpers.missing_data("POST data"));
            else if (!req.file)
                cb(helpers.missing_data("a file"));
            else if (!helpers.is_image(req.file.originalname))
                cb(helpers.not_image());
            else
                // get the album
                album_data.album_by_name(req.params.album_name, cb);
        },
        function (album_data, cb) {
            if (!album_data) {
                cb(helpers.no_such_album());
                return;
            }

            album = new Album(album_data);
            req.body.filename = req.file.originalname;
            album.add_photo(req.body, req.file.path, cb);
        }
    ],
    function (err, p) {
        if (err) {
            helpers.send_failure(res, helpers.http_code_for_error(err), err);
            return;
        }
```

```
        var out = { photo: p.response_obj(),
                    album_data: album.response_obj() };
        helpers.send_success(res, out);
    });
};
```

Adding Some New Pages to the Application

The JSON server is now completely modified to use MongoDB for all its album and photo storage work. What you don't have yet, however, are some pages to let you create new albums or add new photos to albums via the web interface. Let's fix that now.

Defining the URLs for the Pages

Here, you place the two new pages you want to create in */pages/admin/add_album* and */pages/admin/add_photo*. Fortunately, you don't need to modify the URL handlers in the express app for this at all.

Creating an Album

Don't forget that for each page in the Mustache-templated site, you need two files:

- A JavaScript bootstrapper
- A template HTML file

The code to bootstrap the add album page is straightforward; it doesn't even need to load any JSON from the server, only the template. It is shown in Listing 8.3.

Listing 8.3 **admin_add_album.js**

```
$(function(){

    var tmpl,    // Main template HTML
    tdata = {};  // JSON data object that feeds the template

    // Initialize page
    var initPage = function() {

        // Load the HTML template
        $.get("/templates/admin_add_album.html", function (d){
            tmpl = d;
        });

        // When AJAX calls are complete parse the template
        // replacing mustache tags with vars
        $(document).ajaxStop(function () {
```

```
            var renderedPage = Mustache.to_html( tmpl, tdata );
            $("body").html( renderedPage );
        })
    }();
});
```

The code for the HTML page to add the album is a bit more complicated, because you need to write some JavaScript to do the form submission via Ajax. This code is shown in Listing 8.4. The trickery you see with the `dateString` variable ensures that dates are always in the format *yyyy/mm/dd*, and not sometimes *yyyy/m/d*.

Listing 8.4 **admin_add_album.html**

```html
<form name="create_album" id="create_album"
      enctype="multipart/form-data"
      method="PUT"
      action="/v1/albums.json">

 <h2> Create New Album: </h2>
 <dl>
  <dt>Album Name:</dt>
  <dd><input type='text' name='name' id="name" size='30'/></dd>
  <dt>Title::</dt>
  <dd><input id="photo_file" type="text" name="title" size="30"/></dd>
  <dt>Description:</dt>
  <dd><textarea rows="5" cols="30" name="description"></textarea></dd>
 </dl>
 <input type="hidden" id="date" name="date" value=""/>
</form>

<input type="button" id="submit_button" value="Upload"/>

<script type="text/javascript">

  $("input#submit_button").click(function (e) {
      var m = new Date();
      var dateString =
          m.getUTCFullYear() +"/"+
          ("0" + (m.getUTCMonth()+1)).slice(-2) +"/"+
          ("0" + m.getUTCDate()).slice(-2) + " " +
          ("0" + m.getUTCHours()).slice(-2) + ":" +
          ("0" + m.getUTCMinutes()).slice(-2) + ":" +
          ("0" + m.getUTCSeconds()).slice(-2);

      $("input#date").val(dateString);
```

```
    var json = "{ \"name\": \"" + $("input#name").val()
        + "\", \"date\": \"" + $("input#date").val()
        + "\", \"title\": \"" + $("input#title").val()
        + "\", \"description\": \"" + $("textarea#description").val()
        + "\" }";

    $.ajax({
        type: "PUT",
        url: "/v1/albums.json",
        contentType: 'application/json',    // request payload type
        "content-type": "application/json",   // what we want back
        data: json,
        success: function (resp) {
            alert("Success! Going to album now");
            window.location = "/pages/album/" + $("input#name").val();
        }
    });
});
```

```
</script>
```

Adding Photo to Album

To add a photo to the album, you have to write a bit more complicated code. In the bootstrapper, you need a list of all the albums so that the user can select to which album the photo should be added. This code is shown in Listing 8.5.

Listing 8.5   **admin_add_photo.js**

```
$(function () {
    var tmpl,    // Main template HTML
    tdata = {};  // JSON data object that feeds the template

    // Initialize page
    var initPage = function () {
        // Load the HTML template
        $.get("/templates/admin_add_photos.html", function (d) {
            tmpl = d;
        });

        // Retrieve the server data and then initialize the page
        $.getJSON("/v1/albums.json", function (d) {
            $.extend(tdata, d.data);
        });
```

```
        // When AJAX calls are complete parse the template
        // replacing mustache tags with vars
        $(document).ajaxStop(function () {
            var renderedPage = Mustache.to_html( tmpl, tdata );
            $("body").html( renderedPage );
        })
    }();
});
```

And finally, I leave you to look in the *create_album/* folder in the GitHub source for Chapter 8 for the source of the HTML page that shows the form and performs the actual uploads to the server (*static/templates/admin_add_photo.html*). The big thing this file does is use the `FormData` extension to the `XmlHttpRequest` object to allow Ajax file uploads, as shown here:

```
$("input#submit_button").click(function (e) {
    var m = new Date();
    var dateString = /* process m -- see GitHub */
    $("input#date").val(dateString);

    var oOutput = document.getElementById("output");
    var oData = new FormData(document.forms.namedItem("add_photo"));

    var oReq = new XMLHttpRequest();
    var url = "/v1/albums/" + $("#albumid").val() + "/photos.json";
    oReq.open("PUT", url, true);
    oReq.onload = function (oEvent) {
        if (oReq.status == 200) {
            oOutput.innerHTML = "\
Uploaded! Continue adding or <a href='/pages/album/"
                + $("#albumid").val() + "'>View Album</a>";
        } else {
            oOutput.innerHTML = "\
Error " + oReq.status + " occurred uploading your file.<br \/>";
        }
    };

    oReq.send(oData);
});
```

`FormData` is powerful and awesome but is not supported in Internet Explorer versions before 10. Firefox, Chrome, and Safari have all supported it for quite a while. If you must support older IE browsers, you need to look at other methods for uploading files, such as using Flash or otherwise regular old HTML forms.

Recapping the App Structure

The application has gotten a bit more complicated; it is worth spending a few seconds again covering exactly how you've structured it. You've moved all static content into the *static/* folder and the code into the *app/* folder, so you now have the following basic layout:

The *static/* folder contains the following subfolders:

- *albums/*—Contents our albums and their image files
- *content/*—Contains stylesheets and JavaScript bootstrapping files needed to render the page templates
- *templates/*—The HTML templates for rendering pages in the client browser

In the *app/* folder, you have:

- *./*—Contains the core server scripts and *package.json* files
- *data/*—All code and classes related to working with the backend data store
- *handlers/*—Contains the classes that are responsible for handling incoming requests

All of the versions of your application from this point on will use this structure.

Summary

You now have not only a fully updated version of the photo album application that uses MongoDB as its data store for albums and photos but also a couple of more interesting pages in your web application for creating albums and uploading photos to the server.

The only problem is that anybody can view and use these pages and APIs to manipulate albums and photos. So you next need to focus your attention on adding users and requiring that the users be logged in before making these changes.

9

Databases II: SQL (MySQL)

Although the NoSQL databases are surging in popularity, there are still plenty of good reasons to continue using relational databases, and they too remain just as popular as ever, especially the two most common open source variants, MySQL and PostgreSQL. The good news is that the asynchronous nature of Node.js meshes perfectly well with using these databases in your web applications, and there is good npm module support for most of them.

In this chapter, I cover using MySQL with Node, using the *mysql* module from npm. Because you learned how to put your albums and photos in the database in the preceding chapter, you can now turn your focus to registering users in the application and requiring them to be logged in before creating any albums or adding any photos. We leave seeing how albums and users were converted to MySQL as an exercise for the reader to view in the GitHub source code.

Even if you're not planning on using traditional relational databases such as MySQL, it is still worth your while to read through this chapter because I introduce a couple of important features in express, as well as talk about *resource pooling*, a way to control and limit the use of precious system resources. You also update the photo albums sample so that albums and photos will work with MySQL.

Getting Ready

You need to do two things before you can start playing around with MySQL in Node.js: make sure MySQL is installed and install the mysql npm module.

Installing MySQL

If you haven't installed MySQL on your development machine yet, visit *dev.mysql.com/downloads/mysql* and download the version of the community server most appropriate for your machine. For Windows and Mac OS X, you can find downloadable installers, whereas for Linux and other UNIX systems, you can unpack *.tar.gz* archives to your preferred location (most typically /usr/local/mysql).

If you're running the installers for Windows or Mac OS X, they take care of everything for you, whereas for binary distributions only, you have to read the *INSTALL-BINARY* text file and follow the instructions in there to get MySQL fully up and running. When you're done, you should be able to start a new command prompt or terminal and run the `mysql` command:

```
hostname:Learning Node marcw$ /usr/local/mysql/bin/mysql -u root
Welcome to the MySQL monitor. Commands end with ; or \g.
Your MySQL connection id is 1
Server version: 5.7.14 MySQL Community Server (GPL)

mysql>
```

Adding the mysql Module from npm

To install the mysql module for Node.js, you can modify *package.json* and add the following under dependencies:

```
"dependencies": {
  "async": "2.x",
  "mysql": "2.x"
}
```

You should now see *mysql/* under *node_modules/* in your folder. Note that the *2.x* series of the *mysql* module is a significant improvement and departure from the *0.x* series. It is much more robust than previous versions.

Creating a Schema for the Database

When working with MySQL, you need to create a database schema for the application, which you place in *schema.sql*. The first part of this is to create a database with UTF-8 as the default character set and sorting order, as follows:

```
DROP DATABASE IF EXISTS PhotoAlbums;

CREATE DATABASE PhotoAlbums
    DEFAULT CHARACTER SET utf8
    DEFAULT COLLATE utf8_general_ci;

USE PhotoAlbums;
```

You then have to create a schema for your Users table, where you place information for registered users of your photo-sharing app. You only need to require an email address, display name, and password from the user and to store a couple of extra pieces of information, including when the account was created, when it was last modified, and whether or not it's been marked as deleted. The Users table looks as follows:

```
CREATE TABLE Users
(
  user_uuid VARCHAR(50) UNIQUE PRIMARY KEY,
  email_address VARCHAR(150) UNIQUE,

  display_name VARCHAR(100) NOT NULL,
  password VARCHAR(100),

  first_seen_date BIGINT,
  last_modified_date BIGINT,
  deleted BOOL DEFAULT false,

  INDEX(email_address),
  INDEX(user_uuid)
)
ENGINE = InnoDB;
```

Running all these commands in MySQL (`mysql -u user -p secret < schema.sql`) sets up the appropriate database and table structures you need to begin writing code. If you're following along with the code from the GitHub repository, you'll notice that tables have been added for albums and photos as well to keep our app working!

Basic Database Operations

Most of your work with MySQL will be limited to making connections to the MySQL server and executing these queries and statements. This gives you more than enough to run your straightforward web applications and extract much of the power of the database server.

Connecting

To connect to the remote server, you create a connection via the *mysql* module and then call the `connect` function, as follows:

```
conn_props = local.config.db_config;
client = mysql.createClient({
    host:         conn_props.host,
    user:         conn_props.user,
    password:     conn_props.password,
    database:     conn_props.database
});
};
```

You might have noticed that this is a bit different from the `init` method we had in the *db.js* file in the previous chapter for MongoDB. It turns out that MySQL manages its own connections and connects and disconnections whenever it needs to, so you don't need to do the initialization that you did for MongoDB.

If you've passed in bad values or other invalid information, you get an error. If the connection succeeds, you can then use your client object to execute queries with the `query` method. After finishing all your work with the database, you should close the connection by calling the end method:

```
dbclient.end();
```

There is one problem with this code, however—it creates only a single connection. If we have dozens of requests coming in at the same time, attempting to execute database queries for them using the same connection will be extremely slow and cause problems. To get around this, the *mysql* module now includes *connection pooling* (it used to be that you had to use another module instead). Conveniently, we just have to change the method we use to create the *dbclient*, as follows:

```
conn_props = local.config.db_config;
dbpool = mysql.createPool({
    connectionLimit: conn_props.pooled_connections,
    host:           conn_props.host,
    user:           conn_props.user,
    password:       conn_props.password,
    database:       conn_props.database
});
```

The createPool method means that whenever we call the query method, the dbclient will look for an existing connection to the database and reuse it. If none exists, it'll create a new one up to connectionLimit times. If there are no connections left, it'll pause your query until a connection comes free and then execute it. All we have to do in our code is execute the queries, and everything is taken care of for us—we don't have to worry about calling the end method or anything else.

Adding Queries

After connecting to the database server, you can start executing queries with the query method, to which you pass the SQL statements you want executed:

```
dbclient.query("SELECT * FROM Albums ORDER BY date",
                function (err, results, fields) {});
```

If the query succeeds, the results parameter passed to the callback contains data relevant to what you requested, and there is a third parameter, fields, for those cases when you have additional information to specify (it is often empty when you don't have such information). For SELECT statements, the second parameter is an array of queried rows:

```
dbpool.query("SELECT * FROM Albums", function (err, rows) {
    for (var i = 0; i < rows.length; i++) {
        console.log(" -> Album: " + rows[i].name
                    + " (" + rows[i].date + ")");
    }
});
```

If you are using INSERT, UPDATE, or DELETE (to add, change, or remove rows from the specified table correspondingly), the results you get back from the query method look more like the following:

```
{ fieldCount: 0,
  affectedRows: 0,
  insertId: 0,
  serverStatus: 2,
  warningCount: 0,
  message: '',
  changedRows: 0 }
```

You can use this information to make sure that the number of affected rows is what you expected it to be by looking at the affectedRows property, or you can get the autogenerated ID of the last inserted row via the insertId property.

To specify values in your MySQL queries, you use *placeholders*, which are indicated with the ? character, as follows:

```
dbpool.query("INSERT INTO Albums VALUES (?, ?, ?, ?)",
             [ "italy2012",
               "Marc visits Italy",
               "Marc spent a month in Italy!",
               "2012-01-01" ],
             callback);
dbpool.query("SELECT * FROM Albums WHERE albumid = ? ORDER BY album_date DESC",
             [ "australia2010" ],
             callback);
```

The question mark character indicates that the value will be filled in from an array passed as the second parameter to the query method, where the *n*th element in the array replaces the *n*th ? character in the query. Most importantly, these values are *escaped* or *sanitized* for you so that it becomes much harder to fall victim to *SQL Injection* attacks or other ways where malicious data and damage your database.

And that's pretty much all there is to using MySQL in Node.js. Let's put it to some serious use then!

Updating the Photo Sharing Application

We have updated the photo sharing application we are building in this book to work with MySQL instead of MongoDB. We'll leave looking at the differences between these two way of doing things as an exercise to the reader by looking in GitHub. The good news is that 99% of what's new and different is in the *data/* subfolder—most of the serving code and handler code doesn't need to change at all! In this chapter, we will focus on integrating passport into our photo sharing app.

Authenticating via the Database

Back in Chapter 7, we covered adding authentication to our application using the *passport* module. In that sample application, however, we covered only having a hard-coded list of users and passwords, which is not particularly useful in real-world usage.

In this chapter, we're going to add *passport* support to our photo sharing application, and we're going to use the database to store user information, using the Users table we described above.

Our application will support the following user operations:

- Let new users register for the application.

- Require a user to be logged in before using the *admin* pages that allow adding photos or albums.

Updating the API to Support Users

To support a new user subsystem, you need to add a couple of new routes to the API:

```
app.put('/v1/users.json', user_hdlr.register);
app.post('/service/login', /* we'll see this later */);
app.get('/service/logout', /* we'll see this later */);
```

The first is the CRUD method (see "API Design" in Chapter 7, "Building Web Applications with Express") for creating users through the API. The second and third are the way you support logins and authentication for the web browser version of the application. I show the implementations for these two methods later in this chapter.

Examining the Core User Data Operations

To get a connection to the database, go to the *data/* folder for your application and put—in addition to a *backend_helpers.js* file containing some simple error-handling help—a file called *db.js* there. This file is shown in Listing 9.1. Effectively, it provides a function to get a connection to a MySQL database using connection information provided in the file *local.config.json*, as you saw in Chapter 8, "Databases I: NoSQL (MongoDB)."

Listing 9.1 **db.js**

```
var mysql = require('mysql'),
    local = require("../local.config.json");

exports.init = function () {
    conn_props = local.config.db_config;
    exports.dbpool = mysql.createPool({
        connectionLimit: conn_props.pooled_connections,
        host:           conn_props.host,
```

```
        user:           conn_props.user,
        password:       conn_props.password,
        database:       conn_props.database
    });
};

exports.dbpool = null;
```

Whenever we need a database connection to run a query, we can just fetch `db.dbpool`. With this file in place, you can start implementing the back end for the preceding new APIs in *data/user.js*.

Creating a User

The code to register a new user in the database is as follows:

```
exports.register = function (email, display_name, password, callback) {
    var userid;
    async.waterfall([
        // validate the params
        function (cb) {                                        // 1.
            if (!email || email.indexOf("@") == -1)
                cb(backend.missing_data("email"));
            else if (!display_name)
                cb(backend.missing_data("display_name"));
            else if (!password)
                cb(backend.missing_data("password"));
            else
                cb(null);
        },

        function (cb) {
            bcrypt.hash(password, 10, cb);                     // 3.
        },
        function (hash, cb) {
            userid = uuid();                                   // 4.
            db.dbpool.query(                                   // 5a.
                "INSERT INTO Users VALUES (?, ?, ?, ?, UNIX_TIMESTAMP(), NULL, 0)",
                [ userid, email, display_name, hash ],
                cb);
        },

        function (results, fields, cb) {                       // 5b.
            exports.user_by_uuid(userid, cb);
        }
    ],
```

```
    function (err, user_data) {
        if (err) {
            if (err.code
                && (err.code == 'ER_DUP_KEYNAME'
                    || err.code == 'ER_EXISTS'
                    || err.code == 'ER_DUP_ENTRY'))
                callback(backhelp.user_already_registered());
            else
                callback(err);
        } else {
            callback(null, user_data);
        }
    });
};
```

The code does the following:

1. It validates the incoming parameters, in particular making sure the email address is semi-valid. You could be even stricter if you wanted and require activation of an account by sending a link to that address.

2. It gets a connection to the database.

3. It hashes the password using the bcrypt module. Bcrypt is a slow method of generating passwords that makes brute-force attacks on them extremely difficult.

4. You generate a UUID for the user. You can use it later in the API to identify users. These IDs are better than simple integer user IDs because they're harder to guess and have no obvious ordering.

5. You execute the query to register the user in the database and finally ask the database to return that just-created user back to the caller.

You use two new modules in this code: *bcrypt* (for password encryption) and *node-uuid* (to generate the GUID that you use for the user identifier). You thus update the *package.json* file with the following dependencies:

```
"dependencies": {
  "express": "3.x",
  "async": "0.1.x",
  "mysql": "2.x",
  "bcrypt": "0.x",
  "node-uuid": "1.x"
}
}
```

Also note that you store the account creation date as a BIGINT instead of a regular MySQL DATETIME field. I've found that because JavaScript uses time stamps everywhere for dates and times, it can be much easier to just store and manipulate them in databases as well. Fortunately, MySQL provides a few functions to help you work with these dates.

Fetching a User (by Email Address or UUID)

Now that you have a way to save users into the database, you can write the functions to bring them back. First, write a generic function to find a user based on a particular field in the database:

```
function user_by_field (field, value, callback) {
    async.waterfall([
        function (cb) {
            db.dbpool.query(
                "SELECT * FROM Users WHERE " + field
                    + " = ? AND deleted = false",
                [ value ],
                cb);
        },
        function (rows, fields, cb) {
            if (!rows || rows.length == 0)
                cb(backhelp.no_such_user());
            else
                cb(null, rows[0]);
        }
    ],
    callback);
}
```

Now, write the exported functions to fetch a user:

```
exports.user_by_uuid = function (uuid, callback) {
    if (!uuid)
        cb(backend.missing_data("uuid"));
    else
        user_by_field("user_uuid", uuid, callback);
};


exports.user_by_email = function (email, callback) {
    if (!email)
        cb(backend.missing_data("email"));
    else
        user_by_field("email_address", email, callback);
};
```

And that's all you have to do for the data portion of user management. Everything else you do is on the front-end handlers.

Updating the Express Application for Authentication

To update our application to support authentication, we'll add the *passport* module to our *package.json* file, as well as *passport-local* authentication:

```
"dependencies": {
    "body-parser": "1.x",
    "cookie-parser": "1.x",
    "express": "4.x",
    "express-flash": "0.x",
    "express-session": "1.x",
    "mysql": "2.x",
    "morgan": "1.x",
    "multer": "1.x",
    "node-uuid": "1.x",
    "passport": "0.3.x",
    "passport-local": "1.x"
}
```

You'll see that we've also included a few other modules to support cookies, session data, uploads, and flash messages, which we covered back in Chapter 7.

At the top of our *server.js* file, we're going to have to add all the modules we'll need for passport and configuring all the modules, as follows:

```
var express = require('express'),
    cookieParser = require('cookie-parser'),
    session = require('express-session'),
    passport = require("passport"),
    LocalStrategy = require('passport-local').Strategy,
    bodyParser = require('body-parser'),
    flash = require('express-flash'),
    morgan = require('morgan'),
    multer = require('multer');

var db = require('./data/db.js'),
    album_hdlr = require('./handlers/albums.js'),
    page_hdlr = require('./handlers/pages.js'),
    user_hdlr = require('./handlers/users.js'),
    helpers = require('./handlers/helpers.js');

var app = express();
app.use(express.static(__dirname + "/../static"));
```

```
var session_configuration = {
    secret: 'whoopity whoopity whoop whoop',
    resave: false,
    saveUninitialized: true,
    cookie: { secure: true }
};

session_configuration.cookie.secure = false;

app.use(flash());
app.use(session(session_configuration));
app.use(cookieParser('whoopity whoopity whoop whoop'));
app.use(passport.initialize());
app.use(passport.session());

app.use(morgan('dev'));

// Parse application/x-www-form-urlencoded & JSON
app.use(bodyParser.urlencoded({ extended: false }))
app.use(bodyParser.json())

var upload = multer({ dest: "uploads/" });
```

Our initialization code has grown a bit, but our application is doing quite a lot of things now.

Implementing User Authentication

Let's look at the methods we need to implement passport authentication. First, we need to initialize the passport local strategy with a function that validates a given username and password against our approved list of users.

```
passport.use(new LocalStrategy(
    function(username, password, done) {
        user_hdlr.authenticate_user(username, password, (err, user) => {
            if (err && err.code == "invalid_credentials") {
                return done(null, false, {
                    message: 'Incorrect credentials.'
                });
            } else if (err) {
                return done(null, false, {
                    message: `Error (\(err.code\)) while authenticating`
                });
            } else {
                return done(null, user);
            }
        });
    }
));
```

The key new method we have here is the `authenticate_user` method in the *handlers/users.js* file (which we include and call `user_hdlr`). We'll see this in the next section, "Creating the User Handler."

We create three other authentication functions to help us out, as follows:

```
function alwaysAuthenticated(req, res, next) {
    if (req.isAuthenticated()) {
        next();
    } else {
        res.redirect("/pages/login");
    }
}


function pageAuthenticatedOrNot(req, res, next) {
    if ((req.params && req.params.page_name == 'admin')) {
        if (req.isAuthenticated()) {
            next();
        } else {
            res.redirect("/pages/login");
        }
    } else if (req.params && req.params.page_name == "register") {
        if (req.isAuthenticated()) {
            req.logout();
        }
        next();
    } else {
        next();
    }
}


function verifyLoggedOut(req, res, next) {
    if (req.user) {
        req.logout();
    }
    next();
}
```

The first two of these are *middleware* (see Chapter 7 if you've forgotten what these are) functions that allow us to verify if an incoming request has an authenticated user associated with it. For the first, it will always require an authenticated user. For the second, it'll require authentication only if the user is trying to access an *admin* page. Our last function simply makes sure the user is logged out.

With these implemented, we can now implement the user handler, *handlers/users.js*.

Creating the User Handler

To support management of accounts, you can create a new user handler in *handlers/users.js*. Just as you did previously with albums and photos, you create a new `User` class that will help you wrap users and also let you implement a `response_obj` method to filter out things you don't want to return:

```
function User (user_data) {
    this.uuid = user_data["user_uuid"];
    this.email_address = user_data["email_address"];
    this.display_name = user_data["display_name"];
    this.password = user_data["password"];
    this.first_seen_date = user_data["first_seen_date"];
    this.last_modified_date = user_data["last_modified_date"];
    this.deleted = user_data["deleted"];
}

User.prototype.uuid = null;
User.prototype.email_address = null;
User.prototype.display_name = null;
User.prototype.password = null;
User.prototype.first_seen_date = null;
User.prototype.last_modified_date = null;
User.prototype.deleted = false;
User.prototype.check_password = function (pw, callback) {
    bcrypt.compare(pw, this.password, callback);
};
User.prototype.response_obj = function () {
    return {
        uuid: this.uuid,
        email_address: this.email_address,
        display_name: this.display_name,
        first_seen_date: this.first_seen_date,
        last_modified_date: this.last_modified_date
    };
};
```

Creating a New User

Earlier in this chapter, we saw the back-end code needed to create a new user in the database. Let's look at the front-end portion of this. It basically does the following:

1. Checks the incoming data to make sure it's valid.

2. Creates the user account with the back end and gets the raw data back again.

3. Returns the newly created user object back to the caller.

This function looks like this:

```javascript
exports.register = function (req, res) {
    async.waterfall([
        function (cb) {                                          // 1.
            var em = req.body.email_address;
            if (!em || em.indexOf("@") == -1)
                cb(helpers.invalid_email_address());
            else if (!req.body.display_name)
                cb(helpers.missing_data("display_name"));
            else if (!req.body.password)
                cb(helpers.missing_data("password"));
            else
                cb(null);
        },
        function (cb) {                                          // 2.
            user_data.register(
                req.body.email_address,
                req.body.display_name,
                req.body.password,
                cb);
        },
    ],
    function (err, user_data) {                                  // 3.
        if (err) {
            helpers.send_failure(res, helpers.http_code_for_error(err), err);
        } else {
            var u = new User(user_data);
            helpers.send_success(res, {user: u.response_obj() });
        }
    });
};
```

Authenticating a User

We previously saw that we needed a method called `authenticate_user` to allow the passport local strategy to do its thing. Here it is:

```javascript
exports.authenticate_user = function (un, pw, callback) {
    var user_object;
    async.waterfall([
        function (cb) {
            user_data.user_by_display_name(un, cb);        // 1.
        },
```

```
        function (user_data, cb) {
            user_object = new User(user_data);         // 2.
            user_object.check_password(pw, cb);        // 3.
        }
    ],
    function (err, auth_ok) {
        if (!err) {
            if (auth_ok) {
                callback(null, user_object);
            } else {
                callback(helpers.error("invalid_credentials",
                    "The given username/password are invalid."));
            }
        } else {
            callback(err);
        }
    });
};
```

This code basically does the following:

1. Fetches the user object for the given email address (and throws an error if that email address does not exist).

2. Creates a User object to hold that data.

3. Verifies that the user password is correct. If so, it passes back the user object to the caller.

Hooking up Passport and Routes

Now that we have all the plumbing, we need to implement authentication—the back-end user handles, the key passport functions and the user handlers. We can now tie all this into the *express* app routing directives to ensure everything is secured.

First, we want to be sure that the two routes to create albums and add photos to albums require a logged-in user, as follows:

```
app.put('/v1/albums.json', alwaysAuthenticated, album_hdlr.create_album);
app.put('/v1/albums/:album_name/photos.json',
        alwaysAuthenticated,
        upload.single("photo_file"),
        album_hdlr.add_photo_to_album);
```

Here we see the alwaysAuthenticated function we wrote above—we don't want anybody who isn't authenticated to be able to access these API endpoints.

Next, we want to be sure that pages with *admin* in the URL require authentication but that others do not:

```
app.get('/pages/:page_name', pageAuthenticatedOrNot, page_hdlr.generate);
app.get('/pages/:page_name/:sub_page',
        pageAuthenticatedOrNot,
        page_hdlr.generate);
```

Finally, we implement the login and logout POST methods that web pages can call (we call these *services* as a convention to make it clear that they're doing some processing that's not CRUD related), as follows:

```
app.post("/service/login",
         passport.authenticate('local', {
             failureRedirect: '/pages/login?fail',
         }),
         function (req, res) {
             // We want pages to have access to this.
             res.cookie("username", req.user.display_name);
             res.redirect("/pages/admin/home");
         }
         );

app.get('/service/logout', function (req, res) {
    res.cookie("username", "");
    req.logout();
    res.redirect('/');
});
```

We use *passport* to `authenticate` login requests, and to logout, we just call the `logout` method on the incoming *request* object. Now, all we have left to do is provide a user interface for these operations.

Creating the Login and Register Pages

For the new user subsystem, you have two new pages in your application: a login page and a registration page. (We first saw this way of doing things in Chapter 6 if you don't remember it—all of our pages are implemented this way now.) Both are made up of two files, as usual: a JavaScript *bootstrapper* and an HTML file. For both, the JavaScript bootstrapper is quite standard:

```
$(function () {
    var tmpl,    // Main template HTML
    tdata = {};  // JSON data object that feeds the template

    // Initialize page
    var initPage = function() {
```

```
        // Load the HTML template
        $.get("/templates/login OR register.html", function (d) {
            tmpl = d;
        });

        // When AJAX calls are complete parse the template
        // replacing mustache tags with vars
        $(document).ajaxStop(function () {
            var renderedPage = Mustache.to_html( tmpl, tdata );
            $("body").html( renderedPage );
        });
    }();
});
```

The HTML for the registration page is shown in Listing 9.2. Apart from showing the HTML for the registration form, it has some JavaScript to ensure that the user has entered all the fields, verify that the two passwords match, and then submit the data to the back-end server. If the login succeeds, you redirect the user back home; otherwise, you show an error and let the user try again.

Listing 9.2   **The Registration Page Mustache Template (register.html)**

```
<div style="float: right"><a href="/pages/admin/home">Admin</a></div>
<form name="register" id="register">
  <div id="error" class="error"></div>
  <dl>
    <dt>Email address:</dt>
    <dd><input type="text" size="30" id="email_address" name="email_address"/></dd>
    <dt>Username:</dt>
    <dd><input type="text" size="30" id="display_name" name="display_name"/></dd>
    <dt>Password:</dt>
    <dd><input type="password" size="30" id="password" name="password"/></dd>
    <dt>Password (confirm):</dt>
    <dd><input type="password" size="30" id="password2" name="password2"/></dd>
    <dd><input type="submit" value="Register"/>
  </dl>
</form>

<script type="text/javascript">
$(document).ready(function () {
    if (window.location.href.match(/(fail)/) != null) {
        $("#error").html("Failure creating account.");
    }
});

$("form#register").submit(function (e) {
  if (!$("input#email_address").val()
```

```
            || !$("input#display_name").val()
            || !$("input#password").val()
            || !$("input#password2").val()) {
            $("#error").html("You need to enter an email and password.");
        } else if ($("input#password2").val() != $("input#password").val()) {
            $("#error").html("Passwords don't match.");
        } else {
            var info = { email_address: $("input#email_address").val(),
                         display_name: $("input#display_name").val(),
                         password: $("input#password").val() };
            $.ajax({
                type: "PUT",
                url: "/v1/users.json",
                data: JSON.stringify(info),
                contentType: "application/json; charset=utf-8",
                dataType: "json",
                success: function (data) {
                    window.location = "/pages/admin/home";
                },
                error: function (data) {
                    try {
                        var info = JSON.parse(data.responseText);
                        if (info.error && info.message) {
                            alert(info.error + ": " + info.message);
                        }
                    } catch (e) { }
                    var ext = window.location.href.match(/(fail)/)
                        ? "" : "?fail";
                    window.location = window.location + ext;
                    return false;
                }
            });
        }
        return false;
    });
</script>
```

Finally, the code for the login page is shown in Listing 9.3. It is significantly simpler to implement than the register page, as it simply shows a form and submits the results to the server
(via POSTing to */service/login*). The only additional JavaScript on this page is used to look for the
?fail query parameter to our URL, and if it is present, to show an error message on the page.
(This occurs when the user entered invalid credentials.)

Listing 9.3 **The Login Page Mustache Template (login.html)**

```
<div style='float: right'><a href='/pages/register'>Register</a></div>
<form name="login" id="login" method="post" action="/service/login">
  <div id="error" class="error"></div>
  <dl>
    <dt>Username:</dt>
    <dd><input type="text" size="30" id="username" name="username"/></dd>
    <dt>Password:</dt>
    <dd><input type="password" size="30" id="password" name="password"/></dd>
    <dd><input type="submit" value="Login"/>
  </dl>
</form>


<script type="text/javascript">

$(document).ready(function () {
    if (window.location.href.match(/(fail)/) != null) {
        $("#error").html("Invalid login credentials.");
    }
});

</script>
```

With those new files (*data/user.js* and *handlers/users.js*, *login.js* and *login.html*, and *register.js* and *register.html*), you have a complete login system for your web browser front end.

Summary

I threw two new things at you in this chapter: using MySQL databases in your Node applications and adding user authentication to both your web apps and your API servers. For this chapter, I also updated the MongoDB version of the application with the user authentication subsystem in the GitHub tree, so you're welcome to explore how things are done there as well. By creating two parallel authentication systems, you work to create a good user experience for your browser application, while letting API users still get the full simplicity and power of the JSON API.

In closing out this third part of the book, you learned how to add some powerful new technologies to the photo-sharing application including express and databases and created a fully functioning (if basic) project on which you can build. In the last part of the book, I cover some of the details I have been glossing over thus far in the book. First up, in Chapter 10, you learn how to deploy your applications.

Part IV

Getting the Most Out of Node.js

10

Deployment and Development I: Rolling Your Own

With the ability to build nontrivial Node.js applications firmly under your belt, you can now turn your attention to some additional topics on deployment and development of these apps. In this chapter, you start by looking at some of the various ways that people deploy and run their Node apps on production servers, looking at both UNIX/Mac and Windows options. You also see how you can take advantage of multiprocessor machines, despite the fact that Node.js is a single-threaded platform.

You then move on to look at adding support for virtual hosts on the server, as well as securing your applications with SSL/HTTPS support. Finally, you take a quick look at some of the issues with multiplatform development when you have people working on a Node app with both Windows and Linux/Mac machines.

Deployment

To run your Node.js applications thus far, you've just been using the following from the command line:

```
node script_name.js
```

This approach works fine for development. However, for deploying your applications to live servers, you might want to add in an extra layer of reliability to help in those cases when they crash. Although you, of course, strive to avoid bugs in your servers, some will eventually creep in, so you'd like to have your servers recover as quickly as possible from such problems.

Let's look at some of the options now.

Port Numbers

For most of this book, you have been using very high port numbers for your sample apps, most frequently 8080. The reason is that on some operating systems, most notably UNIX/Mac OS X systems, port numbers below 1024 require superuser (administrator) access. So, for simple debugging and testing, 8080 is a great alternative to the more common port 80 for web traffic.

However, when you deploy your live applications, you frequently want them to run on port 80 because this is the default for web browsers. To do this, you need to run the scripts as superuser. The two ways of doing this are

1. Log in to your system as the superuser and run programs that way.

2. Use the `sudo` command, which elevates the process to be executed to superuser privileges when it actually runs. The Windows equivalent of this is to execute your `cmd.exe` shell with Administrator privileges.

Of these two strategies, I most frequently use the latter.

Level: Basic

At the most basic level, you can just use an infinite loop to run your scripts. This loop just automatically restarts the `node` process whenever it crashes. On UNIX and Mac computers running `bash`, the script can be as simple as:

```
#!/bin/bash
while true
do
    node script_name.js
done
```

On Windows, you can use batch files to do the job for you, as follows (save this to *run_script.bat* or something similar and run it):

```
: loop
node script_name.js
goto loop
: end
```

These scripts make sure that your Node process is always restarted if it crashes or is terminated accidentally.

You can actually go one step further and use a command called `tee` to write the standard output of the node process to a log file. You usually *pipe* the output of your process to the `tee` command using the | ("pipe") operator in the command line, and `tee` then reprints the output on the standard output in addition to writing it to the specified log file, as follows:

```
node hello_world.js 2>&1 | tee -a /var/server/logs/important.log
```

The `-a` flag to `tee` tells it to append the output to the specified log file instead of simply overwriting it. The `2>&1` is a bit of shell wizardry to redirect the *stderr* (standard error) output to the same channel as *stdout* (regular output) so they both get sent to `tee`.

Thus, you can improve your deployment one step further by running your scripts as follows:

```
bash ./run_script.sh 2>&1 | tee -a /var/server/logs/important.log
```

Or, on Windows, you can use the following:

```
run_script.bat 2>&1 | tee -a /var/server/logs/important.log
```

See the sidebar "Tee for Windows" for more information on actually making this technique work.

Tee for Windows (and other useful commands)

The Windows shells are not known for being particularly powerful (although PowerShell is a nice step in the right direction). To get around this issue, people often download external utility packs that let them get some of the cool scripting functionality seen on UNIX platforms such as Linux or Mac OS X.

For the `tee` program mentioned in this chapter, two good choices of utilities are

- http://getgnuwin32.sourceforge.net/
- http://unxutils.sourceforge.net/

You can also find specific `tee` utilities for Windows by simply searching for "Windows tee." Indeed, for many of the UNIX-like tools I've been describing throughout this book, perfectly functional Windows alternatives or versions frequently are available for them.

Using screen to Monitor the Output

Although you are always logged in on Windows and can easily log back in to the desktop to see what is going on with your Node servers, on UNIX servers such as Linux or Mac OS X, you frequently want to log out and just leave the servers running. The problem is that when you do this, you lose your standard output (`stdout`) handle, so the output is lost unless you are also writing to a log file. Even then, the log file sometimes is missing important information printed out by either Node or the OS regarding problems they encounter.

To get around this issue, most UNIX systems support a magical little utility called `screen`, which lets you run programs as if they constantly have a controlling terminal (also known as a *tty*), even if you are logged out. Installation is specific to your platform, but Mac OS X has it by default, and most Linux platforms can get it by doing something similar to `apt-get screen`.

Now, before you run your Node server, you can run `screen` and then run Node within that. To detach from `screen`, you press the key sequence Ctrl+A Ctrl+D. To get back into the screen, you run the command `screen -r` (for resume). If you have multiple `screen` sessions running, they each have a name and you also have to type in the name of the session you want to resume.

You use `screen` for every single Node server you have running. It's a great way to come back every once in a while and browse how things are running.

Level: Ninja

The previous scripts for running applications are pretty useful, and you can use them for low-traffic sites that don't crash very often. They do have a couple of serious limitations, however:

1. If an app gets into a state where it is constantly crashing, even when restarted, these scripts blindly keep restarting it, resulting in what is known as a "run-away process." You never get it to start properly, and your server will work itself to death constantly trying.

2. Although these scripts can keep your processes up and running, they don't do a good job of telling you when they're in trouble, specifically if they're using up too much memory. There are still instances where a Node process can consume a bit too much memory or otherwise get into trouble with system resources. It would be great if there were a way to detect this and terminate them and let them start again from scratch.

Thus, in the following sections, you look at a couple of more advanced deployment options, which start to deviate quite greatly for UNIX and Windows at this point.

Linux/Mac

The previous version of your script (when viewed as pseudo-code) was effectively

```
while 1
      run node
end
```

You can upgrade this script now to do something more along the following lines:

```
PID = run node
while 1
      sleep a few seconds
      if PID not running
         restart = yes
      else
        check node memory usage
        if using too much memory
           restart = yes

      if restart and NOT too many restarts
         PID = restart node
end
```

There are two key tasks you need to perform to make this work:

1. Get the process ID (*pid*) of the last-started node server.

2. Figure out how much memory the node process is using.

For the first, you use the `pgrep` command, available on Mac and most UNIX platforms. When used with the `-n` flag, it gives you the process ID of the latest instance of the given process name. You can also use the `-f` flag to tell it to match the name of the script, in case your computer is running multiple Node servers. Thus, to get the *pid* of the latest created Node process running script_name.js, you use

```
pgrep -n -f "node script_name.js"
```

Now, to get the amount of memory that your process is using, you need to use two commands. The first is the `ps` command, which, when given the `wux` flags (`wup` on some platforms—check your documentation), tells you the total virtual memory consumption of the process, as well as the current resident size (the one you want). The output of `ps wux $pid` is as follows:

```
USER    PID  %CPU %MEM    VSZ     RSS   TT  STAT STARTED      TIME COMMAND
marcw  1974   6.6  3.4  4507980  571888   ??  R    12:15AM  52:02.42 command name
```

You want the sixth column (RSS) of the second line of this output. To get this, you have to first run the `awk` command to get the second line only, and then you run it again to get the value in the sixth column, as follows:

```
ps wux $PID | awk 'NR>1' | awk '{print $6}'
```

When you know the amount of memory this process is consuming, you can make a decision as to whether it's using too much and then terminate and restart it if necessary.

I won't print out the full code of the shell script here, but you can see it in the code for Chapter 10 in the GitHub repository, as *node_ninja_runner.sh*. To use it, you can run it as

```
node_ninja_runner.sh server.js [extra params]
```

You do, of course, need to make sure it's elevated to superuser privileges if you're going to listen on a port such as *80* or *443*.

Windows

On Windows, the best way to run your apps in a reliable way that can be monitored would be to use a Windows Service. Node.js itself is not set up to be a Windows Service, but fortunately you can use some tricks to get it to behave like one.

Through the use of a nice little program called `nssm.exe` (the *Non-Sucking Service Manager*) and an `npm` module called *winser*, you can install your Node web applications as services and manage them fully through the Windows Management Console. To set this up, you need to do two things:

1. Install a new custom action in *package.json* for the web application.

2. Download and install winser and have it do its work.

For the first step, you just need to add the following to the *package.json* file:

```
{
  "name": "Express-Demo",
  "description": "Demonstrates Using Express and Connect",
  "version": "0.0.2",
  "private": true,
  "dependencies": {
    "express": "4.x"
  },
    "scripts": {
    "start": "node 01_express_basic.js"
  }
}
```

For the second step, you can just do the following:

```
C:\Users\Mark\LearningNode\Chapter10> npm install winser
```

(Or you can add winser to your dependencies.) Then, when you are ready to install your app as a service, you can go to the project folder holding the *package.json* for the app and run

```
C:\Users\Mark\LearningNode\Chapter10> node_modules\.bin\winser -i
The program Express-Demo was installed as a service.
```

To uninstall the service, just run winser -r, as follows:

```
C:\Users\Mark\LearningNode\Chapter10> node_modules\.bin\winser -r
The service for Express-Demo was removed.
```

You can then go to the Windows Management Console and start, stop, pause, or otherwise manage the service to your heart's content!

Multiprocessor Deployment: Using a Proxy

I've mentioned many times that Node.js effectively operates as a single-threaded process: all the code that your scripts are executing is in the same thread, and you use asynchronous callbacks to get as much efficiency out of your CPU as possible.

However, you must then ask these questions: What do you do on a system with multiple CPUs? How can you extract maximal functionality out of your servers? Many modern servers are nice, powerful 8–16 core machines, and you'd like to use all of them if possible.

Fortunately, the answer is reasonably simple: just run one node process per core you want to utilize (see Figure 10.1). You can choose one of a number of strategies to route incoming traffic to the various different node processes, as suits your requirements.

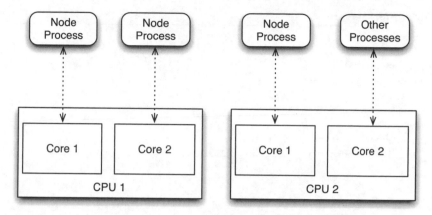

Figure 10.1   Running multiple node processes for the same app

The problem you are now faced with is that you have not one, but *n* Node processes running, all of which must listen on a different port (you can't have multiple people listening on the same port number). How do you get traffic to *mydomain:80* to these servers?

You can solve this problem by implementing a simple round-robin *load balancer* that is given a list of node servers running your particular web application. You then redirect incoming requests to your domain to these other servers, one at a time. You can, of course, experiment with more advanced strategies that monitor load, availability, or responsiveness.

To implement the load balancer, you first compile a list of servers that you are running. Say you have a server with four cores; you give three of them over to the app (and leave the fourth for running other system services). You run these app servers on ports 8081, 8082, and 8083. Thus, your list of servers is

```
{
    "servers": [
        "http://localhost:8081",
        "http://localhost:8082",
        "http://localhost:8083"
    ]
}
```

The code for these simple servers is shown in Listing 10.1. It is the simplest web server that you've seen in this book, with an additional bit of code to get the port number on which it should listen from the command line (you learn more about command-line parameters in Chapter 12, "Command-Line Programming").

Listing 10.1 **Trivial HTTP Server**

```
var http = require('http');

if (process.argv.length != 3) {
    console.log("Need a port number");
    process.exit(-1);
}

var s = http.createServer(function (req, res) {
    res.end("I listened on port " + process.argv[2]);
});

s.listen(process.argv[2]);
```

You can launch your three servers on UNIX/Mac platforms by typing

```
$ node simple.js 8081 &
$ node simple.js 8082 &
$ node simple.js 8083 &
```

On Windows platforms, you can launch them by simply running the following three commands in different command prompts:

```
node simple.js 8081
node simple.js 8082
node simple.js 8083
```

You can now build your proxy server using the npm module *http-proxy*. The *package.json* looks as follows:

```
{
  "name": "Round-Robin-Demo",
  "description": "A little proxy server to round-robin requests",
  "version": "0.0.2",
  "private": true,
  "dependencies": {
    "http-proxy": "1.x"
  }
}
```

The code for the proxy is quite simple, as shown in Listing 10.2. It basically maintains an array of available servers, as shown previously, and then for each request coming to the service, cycles through those available servers and forwards the requests to them.

Listing 10.2   **A round-robin Proxy Load Balancer (roundrobin.js)**

```
var http = require("http"),
    httpProxy = require('http-proxy'),
    fs = require('fs');

var servers = JSON.parse(fs.readFileSync('server_list.json')).servers;

// 1. Create the proxy server.
var proxy = httpProxy.createProxyServer({});

// 2. Create a regular HTTP server.
var s = http.createServer(function (req, res) {
    var target = servers.shift();           // 3. Remove first server
    proxy.web(req, res, { target: target }); // 4. Re-route to that server
    servers.push(target);                    // 5. Add back to end of list
});

s.listen(8080);
```

To put all this in action, you now run `node roundrobin.js`, and you can start to query it as follows:

```
curl -X GET http://localhost:8080
```

As you run this command multiple times, you should see the output showing the actual port number that is being listened to for the current processing server.

Multiple Servers and Sessions

Running multiple servers on different CPUs and servers is a great way to spread the load and give you a cheap path to scalability. (Servers under heavy load? Just add more!) But they create one small complication that you need to address before you can use them effectively: the session data is currently stored per process using local `MemoryStore` objects. (See "POST Data, Cookies, and Sessions" in Chapter 7, "Building Web Applications with Express.") This creates a rather serious problem, as shown in Figure 10.2.

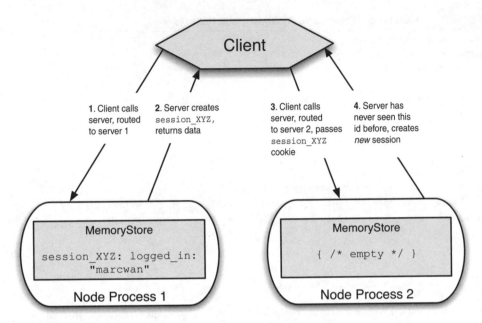

Figure 10.2   Multiple instances of the servers and session data

Because each Node server stores its own record of sessions in its own memory store, when two requests from the same client go to two different node processes, they have different ideas of current state of the session data from the client and quickly get horribly confused. You have two obvious ways to solve this problem:

1. Implement a more advanced router that remembers to which Node server requests from a particular client are being sent and ensure that all traffic continues to be routed in the same way for the same client.

2. Somehow pool the memory stores that the session data uses so that all Node processes can access it.

I prefer the second solution because it is quite simple to implement and much less complicated.

To set up this solution, you need to first choose a pooled memory store. The obvious candidates for this are *memcached* and *Redis*, both of which are effectively large *memory-based key/value stores* that can be spread across different computers. You work with memcached in this chapter because it's entirely adequate for your needs and extremely lightweight. Your setup should look similar to that shown in Figure 10.3.

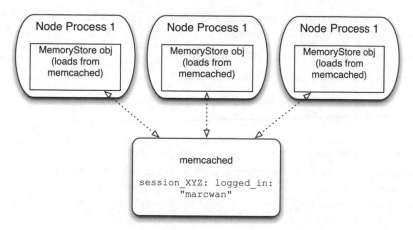

Figure 10.3   Using memory-based key/value stores to implement sessions

Installation on Windows

For Windows users, you can install one of the many binary installers available for memcached that can be found with a simple Internet search. You don't need the latest and greatest version; anything in the 1.2.x series or later is fine. To install it as a service, you run

```
c:\memcached\memcached -d install
```

You can then run the memcached service by typing

```
net start memcached
```

And finally, you can edit HKEY_LOCAL_MACHINE/SYSTEM/CurrentControlSet/Services/memcached Server and modify the ImagePath to be

```
"C:/memcached/memcached.exe" -d runservice -m 25
```

This sets the amount of memory available to memcached to be 25MB, which is usually more than enough for development (you can choose whatever values you want here, of course). It listens on port *11211*.

Installation on Mac and UNIX-like Systems

If you're on a system with some sort of packaging manager, you can often use something like (you might need to run sudo for this)

```
apt-get install memcached
```

and you're good to go. If you want to build from source, you first need to get *libevent* from *http://libevent.org*. Download, build, and install (as superuser) the library. It should place the service in */usr/local/lib*.

Next, visit *memcached.org* and download the latest source tarball (*.tar.gz* file) and configure, build, and install it as well. Again, do so as superuser.

To run memcached after it is installed, run the following command:

```
/usr/local/bin/memcached -m 100 -p 11211 -u daemon
```

This command tells the service to run using 100MB of memory and listen on port *11211*, running as the user *daemon*. It typically refuses to run as *root*.

Getting memcached into express

Now that you have memcached installed and running (assume localhost on port *11211*), you need to get a `MemoryStore` object for it so that you can use it for your session data. Fortunately, the Node.js community is so active that there's already an npm module called *connect-memcached*. So, let's add the following to your dependencies in *package.json*:

```
"connect-memcached": "0.x"
```

Then you can modify your session creation code as follows:

```
var express = require('express'),
    cookieParser = require('cookie-parser'),
    morgan = require('morgan'),
    session = require('express-session');


var port_number = 8080;
if (process.argv.length == 3) {
    port_number = process.argv[2];
}


// pass the session object so it can inherit from MemoryStore
var MemcachedStore = require('connect-memcached')(session);
var mcds = new MemcachedStore({ hosts: "localhost:11211" });


var app = express()
    .use(morgan('dev'))
    .use(cookieParser())
    .use(session({ secret: "cat on keyboard",
                   cookie: { maxAge: 1800000 },
                   resave: false,
                   saveUninitialized: true,
                   store: mcds}))
    .use(function (req, res) {
        var x = req.session.last_access;
        req.session.last_access = new Date();
        res.end("You last asked for this page at: " + x);
    })
    .listen(port_number);
```

Now all the Node servers can be configured to use the same `MemoryStore` for session data and will be able to fetch the correct information, no matter where the request is processed.

Virtual Hosting

Running multiple websites on one server has been a major requirement of web application platforms for many years now, and fortunately Node.js offers a couple of very workable solutions for you when you build your apps with express.

You implement virtual hosting by adding the `Host:` header to the incoming HTTP request, one of the major features in HTTP/1.1 (see Figure 10.4).

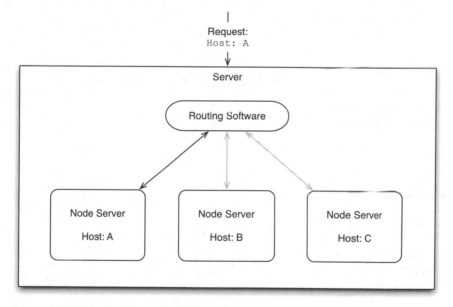

Figure 10.4   The basic idea behind virtual hosting

Express Support

The ability to run multiple virtual hosts used to be built directly into express but is now in a module called (wait for it ...) *express-vhost*. To make it work, you create one express server for each host you want to support and then another "master" server that is given the other virtual servers and routes requests to them as appropriate. Finally, you use the *vhost* connect middleware component to put this all together. The code is shown in Listing 10.3.

Listing 10.3   **Virtual Hosts in Express (vhost_server.js)**

```
var express = require('express'),
    evh = require('express-vhost'),
    morgan = require('morgan');

var one = express();
one.get("/", function (req, res){
    res.send("This is app one!")
});


// App two
var two = express();
two.get("/", function (req, res){
    res.send("This is app two!")
});

// App three
var three = express();
three.get("/", function (req, res){
    res.send("This is app three!")
});


// controlling app
var master_app = express();
master_app.use(evh.vhost());
master_app.use(morgan('dev'));

evh.register("app1", one);
evh.register("app2", one);
evh.register("app3", one);

master_app.listen(8080);
```

Testing Virtual Hosts

Testing virtual hosts can be a bit of a challenge because your servers are all running on local-host, but you need to somehow get the server to recognize the name of the requested server.

If you're testing from the command line using `curl`, you can just add a header to your request to specify which host you are requesting, as follows:

```
curl -X GET -H "Host: hostname1.com" http://localhost:8080
```

However, if you want to test things out in the browser, you need to modify the DNS entries on your machine. The most common way to do this is to edit */etc/hosts* (on UNIX/Mac machines) or *C:\Windows\System32\drivers\etc\hosts*. You must do this with elevated permissions. On UNIX/Mac, you launch your editor with `sudo`, whereas on Windows, you can simply use Notepad, but make sure you run it with Administrator privileges.

Then you can add entries of the following format to the file:

```
127.0.0.1        hostname
```

Here, *127.0.0.1* is the IPv4 address for your local computer, and next to it, you just put the name you want to map to that address. You can add as many lines for as many hosts as you want (for example, *app1*, *app2*, and *app3*).

Between these two options, you should have no problems testing virtual hosts, either from the command line or the browser.

Securing Your Projects with HTTPS/SSL

For those parts of your application that handle sensitive data such as user passwords, personal data, bank accounts, or payment information, or indeed anything else somewhat private in nature, you should secure your applications with SSL-encrypted HTTPS traffic. Although there is some overhead in creating the SSL connection and encrypting the traffic, the security benefits are, of course, of paramount importance.

To add support for SSL/HTTPS to your applications, you need to first generate some test certificates and then add support for the encrypted traffic to the application. For the latter, you again have two ways of doing this: either through built-in support in express or by using a proxy server.

Generating Test Certificates

To work with encrypted traffic on your development machines, you need to generate some test certificates. You need to generate two files—*privkey.pem* and *newcert.pem*—the private key and certificate, respectively. All UNIX/Mac machines come with a tool called `openssl` that you can use to generate these two files.

For Windows users, you can download a Win32 version of `openssl.exe` by visiting *http://gnuwin32.sourceforge.net/packages/openssl.htm*. Then the commands you run are the same as on the other platforms.

To generate the two certificate files, run the following three commands:

```
openssl genrsa -out privkey.pem 1024
openssl req -new -key privkey.pem -out certreq.csr
openssl x509 -req -days 3650 -in certreq.csr -signkey privkey.pem -out newcert.pem
```

With these two files in hand, you can work on using them in your apps. Note that you should never use them in production sites; if you attempt to view a website in a browser secured with these certificates, you get a horribly loud and dangerous-sounding warning about how they are not to be trusted at all. You typically have to purchase production certificates from a trusted certificate authority.

Built-in Support

Not surprisingly, Node.js and express provide support for SSL/HTTPS streams right out of the box, via the built-in https module provided by Node. You can actually run an https module server to do the listening on the HTTPS port (by default 443, but for development, you can use 8443 to avoid having to elevate the permissions of your Node process), and then it routes traffic to the express server after the encrypted stream has been negotiated and created.

You create the HTTPS server and pass in as options the locations of the private key and certificate file you plan to use to sign the site. You also give it the express server to which it can send traffic after encryption is established. The code for this support is shown in Listing 10.4.

Listing 10.4   Express/https Module SSL Support (https_express_server.js)

```
var express = require('express'),
    https = require('https'),
    fs = require('fs');

// 1. Load certificates and create options
var privateKey = fs.readFileSync('privkey.pem').toString();
var certificate = fs.readFileSync('newcert.pem').toString();

var options = {
    key : privateKey,
    cert : certificate
}

// 2. Create express app and set up routing, etc.
var app = express();
app.get("*", function (req, res) {
    res.end("Thanks for calling securely!\n");
});


// 3. start https server with options and express app.
https.createServer(options, app).listen(443, function () {
    console.log("Express server listening on port " + 443);
});
```

You can view these encrypted pages in a web browser by entering `https://localhost:443` in the address bar. The first time you view them, you get a scary warning about how insecure your test certificates are.

Proxy Server Support

As with many of the other things you're investigating in this chapter, you can also use the remarkably powerful *http-proxy* module to handle SSL/HTTPS traffic for you. Using this module has a couple of key advantages over using built-in support for HTTPS in that you let the actual app servers run as regular HTTP servers, leaving them "hidden" behind the HTTPS proxy server and freeing them from tedious encryption work. You can then also run as many as you want using round-robin load balancing seen previously or look at other creative ways to set up your configuration.

The methodology for this support isn't terribly different from that used in the previous example with express; you create an instance of Node's built-in HTTPS server class and also create an instance of a proxy server that knows to route traffic to a regular HTTP server (the app server). You then run the HTTPS server, and when it has established the secure connection, it passes the request to the proxy server, which in turn passes it to the app server(s). The code for this support is shown in Listing 10.5.

Listing 10.5 `http-proxy SSL Support (https_proxy_server.js)`

```
var httpProxy = require('http-proxy'),
    https = require('https'),
    fs = require('fs');

// 1. Get certificates ready.
var privateKey = fs.readFileSync('privkey.pem').toString();
var certificate = fs.readFileSync('newcert.pem').toString();

var options = {
    key : privateKey,
    cert : certificate
}

// 2. Create an instance of HttpProxy to use with another server
var proxy = httpProxy.createProxyServer({});

// 3. Create https server and start accepting connections.
https.createServer(options, function (req, res) {
    proxy.web(req, res, { target: "http://localhost:8081" });
}).listen(443);
```

This may seem like a lot of routing and redirecting, but the Node development group is almost fanatical about performance, and these components are sufficiently lightweight that they shouldn't add much perceptible delay to the processing of requests for your web applications.

Multiplatform Development

One of the great strengths of Node.js is not only its strong support for UNIX and Mac-like computers but also its ability to run on Windows machines. As I was writing this book, I played around with all the samples and ran things on Windows without much trouble at all.

Indeed, you can have people on your projects developing on whatever platforms they want, as long as you take care to prepare for a couple of minor issues that will crop up: differences in configurations and path differences.

Locations and Configuration Files

Windows and UNIX-like operating systems naturally keep things in different places. One way that you can mitigate this problem is to use a configuration file to store these locations. Then your code can be made flexible enough to know where to find things without having to handle each platform separately.

You actually first used this technique in Chapter 8, "Databases I: NoSQL (MongoDB)," and Chapter 9, "Databases II: SQL (MySQL)," where you put database configuration information in a file called *local.config.json*. You can continue to follow this technique expand on it, and generally put any information that affects the running of your application into that file. Indeed, you don't need to restrict it simply to file locations or paths, but you can configure port numbers or build types from there as well:

```
{
  "config": {
    "db_config": {
        "host": "localhost",
        "user": "root",
        "password": "",
        "database": "PhotoAlbums",

        "pooled_connections": 125,
        "idle_timeout_millis": 30000
    },

    "static_content": "../static/",
    build_type: "debug"
  }
}
```

What you normally do is actually check this file in to the version control system (such as GitHub) as *local.config.json-base* and not have a *local.config.json* in the source tree. To run the application, you then copy this base file over to *local.config.json*, update the values as appropriate for your local running setup, and then run it that way. Any time you want to use these local configuration variables, you just add

```
var local = require('local.config.json');
```

Then, in code, you're free to refer to `local.config.variable_xyz` as you need.

Handling Path Differences

The other major difference between Windows and UNIX-like operating systems is paths. How do you code for things such as `require` when you have handlers in subfolders of your current project directory and so on?

The good news is that a vast majority of the time, you'll find that Node accepts the forward slash (/) character. When you require modules from relative paths (such as "*../path/to/sth*"), it just works as you would expect it to. Even for cases in which you're using the *fs* module APIs, most of them are also able to handle the differences in path types between the platforms.

For those cases in which you absolutely need to work with the different path styles, you can use the `path.sep` property in Node.js and some clever use of array joining and splitting, for example:

```
var path = require('path');
var comps = [ '..', 'static', 'photos' ];
console.log(comps.join(path.sep));
```

The `process` global in Node.js always tells you what platform you're running on and can be queried as follows:

```
if (process.platform === 'win32') {
    console.log('Windows');
} else {
    console.log('You are running on: ' + process.platform);
}
```

Summary

In this chapter, you looked at how to take your Node applications and run them in production environments, investing execution scripts, load balancing, and multiprocess applications. This chapter also showed you how to secure your web applications using HTTPS over SSL and finally described multiplatform development, showing that it's not nearly as scary as you might fear.

You now have a pretty hefty set of tools that enable you to build and deploy Node.js applications. In the next chapter, we're going to look at other options for deploying your applications, notably public hosting services such as Heroku and Microsoft Azure. These give you the flexibility and power of full production-ready servers, without requiring you to buy the hardware or become system administrators.

11

Deployment and Development II: Heroku and Azure

In the previous chapter you looked at how to deploy your Node.js applications to servers and what strategies to use to monitor them and keep them running. However, you don't always have access to your own server or may find that it's not terribly cost-effective to maintain one. Thus in this chapter you'll take a look at how you can use some of the application hosting environments available to run your applications for us.

While they'll require that you make some changes to your application, they are often free to start with and will give you a production-quality environment in which to deploy your code. You'll start by taking a look at Heroku, which supports Node.js as a first-class programming environment. You'll see how to deploy your app to Heroku and then address a couple of problems that will come when working in cloud environments. You'll then take a look at how this differs from deploying to Microsoft's Azure platform. (Fortunately, it largely doesn't!)

Deploying to Heroku

Heroku is an application deployment platform that originally started out supporting Ruby-on-Rails developers but has since expanded to all sorts of languages and platforms—most interestingly for you Node.js. Applications run in secure execution environments called *dynos*, which are not entirely unlike lightweight virtual machines. It's extremely easy to get started with and will let you deploy free applications that, while not likely to be appropriate for high-traffic web sites, are plenty useful for smaller purposes and development. As your traffic and needs grow, you can scale your application to be given more processing power and dedicated server resources, which are available on a pay-as-you-go model.

Let's work our way through the process of getting your photo albums application up and running on Heroku.

Before We Begin

You'll need to do a couple of things before you begin deploying your application to Heroku.

Sign Up for a Heroku Account

Go to *heroku.com* and sign up for an account if you do not have one. Accounts are free and quick to get.

Download the Heroku CLI Tools

You'll next need to download the Heroku CLI (command-line interface) tools (formerly called the Heroku Toolbelt) appropriate for your platform. You can find the installer for these at *https://devcenter.heroku.com/articles/heroku-command-line*. When you're done, verify that the installation worked by typing `heroku`—the output should look something as follows:

```
hostname:simple_node_project marcw$ heroku
 ▸    Add apps to this dashboard by favoriting them with heroku apps:favorites:add
See all add-ons with heroku addons
See all apps with heroku apps --all

See other CLI commands with heroku help. The display on your machine will be a little
different.
```

Get the Updated Photo Sharing App for Heroku

We have a special version of our photo sharing application for Heroku, which we'll explain in greater detail in the next sections. However, you'll want to clone this from GitHub by grabbing the repository at *github.com/marcwan/NodePhotoSharingHeroku.git*.

Preparing Your Deployment

Let's get started, shall we?

1. Log In

Log in to Heroku as follows:

```
hostname:simple_node_project marcw$ heroku login
Enter your Heroku credentials.
Email: marcwan@gmail.com
Password (typing will be hidden):
Logged in as marcwan@gmail.com
```

2. Go to Your NodePhotoSharingHeroku Git Folder

Change into the directory for the repository you just pulled down from GitHub. I'll assume it's called *photo_sharing_heroku/* from now on.

3. Look at the Changes We've Made

In order to make our application work on Heroku, we've had to make a few changes. Let's take a look at what those are.

First and foremost, we've changed the directory hierarchy a little bit. We've moved our main script and its subfolders into the root folder. This will make it a bit easier to find things in the Heroku execution environment. Our folder structure now looks like the following:

```
Procfile
README.md
app.json
basic.html
data/
handlers/
local.config.json
package.json
schema.sql
server.js
static/
test.jpg
uploads/
```

All of our files and folders are still there, just laid out a bit differently.

There are two new files of note, however: *Procfile* and *app.json*. *Procfile* looks like this:

```
web: node server.js
```

Very simply, it tells Heroku how to run our (web) application: simply run `node` with the *server.js* script!

The *app.json* file is a bit more involved, as follows:

```
{
  "name": "Node.js Photo Sharing on Heroku",
  "description": "A Node.js app using Express 4",
  "repository": "https://github.com/marcwan/simple_node_project",
  "logo": "http://node-js-sample.herokuapp.com/node.svg",
  "keywords": ["node", "express", "static"],
  "image": "heroku/nodejs"
}
```

This file provides metadata for Heroku about your application, including the GitHub repository from which it is running.

We've made one other small change—if you look in *package.json*, you'll see the following at the bottom now:

```
"engines" : {
  "node" : "6.x"
}
```

This will tell Heroku to use version *6.x* of Node.js to run our application, which is great, because that's what we've been developing with!

And that's basically all we had to change (add) to get our application ready for Heroku.

Create and Deploy the Application on Heroku

In order to do anything with your application, you'll need to create a Heroku app and then deploy it. You can then configure other missing parts which you'll see in subsequent sections.

1. Create Your Heroku Application

To create your application, you run:

```
heroku create
```

This will give you an application name that is semi-random, like *shrouded-earth-22708* below.

```
hostname:simple_node_project marcw$ heroku create
Creating app... done, shrouded-earth-22708
https://shrouded-earth-22708.herokuapp.com/ | https://git.heroku.com/ shrouded-
earth-22708.git
Git remote Heroku added
```

You can, if you want, give it your own name, and if it is not already taken, can use that instead. Deploy the application to set up everything you need in Heroku:

```
hostname:photo_sharing_heroku marcw$ git push heroku master
Counting objects: 65, done.
Delta compression using up to 8 threads.
Compressing objects: 100% (60/60), done.
Writing objects: 100% (65/65), 74.46 KiB | 0 bytes/s, done.
Total 65 (delta 18), reused 0 (delta 0)
remote: Compressing source files... done.
remote: Building source:
remote:
remote: -----> Node.js app detected
remote:
remote: -----> Creating runtime environment
remote:
remote:        NPM_CONFIG_LOGLEVEL=error
remote:        NPM_CONFIG_PRODUCTION=true
remote:        NODE_ENV=production
remote:        NODE_MODULES_CACHE=true
remote:
```

```
remote: -----> Installing binaries
remote:         engines.node (package.json):  6.x
remote:         engines.npm (package.json):   unspecified (use default)
remote:
remote:         Resolving node version 6.x via semver.io...
remote:         Downloading and installing node 6.5.1...
remote:         Using default npm version: 3.10.3
remote:
remote: -----> Restoring cache
remote:         Skipping cache restore (new runtime signature)
remote:
remote: -----> Building dependencies
<<< I've deleted a lot of node package installation stuff here >>>
remote:
remote:
remote: -----> Discovering process types
remote:         Procfile declares types -> web
remote:
remote: -----> Compressing...
remote:         Done: 13.5M
remote: -----> Launching...
remote:         Released v3
remote:         https://shrouded-earth-27708.herokuapp.com/ deployed to Heroku
remote:
remote: Verifying deploy... done.
To https://git.heroku.com/shrouded-earth-27708.git
 * [new branch]      master -> master
```

2. Open and Test the Application in the Browser

Open the application in your browser by running:

```
heroku open
```

You should see a browser pop open with your application running in it! It will say there are no albums, and furthermore, if you try to do anything with it, it will break. Why? Because you haven't configured the database yet! Let's do that now.

3. Configure the ClearDB MySQL Database Add-On

Before you can start really using your application, you have to prepare your MySQL database. You don't have a local database in a Heroku application, so you need to configure what's called an "add-on" in Heroku. Fortunately, there's a MySQL add-on called *ClearDB* that will let you work with a small database for free when starting out. Add that to your Heroku app now.

```
hostname:photo_sharing_heroku marcw$ heroku addons:create cleardb:ignite
Creating cleardb:ignite on shrouded-earth-27708... free
Created cleardb-metric-77672 as CLEARDB_DATABASE_URL
Use heroku addons:docs cleardb to view documentation
```

You now have a MySQL database ready for you to use. You'll now need to get some critical information to update your *local.config.json* file: The server name, user name, password, and database name. You get this by running the following:

```
hostname:photo_sharing_heroku marcw$ heroku config | grep CLEARDB
CLEARDB_DATABASE_URL: mysql://bde4e0dd77d8d0:ce05cb42@us-cdbr-iron-east-08.cleardb.
net/heroku_9039bbf50c4c7a9?reconnect=true
```

Windows users will use `findstr` instead of `grep` in the above command, but otherwise it's the same.

You'll see four things that are bold italic:

1. `us-cdbr-iron-east-08.cleardb.net`—the database server address.

2. `heroku_9039bbf50c4c7a9`—the database name.

3. `bde4e0dd77d8d0`—the user name.

4. `ce05cb42`—the password.

With this, you now have enough to update your *local.config.json* file with the database connection information, as follows:

```
{
    "config": {
        "db_config": {
            "host": "us-cdbr-iron-east-08.cleardb.net",
            "user": "bde4e0dd77d8d0",
            "password": "ce05cb42",
            "database": "heroku_9039bbf50c4c7a9",
            "pooled_connections": 125,
            "idle_timeout_millis": 30000
        },

        "static_content": "/static/"
    }
}
```

Now, you have to run the *schema.sql* file to create the contents of the database! You'll change the top of the *schema.sql* file to look like the following:

```
DROP DATABASE IF EXISTS heroku_9039bbf50c4c7a9

CREATE DATABASE heroku_9039bbf50c4c7a9
    DEFAULT CHARACTER SET utf8
    DEFAULT COLLATE utf8_general_ci;

USE heroku_9039bbf50c4c7a9;
```

Now you can run the script with the following command:

```
mysql --host=us-cdbr-iron-east-08.cleardb.net --user=bde4e0dd77d8d0 \
     --password=ce05cb42 heroku_9039bbf50c4c7a9 < schema.sql
```

Now you have your database all setup!

Commit, redeploy, and open your application, as follows:

```
git commit -a -m "updated db conn info" && git push heroku master && heroku open
```

(The `&&` in the above command is a way of joining multiple commands into one—the command after `&&` is executed only if the previous command completes without any errors.) Indeed, you'll use this command line (three commands at once) to quickly push and deploy your application all the time.

You'll now see the same application, except that it will work! You can register, login, create an album, and then upload a photo.

We Have a Problem

We have a rather serious problem with your application, however. This is due to the rather ephemeral nature of Heroku *dynos*, the environment in which your applications run. These are temporary execution environments that Heroku manages for us. They do have a decent amount of disk space, but every time you restart one of these, *this disk space is completely reset*!

Thus, all photo files you have uploaded are deleted every time you restart the application! The database records for them are still there, but the actual images are gone! To see this in action, just make a quick change to your code somewhere, and then run the `git commit/ git push / heroku open` commands above. You'll notice your image files are gone.

This is where you'll need to use another Heroku add-on to handle cloud storage for us—you'll keep all the images that users upload to your application in a remote file storage application. The one you'll use is called *Cloudinary*, which is free for small amounts of files with very little traffic—perfect for your development environment!

To work with these, you'll need to do the following things:

1. Add *cloudinary* to your Heroku application.

2. Update your *package.json* to include the Cloudinary uploader.

3. Update your *album.js* data class to use this instead of local file storage.

4. Update your *album.js* page bootstrapper (in *static/content/abum.js*) to use the Cloudinary URL instead of a local URL to static files on your server.

Let's do these one by one.

1. Add Cloudinary to your Heroku Application

You'll use the same command you used for adding CloudDB to add Cloudinary, as follows:

```
hostname:photo_sharing_heroku marcw$ heroku addons:create cloudinary
Creating cloudinary on • shrouded-earth-27708... free
Created cloudinary-rectangular-70140 as CLOUDINARY_URL
Use heroku addons:docs cloudinary to view documentation
```

If you want to see the configuration information for Cloudinary, you can just run the following command (Windows users, don't forget to use `findstr` instead of `grep`):

```
heroku config | grep CLOUDINARY
```

But the good news is that you won't need to use this at all; the *cloudinary* module will just work by using environment variables to figure out where to go.

2. Update Your package.json to Include Cloudinary

This step is pretty straightforward—you simply need to include a new dependency as follows:

```
"dependences" : {
  … etc …
  "cloudinary" : "",
  … etc …
}
```

You'll see you just grab the latest version of the *cloudinary* module.

3. Update Your album.js Data Handler for Cloudinary

Basically, you need to modify *data/album.js* in two places to make it compatible with Cloudinary. First, in `exports.create_album`, you'll remove all references to `mkdir`, since you won't need album folders any more. So, you'll get rid of the following lines: in `create_album`:

```
// make sure the folder exists.
function (results, fields, cb) {
    write_succeeded = true;
    fs.mkdir('.' + local.config.static_content
             + "albums/", cb);
},
```

You can just copy over *data/cloudinary/album*.js to *data/album.js* to save yourself having to type in all this. You'll also note that the next function argument list changes because of the deletion of code.

Next, you need to get rid of the file copying in `exports.add_photo_to_album`. In the older version of `add_photo_to_album`, after the `db.dbpool.query`, you have the following code:

```
// make sure the folder exists!!!!
function (results, fields, cb) {
    write_succeeded = true;
    fs.mkdir(basepath, function () { cb(null); });
},
```

```
function (cb) {
    var pttth = basepath + photo_data.albumid + "/";
    fs.mkdir(pttth, function () { cb(null); });
},

// now copy the temp file to static content
function (cb) {
    write_succeeded = true;
    var save_path = '.' + local.config.static_content + "albums/"
        + photo_data.albumid + "/" + base_fn;
    backhelp.file_copy(path_to_photo, save_path, true, cb);
},
```

You'll get rid of all of these, and instead add the following function to the *async* waterfall before the db.dbpool.query:

```
function (cb) {
    cloudinary.uploader.upload(path_to_photo, function (results) {
        cb(null, results);
    });
},

function (results, cb) {
    db.dbpool.query(
        "INSERT INTO Photos VALUES (?, ?, ?, ?)",
        [ photo_data.albumid, results.secure_url, photo_data.description,
          photo_data.date ],
        cb);
},
```

(You'll probably also notice that you need to require *cloudinary* at the top of this file now since you're using the module here!)

You'll see that uploading a file to Cloudinary is as simple as calling cloudinary.uploader. upload with the path to the local file. Once it has uploaded, you'll get the URL to refer to this file in your web applications back in the results. You'll use the secure_url version (there's also just url) since you should always plan to deploy HTTPS versions of your application.

You then update your SQL query to use that secure_url instead of a file path, which means you now have in the database everything you need to get at your pictures!

4. Update Your Album Page Bootstrapper

Your last task to make your application use cloud storage is to update the *album.js* album page bootstrapper to use this new URL instead of a constructed local file URL.

In the massage_album function, you'll change the line:

```
var url = "/albums/" + a.name + "/" + p[i].filename;
```

to be simply:

```
var url = p[i].filename
```

Since the filename is just the complete URL.

And That's It!

Without too much hassle, you've been able to take your photo sharing application and upload, deploy, and adapt it to the cloud execution world of Heroku. You're still not quite done yet—you'll definitely want to look at improving session storage, and configuring your application to handle more load and requests, but you've made a great start and without really having to know much about server execution environments yourselves!

Deploying to Microsoft Azure

If you're a Windows user or simply more partial to Microsoft's Azure cloud platform, you're in luck—deploying Node.js applications to Azure isn't a whole lot much more difficult than it was for you to deploy to Heroku above, and indeed you'll be able to take advantage of some of the same add-ons such as CloudDB and Cloudinary to handle MySQL and image storage for us.

Before We Begin

We'll need to do a couple of things before we begin deploying your application to Azure.

Sign Up for an Azure Account

Go to *azure.microsoft.com* and sign up for an account if you do not have one. They give you some free credit to start using and developing with the platform, which will be plenty for your purposes in this book. (Indeed, we didn't use any of our balance while writing this book!) You will probably have to enter a phone number and credit card information, but your card won't get charged until you scale beyond a certain level, which you won't be doing here.

Download the Azure CLI Tools

There are command-line tools for Azure for most major platforms, including Windows, Mac OS X, and Linux. You will use the Windows ones here.

First, go and visit *https:///azure.microsoft.com/en-us/documentation/articles/xplat-cli-install*. From here click on the "Azure CLI" tab and then pick and download the version of the tools most appropriate for your platform.

To test if they're working, run the following command in `cmd.exe`:

```
C:\src\AzureTest> azure
```

You'll probably see something similar to Figure 11.1. If not, check your installation and make sure you can see this screen.

Figure 11.1   Running azure

Download the Updated Photo Sharing App for Azure

We have a special version of our Photo Sharing application for Azure, which we'll explain in
greater detail in the next sections. However, you'll want to *download* (not clone) this from
GitHub by grabbing the repository at *github.com/marcwan/NodePhotoSharingAzure.git*. You'll see
why you download instead of clone this in a little bit.

Preparing Your Deployment

Deploying to Azure is going to feel awfully familiar if you've already done the Heroku part of
this chapter. If not, then just follow along with the instructions!

1. Login to Azure

To login to Azure, run the following command in `cmd.exe`:

```
C:\src\AzureTest> azure login

info:   Executing command login
-info:  To sign in, use a web browser to open the page https://aka.ms/devicelogin.
Enter the code ABC123DEF to authenticate.
```

Follow the instructions in the browser and then switch back to your `cmd.exe` window. You should then see:

```
|info:    Added subscription Free Trial
+info:    login command OK
```

Of particular importance is the "Added subscription" line. If you do *not* see this in your output, lots of other things are going to fail with vague subscription errors. This is almost always because you did not complete the Microsoft Azure sign-up and verification process. Please go back and complete the full sign-up to Azure, and complete the phone and credit card verification. Then you can re-execute the `azure login` command to make sure it's all okay.

2. Put Your Downloaded Git Source in a Folder

Create a directory on your local machine and unzip the source you downloaded from GitHub into it. I'll assume it's called *C:\src\photo_sharing_azure* from now on.

3. Look at the Changes We've Made

In order to make our application run more smoothly on Azure, we've had to make a few changes. Let's take a look at what those are.

First and foremost, we've changed the directory hierarchy a little bit. We've moved our main script and its subfolders into the root folder. This will make it a bit easier to find things in the Azure execution environment. Our folder structure now looks as follows:

```
README.md
basic.html
data/
handlers/
local.config.json
package.json
schema.sql
server.js
static/
test.jpg
uploads/
```

All of our files and folders are still there, just laid out a bit differently.

Look in server.js, near the end. Instead of the following:

```
db.init();
app.listen(8080);
```

we now have the following:

```
var port = process.env.PORT || process.env.port || 5000;
db.init();
app.listen(port);
```

Azure will tell you what port to listen on via *environment variables*, which we can see via the `process` object in Node. Environment variables are usually system configuration settings that we can access within our application, and they tell you more about our execution environment.

We've made one other small change—if you look in *package.json*, you'll see the following at the bottom now:

```
"engines" : {
  "node" : "6.x"
}
```

This will tell Azure to use version *6.x* of Node.js to run our application, which is great, because that's what we've been developing with!

Create and Deploy the Application on Azure

In order to do anything with your application, you'll need to create an Azure app and then deploy it. You can then configure other missing parts which you'll see in subsequent sections.

1. Create Your Azure Application

To create your application, you run:

```
azure site create --git marcwandphotosharingapp111
```

For this example, you'll pick your own application name, so we've chosen something pretty unique for your photo sharing application.

Remember how you just downloaded your source code from GitHub before? You did this because Azure gives you your own Git repository that it manages for us, not using GitHub. That is what the --git flag does for us.

```
C:\src\photo_sharing_azure> azure site create --git marcwandphotosharingapp111
info:    Executing command site create
+ Getting sites
+ Getting locations
help:    Location:
  1) South Central US
  2) North Europe
  3) West Europe
  4) Southeast Asia
  5) East Asia
  6) West US
  7) East US
  8) Japan West
  9) Japan East
  10) East US 2
  11) North Central US
  12) Central US
  13) Brazil South
  14) Canada Central
  15) Canada East
```

```
 16)  West Central US
 17)  West US 2
 18)  UK West
 19)  UK South
: 3
info:      Creating a new web site at marcwandphotosharingapp111.azurewebsites.net
/info:     Created website at marcwandphotosharingapp111.azurewebsites.net
+
+ Getting locations
info:      Initializing remote Azure repository
+ Updating site information
info:      Remote azure repository initialized
+ Getting site information
+ Getting user information
info:      Executing 'git remote add azure https://marcwan_nt1@ marcwandphotosharing
app111.scm.azurewebsites.
net/marcwandawesome11111.git'
info:      A new remote, 'azure', has been added to your local git repository
info:      Use git locally to make changes to your site, commit, and then use 'git push
azure master'
to deploy to Azure
info:      site create command OK
```

And with that, you have your application created on Azure!

3. Deploy Your Application to Your Site

Let's deploy the code to the server and open up the home page. First you'll add all your
files to the Git repository you created along with your project in the previous step and then
push your changes to Azure. You'll execute the following commands:

```
C:\src\photo_sharing_azure> git add .
C:\src\photo_sharing_azure> git commit -a -m "initial checkin"
C:\src\photo_sharing_azure> git push azure master
```

After a lengthy bit of output, your application should be ready to go. To view it, you now do:

```
C:\src\photo_sharing_azure> azure site browse
```

And a browser will pop up with your website in it. It will have no albums, and furthermore,
nothing will work!

This is because you haven't added database support to your application yet. We do that now.

3. Configure the ClearDB MySQL Database Add-On

Before you can start really using your application, you have to prepare your MySQL database.
You don't have a local database in an Azure application, so you need to configure what's called
a service. Fortunately, there's a MySQL add-on called *ClearDB* (just as there was for Heroku
above) that will let you work with a small database for free when starting out. Add that to your
Azure app now.

Figure 11.2   Adding ClearDB

You'll need to do this via the web browser, so visit *azure.microsoft.com* again, and click on the "+ New" button in the top left. You'll then get a search box into which you can type "ClearDB" (see Figure 11.2).

NAME		PUBLISHER
ClearDB		
Results		
NAME	^	PUBLISHER
MySQL Database		ClearDB
Web App + MySQL		Microsoft

Figure 11.3   Choosing ClearDB

You'll see a match and then you can click on that to go to the results page (see Figure 11.3) where "MySQL Database" by publisher "ClearDB" will be an option. Click on that and then click "Create" to create your database. Give it a name, like "marcwand_photo_sharing_1", choose "Free Trial" for subscription, "Shared" for database type, and then create a new resource group called "learning_node_resources." For location, pick something appropriate (I chose West Europe since that's closest to where I am), and then choose Mercury for the pricing tier and accept the legal terms (see Figure 11.4).

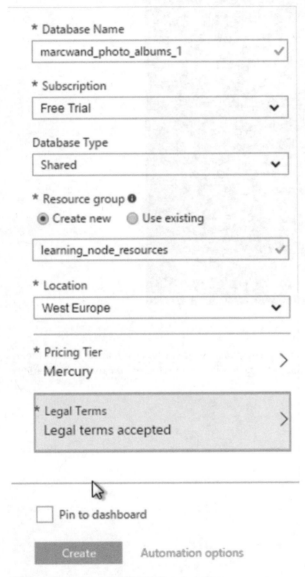

Figure 11.4   Setting ClearDB parameters

You then click "Create" again, and your database will soon be ready to go! It'll take a few minutes for the initialization to complete, but once it does, you'll be able to click into your new database to see the parameters you'll need to make the connection.

You'll see your connection parameters in a panel like that shown in Figure 11.5. You'll want to specify the *hostname*, *username*, and *password*. (Your database name is the one you chose above, `marcwand_photo_sharing_1`.)

Figure 11.5   **Your connection parameters**

With this, you now have enough to update your *local.config.json* file with the database connection information, as follows:

```
{
    "config": {
        "db_config": {
            "host": "us-cdbr-iron-east-08.cleardb.net",
            "user": "53c8ab8ffe",
            "password": "488ae",
            "database": "marcwand_photo_sharing_1",
            "pooled_connections": 125,
            "idle_timeout_millis": 30000
        },

        "static_content": "/static/"
    }
}
```

Now, you have to run the *schema.sql* file to create the contents of the database! You'll change the top of the *schema.sql* file to look as follows:

```
DROP DATABASE IF EXISTS marcwand_photo_sharing_1

CREATE DATABASE marcwan_photo_sharing_1
    DEFAULT CHARACTER SET utf8
    DEFAULT COLLATE utf8_general_ci;

USE marcwand_photo_sharing_1;
```

Now you can run the script with the following command:

```
C:\Users\marcwan> mysql --host= us-cdbr-iron-east-08.cleardb.net --user=53c8ab8ffe
--password=488ae marcwand_photo_sharing_1 < schema.sql
```

Now you have your database all setup!

Commit and redeploy your application, as follows:

```
C:\src\photo_sharing_azure> git commit -a -m "updates"
C:\src\photo_sharing_azure> git push azure master
```

We Have a Problem (and Déja Vu!)

Much like for the Heroku-deployed version of your application above, we have a rather serious problem with your application, however. The problem is caused by the rather ephemeral nature of an Azure execution environment, the environment in which your applications run. You cannot rely on the disk space backing these environments not to change or be erased periodically.

Thus, all photo files you have uploaded can disappear at inconvenient times! The database records for them are still there, but the actual images will not be.

You'll use another service to handle image storage for us—you'll keep all the images that users upload to your application in a remote file storage application. The one you'll use is called *Cloudinary*, and is free for small amounts of files with very little traffic; perfect for your development environment!

To work with these, you'll need to do the following things:

1. Create a Cloudinary (free) account.

2. Update your *package.json* to include the Cloudinary uploader.

3. Update *server.js* with your connection information.

4. Update your *album.js* data class to use this instead of local file storage.

5. Update your *album.js* page bootstrapper (in *static/content/abum.js*) to use the Cloudinary URL instead of a local URL to static files on your server.

Let's do these one by one.

1. Create a (Free) Cloudinary Account

While there once was a service in the Azure marketplace for Cloudinary, it no longer appears to be there. Fortunately, that won't stop you from using Cloudinary in your photo sharing application—you just have to visit *cloudinary.com* and sign up for a free account. Once you've done that, you'll need to remember three things from the Cloudinary dashboard:

1. Cloud name

2. API Key

3. API Secret

You'll use all of these in step 3 below. You can see an example of the Cloudinary dashboard / console where you'd get these values in Figure 11.6.

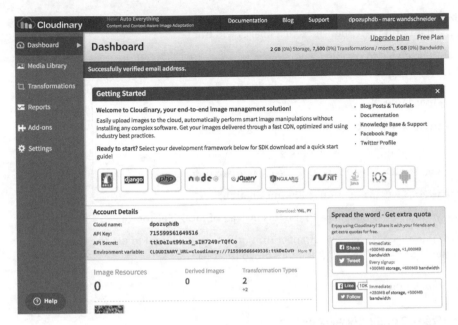

Figure 11.6   Your Cloudinary parameters

2. Update Your package.json to Include Cloudinary

This step is pretty straightforward—you simply need to include a new dependency as follows:

```
"dependences" : {
  … etc …
  "cloudinary" : "",
  … etc …
}
```

You'll see you just grab the latest version of the *cloudinary* module.

3. Update server.js with Your Connection Information

Remember those three values you saved when you created your Cloudinary account? You need those now. Modify your *server.js* file to require the *cloudinary* module at the very top, and then add the following:

```
cloudinary.config({
    cloud_name: "SAVED_CLOUD_NAME",
    api_key: "SAVED_API_KEY",
    api_secret: "SAVED_API_SECRET"
});
```

4. Update Your album.js Data Handler for Cloudinary

Basically, you need to modify *data/album.js* in two places to make it compatible with Cloudinary. First, in `exports.create_album`, you'll remove all references to `mkdir`, since you won't need album folders any more. So, you'll get rid of the following lines: in `create_album`:

```
// make sure the folder exists.
function (results, fields, cb) {
    write_succeeded = true;
    fs.mkdir('.' + local.config.static_content
                + "albums/", cb);
},
```

You can just copy over *data/cloudinary/album.js* to *data/album.js* to save yourself having to type in all this. You'll also note that the next function argument list changes because of the deletion of code.

Next, you need to get rid of the file copying in `exports.add_photo_to_album`. In the older version of `add_photo_to_album`, after the `db.dbpool.query`, you have the following code:

```
// make sure the folder exists!!!!
function (results, fields, cb) {
    write_succeeded = true;
    fs.mkdir(basepath, function () { cb(null); });
},
function (cb) {
    var pttth = basepath + photo_data.albumid + "/";
    fs.mkdir(pttth, function () { cb(null); });
},

// now copy the temp file to static content
function (cb) {
    write_succeeded = true;
    var save_path = '.' + local.config.static_content + "albums/"
        + photo_data.albumid + "/" + base_fn;
    backhelp.file_copy(path_to_photo, save_path, true, cb);
},
```

You'll get rid of all of these, and instead, add the following function to the *async* waterfall before the `db.dbpool.query`:

```
function (cb) {
    cloudinary.uploader.upload(path_to_photo, function (results) {
        cb(null, results);
    });
},
```

```
function (results, cb) {
    db.dbpool.query(
        "INSERT INTO Photos VALUES (?, ?, ?, ?)",
        [ photo_data.albumid, results.secure_url, photo_data.description,
          photo_data.date ],
        cb);
},
```

(You'll probably also notice that you need to require *cloudinary* at the top of this file now since you're using the module here!)

You'll see that uploading a file to Cloudinary is as simple as calling `cloudinary.uploader.upload` with the path to the local file. Once it has uploaded, the results will return to you the URL you'll need to refer to the file in your web application. You'll use the `secure_url` version (there's also just `url`), since you should always plan to deploy HTTPS versions of your application.

You then update your SQL query to use that `secure_url` instead of a file path, which means you now have in the database everything you need to get at your pictures!

5. Update Your Album Page Bootstrapper

Your last task to make your application use cloud storage is to update the *album.js* Album page bootstrapper to use this new URL instead of a constructed local file URL.

In the `massage_album` function, you'll change the line:

```
var url = "/albums/" + a.name + "/" + p[i].filename;
```

to be simply:

```
var url = p[i].filename
```

Since the filename is just the complete URL.

And That's It!

Recommit, and then execute:

```
C:\src\photo_sharing_azure> git commit -a -m "cloudinary updates"
C:\src\photo_sharing_azure> git push azure master
```

Running `azure site browse` should now show you a perfectly working web application with persistent file storage and a working database!

Microsoft Azure provides a robust cloud platform for you to deploy your Node.js applications, and in this part of the book, you've seen that it's not particularly difficult to modify your application to work with Azure.

Summary

In this chapter you've taken the MySQL version of your photo sharing application and deployed it to two different cloud platforms, Heroku and Microsoft Azure. The process for doing so was pretty straightforward for both and remarkably similar! You're even able to use most of the same services for things like databases and image storage on the backend! This will give you maximum flexibility later when you want to scale and grow your servers.

In the next chapter, you're going to change gears briefly and see how you can use Node.js not just to develop powerful web applications but also to do synchronous tasks that lend themselves to doing command-line programming and scripting.

12

Command-Line Programming

After spending so much time in this book discussing how Node.js is a powerful asynchronous, nonblocking platform for creating applications, I'm now going to show you how sometimes using regular synchronous, blocking IO is also cool in Node—writing command-line programs. It turns out that writing JavaScript code is so much fun that people are starting to write a lot of their day-to-day scripts and other quick programs in Node as well.

In this chapter, you look at the basics of running command-line scripts in Node, including looking at some of the synchronous file system APIs available to you. You then look at how you can interact with the user directly via buffered and unbuffered input, and finally look at process creation and execution.

Running Command-Line Scripts

You have quite a few options to run Node.js scripts from the command line, for both UNIX-like and Mac operating systems as well as Windows. You are able to make them appear as regular operating system commands and pass command-line parameters to them as well.

UNIX and Mac

On UNIX-like operating systems such as Linux or Mac OS X, a majority of command-line users use the Bourne Shell, sh (or the popular modern variant, bash). Although the shell scripting language it comes with is quite full featured and powerful, it can sometimes still be more fun to write scripts in JavaScript instead.

You have two ways to run your Node programs in the shell. The easiest is to just run a program as you always have—by specifying the node program and the script to run (the .js extension is optional, actually):

```
node do_something
```

The second is to directly make the script an executable file by changing the first line as follows:

```
#!/usr/local/bin/node
```

The first two characters are known as a *shebang* and tell the operating system that what comes directly after it is the path of the program to execute with this file as a given argument. In the preceding example, the operating system knows to go to */usr/local/bin*, look for the executable node, run it, and pass in the file as an argument to Node. The Node interpreter is smart enough to ignore this first line starting with #! because it realizes that this line is for operating system use.

So, you can write the following *hello world* executable in Node:

```
#!/usr/local/bin/node
console.log("Hello World!");
```

To run the program as an executable, you also need to mark it as an executable file by using the chmod command:

```
chmod 755 hello_world
```

Now you can directly execute the script by typing (the ./ tells the shell to look in the current folder for the script)

```
$ ./hello_world
Hello World!
$
```

There is one small problem with this approach: what happens when you take your script to other machines and node is not in */usr/local/bin*, but instead in */usr/bin*? The common solution is to change the shebang line as follows:

```
#!/usr/bin/env node
```

The env command then looks through your PATH environment variable to find the first instance of the node program and then runs that. All UNIX-like and Mac machines have env in /usr/bin, so as long as node is in the system PATH somewhere, this is more portable.

If you poke around in your various operating system executable directories or other places where you have installed software, you see that a lot of programs you use on a regular basis are, in fact, scripts of some sort.

One small bonus: the Node interpreter is smart enough, even on Windows, to ignore the #! syntax, so you can still write scripts that can be run as executables on both platforms!

Windows

Microsoft Windows has never really had a fantastic scripting environment available to it. Windows Vista and 7 introduced the PowerShell, which is a nice improvement on previous ones, but it still never quite feels as powerful and easy to use as the shells available on UNIX-like platforms. The good news, however, is that this doesn't hurt you that much because your primary goal is just to get your scripts launched and executing, and the features available in all modern (and semimodern) versions of Windows are more than enough.

You can run your scripts with batch files (carrying the extension .bat). If you have the simple *hello_world.js* you saw in the previous section, you could create *hello_world.bat*, as follows:

```
@echo off
node hello_world
```

By default, Windows echoes every command it sees in a batch file. The `@echo off` tells it to stop that. Now, to run the program, you could just type

```
C:\Users\Mark\LearningNode\Chapter11\> hello_world
Hello World!
C:\Users\Mark\LearningNode\Chapter11\>
```

But there is a bug in this program! What if *hello_world.bat* and *hello_world.js* are in the same folder, but you are executing the batch file from somewhere else, as shown here:

```
C:\Users\Mark\LearningNode\Chapter11\> cd \
C:\> \Users\Mark\LearningNode\Chapter11\hello_world
module.js:340
    throw err;
          ^
Error: Cannot find module 'C:\hello_world'
    at Function.Module._resolveFilename (module.js:338:15)
    at Function.Module._load (module.js:280:25)
    at Module.runMain (module.js:492:10)
    at process.startup.processNextTick.process._tickCallback (node.js:244:9)
```

Because you don't specify the full path to *hello_world.js*, Node doesn't know where to look for it and gets lost. You fix that problem by changing the *hello_world.bat* script to be as follows:

```
@echo off
node %~d0\%~p0\hello_world
```

Here, you make use of two handy little batch file macros, `%-pXX` and `%~dXX`, to give you the drive letter and path, respectively, of the *n*th argument (here, the 0th, or the name of the script being run). Now you can run *hello_world* from wherever you want on your computer and it'll work properly:

```
Z:\> C:\Users\Mark\LearningNode\Chapter11\hello_world
Hello World!
```

Scripts and Parameters

To be able to do interesting things with your scripts, you need to pass them parameters. In this case you need to worry about two problems: how to pass these parameters to your scripts and how to access them within the script.

If you run your Node scripts by calling the interpreter all the time (which works on all platforms), you need to do nothing extra—the arguments are passed directly to the executing script:

```
node script_name [args]*
```

Passing Parameters on UNIX/Mac

On UNIX-like operating systems where you use the #! syntax to launch your scripts, these parameters are passed directly to your scripts when you run them. So even here you don't have to do anything else.

Passing Parameters on Windows

On Windows, you mostly run your Node scripts via batch files with the *.bat* extension. You can pass parameters to these batch files, and they can, in turn, pass them on to your Node.js scripts by using the macro %*. So, the batch file would look as follows:

```
@echo off
node %~d0\%~p0\params %*
```

Accessing Parameters in Node

All parameters passed to your scripts are appended to the argv array on the process global object. The first two items in this array are always the node interpreter running and the script being run. So, any additional arguments passed to the script start at the third element, index *2*. Now run the following:

```
#!/usr/local/bin/node
console.log(process.argv);
```

You should see the output roughly as follows:

```
Kimidori:01_running marcw$ ./params.js 1 2 3 4 5
[ '/usr/local/bin/node',
  '/Users/marcw/src/misc/LearningNode/Chapter11/01_running/params.js',
  '1',
  '2',
  '3',
  '4',
  '5' ]
```

Working with Files Synchronously

For nearly every single API you have seen in the file system module (*fs*), both asynchronous and synchronous versions are available. You have mostly been using the asynchronous versions thus far, but the synchronous versions can be extremely useful to you when writing command-line programs. Basically, for a vast majority of APIs in *fs* with the name func, there is a corresponding API called funcSync.

In the following sections, you look at a few examples of how you can use some of these synchronous APIs.

Basic File APIs

The *fs* module doesn't have a file copy function, so you can write one yourself. For the `open`, `read`, and `write` APIs, you use the synchronous versions: `openSync`, `readSync`, and `write-Sync`. In the synchronous versions, they throw an error if anything goes wrong. You can use a buffer to hold the data as you copy from location *a* to *b*. Be sure to close everything when you're done:

```
var BUFFER_SIZE = 1000000;

function copy_file_sync (src, dest) {
    var read_so_far, fdsrc, fddest, read;
    var buff = new Buffer(BUFFER_SIZE);

    fdsrc = fs.openSync(src, 'r');
    fddest = fs.openSync(dest, 'w');
    read_so_far = 0;

    do {
        read = fs.readSync(fdsrc, buff, 0, BUFFER_SIZE, read_so_far);
        fs.writeSync(fddest, buff, 0, read);
        read_so_far += read;
    } while (read > 0);

    fs.closeSync(fdsrc);
    return fs.closeSync(fddest);
}
```

To call this function, you can write a *file_copy.js* script that makes sure it gets enough arguments, calls the copy function, and then handles any errors that are thrown during the process:

```
if (process.argv.length != 4) {
    console.log("Usage: " + path.basename(process.argv[1], '.js')
                + " [src_file] [dest_file]");
} else {
    try {
        copy_file_sync(process.argv[2], process.argv[3]);
    } catch (e) {
        console.log("Error copying file:");
        console.log(e);
        process.exit(-1);
    }

    console.log("1 file copied.");
}
```

You can see here that you also make use of a new function, `process.exit`. This function terminates the Node.js program immediately and passes the return code back to the calling program (often a shell interpreter or command prompt). The standard in Bourne shell (`sh`) or its improved version Bourne Again Shell (bash) is to return 0 on success and nonzero when something bad happens. You return *–1* when something goes wrong with the copy.

You can trivially change this copy function to a move function by first performing the file copy operation and then deleting the source file when you're sure the destination has been fully written and successfully closed. You perform this deletion by using the function unlinkSync:

```
function move_file_sync (src, dest) {
    var read_so_far, fdsrc, fddest, read;
    var buff = new Buffer(BUFFER_SIZE);

    fdsrc = fs.openSync(src, 'r');
    fddest = fs.openSync(dest, 'w');
    read_so_far = 0;

    do {
        read = fs.readSync(fdsrc, buff, 0, BUFFER_SIZE, read_so_far);
        fs.writeSync(fddest, buff, 0, read);
        read_so_far += read;
    } while (read > 0);

    fs.closeSync(fdsrc);
    fs.closeSync(fddest);
    return fs.unlinkSync(src);
}
```

The rest of the script remains the same, except you change the call to copy_file_sync to move_file_sync.

Files and Stats

You create folders in Node by using the mkdir function in the file system module. In the scripts shown here, you use the mkdirSync variation of it. Now you're ready to write a program that behaves the same as the mkdir -p command in UNIX shells: you specify a full path, and it creates that directory and also any missing intermediary directories that do not yet exist.

The work takes place in two steps:

1. You break apart the path and then, starting at the top, see which directories already exist or not. If something exists at the given location but isn't a directory (that is, you want to use mkdir a/b/c, but a/b already exists and is a regular file), you throw an error. To determine the existence of a file, you use the existsSync function and then call the statsSync function, which gives you a Stats object that can tell you whether or not the object is a directory.

2. For all those entries that have not yet been created, you iterate through and create them.

Here's the code for the mkdirs function:

```
function mkdirs (path_to_create, mode) {
    if (mode == undefined) mode = 0777 & (~process.umask());

    // 1. What do we have already or not?
    var parts = path_to_create.split(path.sep);
    var i;
    for (i = 0; i < parts.length; i++) {
        var search;
        search = parts.slice(0, i + 1).join(path.sep);
        if (fs.existsSync(search)) {
            var st;
            if ((st = fs.statSync(search))) {
                if (!st.isDirectory())
                    throw new Error("Intermediate exists, is not a dir!");
            }
        } else {
            // doesn't exist. We can start creating now
            break;
        }
    }

    // 2. Create whatever we don't have yet.
    for (var j = i; j < parts.length; j++) {
        var build = parts.slice(0, j + 1).join(path.sep);
        fs.mkdirSync(build, mode);
    }
}
```

The first line of this function, to set up the mask (the default permissions for file system objects), is just a way for you to choose reasonable permissions for the new directories. The caller of this function can specify them directly or can use what is known as the umask to filter out those permissions that the shell environment variable of the current user does not want to give to new files (or directories). On Windows machines, umask returns 0, indicating that it does not want to mask anything out at all; Windows uses a completely different mechanism for file permissions.

Listing Contents of Directories

To list the contents of a directory, you can use the readdirSync function, which returns an array of all filenames in the specified folder, excluding "." and "..":

```
#!/usr/local/bin/node
var fs = require('fs');

var files = fs.readdirSync(".");
console.log(files);
```

Interacting with the User: stdin/stdout

You might be familiar with the trio of IO handles given to all processes, `stdin`, `stdout`, and `stderr`, representing input, normal output, and error output, respectively. These are all available to the Node.js scripts and hang off the `process` object. In Node, they are all instances of `Stream` objects (see Chapter 6, "Expanding Your Web Server").

The `console.log` function, in fact, is just the equivalent of

```
process.stdout.write(text + "\n");
```

Whereas `console.error` is basically

```
process.stderr.write(text + "\n");
```

Input, however, gives you a few more options, so in the following sections, you look at buffered (line-by-line) input versus unbuffered (type a character and immediately see something) input.

Basic Buffered Input and Output

By default, the stream you get for `stdin` reads and buffers one line at a time. Thus, if you try to read from `stdin`, nothing happens until the user presses the Enter key, and then your program is given the entire line read from the input stream. You listen for these events by adding a handler for the `readable` event on `stdin`, as follows:

```
process.stdin.on('readable', function () {
    var data = process.stdin.read();
    // do something w input
});
```

Let's write a little program that reads in a line of input and then generates and prints out an *md5* hash of this input, looping until the user either presses Ctrl+C or enters a blank line:

```
process.stdout.write("Hash-o-tron 3000\n");
process.stdout.write("(Ctrl+C or Empty line quits)\n");
process.stdout.write("data to hash > ");

process.stdin.on('readable', function () {
    var data = process.stdin.read();
    if (data == null) return;
    if (data == "\n") process.exit(0);

    var hash = require('crypto').createHash('md5');
    hash.update(data);
    process.stdout.write("Hashed to: " + hash.digest('hex') + "\n");
    process.stdout.write("data to hash > ");
});

process.stdin.setEncoding('utf8');
```

Most of the work happens when the user presses Enter: you check to see whether the input is nonempty. If it is, you hash it, print out the result, and then print another prompt and wait for the user to type in something else. Because stdin is not in the paused state, the Node program does not exit. (If you were to pause it, it would exit if there was nothing else to do.)

Unbuffered Input

For those situations in which you want to let the user simply press a key and have something happen immediately, you can turn on *raw mode* on the stdin stream, using the setRawMode function, which takes a Boolean indicating whether or not it should turn on (true) raw mode.

Update your hash generator for the previous section to let the user select which type of hash she would like. After the user enters a line of text and presses Enter, you ask her to press a number between 1 and 4 to choose which algorithm she'd like. The complete listing for this program is shown in Listing 11.1.

Listing 11.1   **Using Raw Mode on Stdin (raw_mode.js)**

```
process.stdout.write("Hash-o-tron 3000\n");
process.stdout.write("(Ctrl+C or Empty line quits)\n");
process.stdout.write("data to hash > ");

process.stdin.on('readable', function (data) {
    var data = process.stdin.read();
    if (!process.stdin.isRaw) {                      // 1.
        if (data == "\n") process.exit(0);
        process.stdout.write("Please select type of hash:\n");
        process.stdout.write("(1 - md5, 2 - sha1, 3 - sha256, 4 - sha512) \n");
        process.stdout.write("[1-4] > ");
        process.stdin.setRawMode(true);
    } else {
        var alg;
        if (data != '^C') {                          // 2.
            var c = parseInt(data);
            switch (c) {
                case 1: alg = 'md5'; break;
                case 2: alg = 'sha1'; break;
                case 3: alg = 'sha256'; break;
                case 4: alg = 'sha512'; break;
            }
            if (alg) {                               // 3.
                var hash = require('crypto').createHash(alg);
                hash.update(data);
                process.stdout.write("\nHashed to: " + hash.digest('hex'));
                process.stdout.write("\ndata to hash > ");
                process.stdin.setRawMode(false);
```

```
        } else {
            process.stdout.write("\nPlease select type of hash:\n");
            process.stdout.write("[1-4] > ");
        }
    } else {
        process.stdout.write("\ndata to hash > ");
        process.stdin.setRawMode(false);
    }
  }
});
```

```
process.stdin.setEncoding(;'utf8')
```

Because this script receives input from `stdin` both when it is buffered (when you're asking for the text to hash) and when it is unbuffered (when you ask for the hashing algorithm to use), it's a bit more involved. Let's see how it works:

1. You first check to see whether the input you received is buffered or unbuffered. If the former, it's a line of text to hash, and you should print out the request to choose which algorithm to use. Because you want the user to just be able to press a number between 1 and 4, you switch `stdin` to raw mode now so that pressing any key triggers the `readable` event.

2. If the stream is in raw mode, it means the user has pressed a key in response to your request for a hash algorithm. For the first line here, you check to see whether this key is Ctrl+C. (Note that this can be tricky to enter into a text editor; in Emacs, you can press Ctrl+Q and then Ctrl+C, and it types the ^C for you. Every editor is slightly different.) If the user pressed Ctrl+C, you abort the input request and go back to the hash prompt.

   If the user entered some other key, you first make sure it's a valid key (1–4) or else you squawk and make the user try again.

3. Finally, depending on the algorithm selected, you generate the hash, print it out, and then go back to the normal enter data prompt. You must be sure to turn off raw mode here so that you go back to line-buffered input!

Because we are working with `stdin` in this program, it does not exit until you call `process.exit`, the user enters a blank line, or the user presses Ctrl+C during buffered input (which causes Node to just terminate).

The readline Module

One other way to work with input in Node.js is to use the *readline* module. It has a couple of neat features that you can use in your programs.

To turn on the readline module, call the `createInterface` method on it, specifying as options the `stdin` and `stdout` streams to use:

```
var readline = require('readline');

var rl = readline.createInterface({
    input: process.stdin,
    output: process.stdout
});
```

After you do this, your program does not exit until `rl.close` is called!

Line-by-Line Prompting

If you call the `prompt` method in *readline*, the program waits for a line of input (followed by Enter). When the program gets this keypress, it sends the `line` event on the `readline` object. The event can process it as needed:

```
rl.on("line", function (line) {
    console.log(line);
    rl.prompt();
});
```

To continue listening, you call the `prompt` method again. One of the nice things about the readline interface is that if the user presses Ctrl+C, you get the `SIGINT` event called, and you can either shut things down there or do other things to reset the state and continue. Here, by closing the readline interface, you cause the program to stop listening for input and exit:

```
rl.on("SIGINT", function () {
    rl.close();
});
```

Now you're ready to write a little reverse Polish notation calculator using the *readline* module. The code for this calculator is shown in Listing 11.2.

If you've never heard of reverse Polish notation or forgotten how it works, it's basically a postfix mathematical notation format. Instead of writing 1 + 2, you write 1 2 +. To write 5 * (2 + 3), you write 5 2 3 + *, and so on. The little calculator takes a string at a time, splits it up based on spaces, and does simple calculations.

Listing 11.2 **Simple postfix calculator using readline (readline.js)**

```
var readline = require('readline');
var rl = readline.createInterface({
    input: process.stdin,
    output: process.stdout
});
```

```
var p = "postfix expression > "
rl.setPrompt(p, p.length);
rl.prompt();                                      // 1.

rl.on("line", function (line) {                   // 2.
    if (line == "\n")  {
        rl.close(); return;
    }

    var parts = line.split(new RegExp("[ ]+"));
    var r = postfix_process(parts);
    if (r !== false)
        process.stdout.write("Result: " + r + "\n");
    else
        process.stdout.write("Invalid expression.\n");
    rl.prompt();                                  // 3.
});

rl.on("SIGINT", function () {                      // 4.
    rl.close();
});

// push numbers onto a stack, pop when we see an operator.
function postfix_process(parts) {
    var stack = [];
    for (var i = 0; i < parts.length; i++) {
        switch (parts[i]) {
          case '+': case '-': case '*': case '/':
            if (stack.length < 2) return false;
            do_op(stack, parts[i]);
            break;
          default:
            var num = parseFloat(parts[i]);
            if (isNaN(num)) return false;
            stack.push(num);
            break;
        }
    }
    if (stack.length != 1) return false;
    return stack.pop();
}

function do_op(stack, operator) {
    var b = stack.pop();
    var a = stack.pop();
    switch (operator) {
      case '+': stack.push(a + b); break;
      case '-': stack.push(a - b); break;
```

```
        case '*': stack.push(a * b); break;
        case '/': stack.push(a / b); break;
        default:  throw new Error("Unexpected operator");
    }
}
```

This program works as follows:

1. You create the *readline* module object, set the default prompt text on it, and then tell *readline* to show that prompt and wait for a line of input.

2. When you receive a line of input, you check to see whether it's empty (in which case you close down the program by closing the *readline* interface), or else you parse the input string and pass it to the little calculating function. You print out the results (good or bad).

3. You complete the loop by telling *readline* to print out the prompt and wait again.

4. If the user presses Ctrl+C, you close down *readline*, which causes the program to exit gracefully.

Now you can test it:

```
hostnameKimidori:03_stdinout marcw$ node readline_rpn.js
postfix expression > 1 2 +
Result: 3
postfix expression > 2 3 4 + *
Result: 14
postfix expression > cat
Invalid expression.
postfix expression > 1 2 4 cat dog  3 4 + - / *
Invalid expression.
postfix expression > 2 3 + 5 *
Result: 25
postfix expression >
```

Questions

The other major functionality in the *readline* module is the ability to ask questions and receive the answers directly in a callback. The basic format is

```
rl.question("hello? ", function (answer) {
    // do something
});
```

Next, you write a little program that performs a survey: it takes an array of questions (which you could put in a file if you wanted to make it configurable) and asks the user to answer them one at a time. It then writes the user's answers to *answers.txt* using `appendFileSync` on the fs module.

Note that because the question function is asynchronous, you have to use `async.`
`forEachSeries` to iterate over each of the questions in the survey! The code for the survey
program is shown in Listing 11.3.

Listing 11.3 **Survey program (questions.js)**

```
var readline = require('readline'),
    async = require("async"),
    fs = require('fs');

var questions = [ "What's your favorite color? ",
                  "What's your shoe size? ",
                  "Cats or dogs? ",
                  "Doctor Who or Doctor House? " ];

var rl = readline.createInterface({                    // 1.
    input: process.stdin,
    output: process.stdout
});

var output = [];
async.forEachSeries(
    questions,
    function (item, cb) {                              // 2.
        rl.question(item, function (answer) {
            output.push(answer);
            cb(null);
        });
    },
    function (err) {                                   // 3.
        if (err) {
            console.log("Hunh, couldn't get answers");
            console.log(err);
            return;
        }
        fs.appendFileSync("answers.txt", JSON.stringify(output) + "\n");
        console.log("\nThanks for your answers!");
        console.log("We'll sell them to some telemarketer immediately!");
        rl.close();
    }
);
```

The program performs the following tasks:

1. It initializes the *readline* module and sets up the stdin and stdout streams.

2. Then for each question in the array, you call the question function on readline (using
   `async.forEachSeries` because question is an asynchronous function) and add the
   result to the output array.

3. Finally, after all the questions have been asked and `async` calls the results function, you either print the error if there was one or append the user's output to the *answers.txt* file and then close the `readline` object to exit the program.

Working with Processes

One other thing you can do from the command line (or even from within your web applications) in Node is to launch other programs. You have a couple of options for this using the *child_process* module, with varying degrees of complexity. In the following sections, you start with the easier option, `exec`.

Simple Process Creation

The `exec` function in the child_process module takes a command and executes it in the system shell (sh/bash on UNIX/Mac, or `cmd.exe` on Windows). Thus, you can specify something simple like `"date"` as the program to run, or something complicated like `"echo 'Mancy' | sed s/M/N/g"`. All commands are run, and all output is buffered and passed back to the caller after the command finishes.

The basic format is

```
exec(command, function (error, stdout, stderr) {
    // error is non-null if an error occurred
    // stdout and stderr are buffers
});
```

After the command finishes executing, the callback is called. The first parameter is non-null only if an error occurred. Otherwise, `stdout` and `stderr` are set to `Buffer` objects with the full contents of anything written to the respective output stream.

Now write a program that uses the `exec` function to run the `cat` program (`type` on Windows). It takes the name of a file to print out. It uses the `exec` function to launch the `cat/type` program and then prints out all the output when you're done:

```
var exec = require('child_process').exec,
    child;

if (process.argv.length != 3) {
    console.log("I need a file name");
    process.exit(-1);
}

var file_name = process.argv[2];
var cmd = process.platform == 'win32' ? 'type' : "cat";
child = exec(cmd + " " + file_name, function (error, stdout, stderr) {
    console.log('stdout: ' + stdout);
    console.log('stderr: ' + stderr);
```

```
    if (error) {
        console.log("Error exec'ing the file");
        console.log(error);
        process.exit(1);
    }
});
```

Advanced Process Creation with Spawn

A more advanced way of creating processes is to use the spawn function available in the *child_process* module. This function gives you complete control over the stdin and stdout of the child processes you create and permits some fantastic functionality, such as piping output from one child process to another.

Start by writing a program that takes the name of a JavaScript file and runs it with the node program:

```
var spawn = require("child_process").spawn;
var node;

if (process.argv.length != 3) {
    console.log("I need a script to run");
    process.exit(-1);
}

var node = spawn("node", [ process.argv[2] ]);
node.stdout.on('readable', print_stdout);
node.stderr.on('readable', print_stderr);
node.on('exit', exited);

function print_stdout() {
    var data = process.stdout.read();
    console.log("stdout: " + data.toString('utf8'));
}
function print_stderr(data) {
    var data = process.stderr.read();
    console.log("stderr: " + data.toString('utf8'));
}
function exited(code) {
    console.error("--> Node exited with code: " + code);
}
```

When you want to call spawn, the first argument is the name of the command to execute, and the second is an array of parameters to pass to it. You can see that any output written to stdout or stderr by the child process immediately triggers an event on the appropriate stream, and you can see what's happening right away.

Now you're ready to write something a bit more advanced. In the preceding chapter, you saw a way to effectively do the following in shell scripts or command prompts:

```
while 1
    node script_name
end
```

Write that same code, but in JavaScript, using the spawn function. Using this function is actually a bit more work than writing it as a shell script, but it's instructive and sets you up to do more work and monitoring as you want later. The code for the new launcher is shown in Listing 11.4.

Listing 11.4   **An all-node node runner (node_runner.js)**

```
var spawn = require("child_process").spawn;
var node;

if (process.argv.length < 3) {
    console.log("I need a script to run");
    process.exit(-1);
}

function spawn_node() {
    var node = spawn("node", process.argv.slice(2));
    node.stdout.on('readable', print_stdout);
    node.stderr.on('readable', print_stderr);
    node.on('exit', exited);
}

function print_stdout() {
    var data = process.stdout.read();
    console.log("stdout: " + data.toString('utf8'));
}
function print_stderr(data) {
    var data = process.stderr.read();
    console.log("stderr: " + data.toString('utf8'));
}
function exited(code) {
    console.error("--> Node exited with code: " + code + ". Restarting");
    spawn_node();
}

spawn_node();
```

This program works by listening for the exit event on the spawned process. Whenever it sees that, it restarts the node interpreter with the script you want to run.

I leave it to you as an exercise to update this script to behave like the full *node_ninja_runner* you wrote in Chapter 10. You can get the output of the `ps  aux` command by using the `exec` function; the resulting buffer can easily be parsed in JavaScript. Finally, you can kill a child process by calling the `kill` method on it if you detect that it's getting too large.

Summary

Now you've seen that Node is not only great for writing networked applications, but is also extremely powerful and fun for command-line synchronous applications. After this tour of creating and running scripts and passing parameters to them, you should now be pretty comfortable manipulating input and output in your program and even be able switch between buffered and unbuffered input when necessary. Finally, you should be able to create and run programs in your Node.js scripts with `exec` and `spawn`.

To finish this treatment of programming JavaScript in Node.js, it's time now to turn your attention to testing your scripts and applications.

13

Testing

With all the code you have written so far, you're now ready to look at how to test it to make sure it works. There are many models and paradigms through which this is done, and Node.js supports most of them. This chapter looks at some of the more common ones and then looks at how you can do functional testing of not only synchronous APIs but also Node's asynchronous code and then add some testing to your photo album application.

Choosing a Framework

A few common models of testing are available, including *test-driven development* (TDD) and *behavior-driven development* (BDD). The former focuses highly on making sure that all your code is properly exposed to testing (indeed, in many cases, demanding that you write no code until you've written the tests for it), whereas the latter focuses more on the business requirements of a particular unit or module of code and encourages testing to be a bit more holistic than simple unit testing.

Regardless of the model to which you subscribe (or will subscribe, if this is your first time writing tests), adding tests to your code base is always a good idea, because you want to make sure not only that what you have written works but also that future changes you make to your code base don't break things. Adding testing to your Node applications adds a few challenges because you frequently need to mix synchronous, asynchronous, and RESTful server API functionality together, but the Node.js platform is sufficiently robust and advanced already that there are options for all your needs.

Of the many frameworks available today, two stand out in popularity:

- *nodeunit*—This is a simple and straightforward test runner for testing both in Node and in the browser. It's extremely easy to work with and gives you a lot of flexibility for setting up your testing framework.

- *Mocha*—Based on an older testing framework called Expresso, Mocha is basically a more feature-rich framework for Node that focuses on being easier to use and more enjoyable to code. It has some cool features for asynchronous testing and an API for output formatting.

Although all they work perfectly fine and have their places, for the first part of this chapter you can stick with the reasonably straightforward *nodeunit*, largely because it's really easy to work with and demonstrate. You'll then take a quick look at some black-box API testing using *Mocha*.

Installing *Nodeunit*

For your projects now, you can create a *test/* subfolder into which you put all the files, samples, and data files related to the testing of your various projects. The first file to put in is *package.json*, as follows:

```
{
  "name": "API-testing-demo",
  "description": "Demonstrates API Testing with nodeunit",
  "version": "0.0.2",
  "private": true,
  "dependencies": {
    "nodeunit": "0.x"
  }
}
```

When you run `npm update`, nodeunit is installed, and you can begin writing and running tests.

Writing Tests

The nodeunit framework organizes tests into modules, with each exposed function acting as a test and each exposed object acting as a group of tests. To each test, you are given an object that will help you perform the tests and tell nodeunit when you are done:

```
exports.test1 = function (test) {
    test.equals(true, true);
    test.done();
}
```

You must call `test.done` at the end of every single test; otherwise, nodeunit does not know when it is finished. To run this test, save it to a file called *trivial.js* and then run the provided running script in the *node_modules/.bin* folder. On both UNIX/Mac platforms and Windows, you run (switch the / characters for \ characters on Windows, of course)

```
node_modules/.bin/nodeunit trivial.js
```

You see something similar to

```
C:\Users\Mark\a> node_modules\.bin\nodeunit.cmd trivial.js

trivial.js
(✔)test1

OK: 1 assertions (0ms)

C:\Users\Mark\a>
```

Simple Functional Tests

For each test you write, you want to do three things:

1. Call the `expect` method on the provided test parameter with the number of conditions nodeunit should expect you to verify in this particular test. This step is optional, but completing it is a good idea in case some of the code accidentally skips over a test.

2. For each condition you want to verify, you should call some sort of assertion function (see Table 12.1) to verify you're seeing what you expect to see. The first example you've seen of this is `test.equals`.

3. Call `test.done` at the end of every single test to tell nodeunit you are finished.

Now take the code you wrote for a reverse Polish notation calculator in the preceding chapter and put it in a file called rpn.js (see Listing 13.1).

Listing 13.1   **The rpn.js file**

```
// push numbers onto a stack, pop when we see an operator.
exports.version = "1.0.0";

exports.compute = function (parts) {
    var stack = [];
    for (var i = 0; i < parts.length; i++) {
        switch (parts[i]) {
          case '+': case '-': case '*': case '/':
            if (stack.length < 2) return false;
            do_op(stack, parts[i]);
            break;
          default:
            var num = parseFloat(parts[i]);
            if (isNaN(num)) return false;
            stack.push(num);
            break;
        }
    }
    if (stack.length != 1) return false;
    return stack.pop();
}

function do_op(stack, operator) {
    var b = stack.pop();
    var a = stack.pop();
    switch (operator) {
      case '+': stack.push(a + b); break;
      case '-': stack.push(a - b); break;
      case '*': stack.push(a * b); break;
```

```
    case '/': stack.push(a / b); break;
    default:  throw new Error("Unexpected operator");
    }
}
```

Now, write some tests for it (don't forget to use `require` in the rpn.js file in your test file):

```
exports.addition = function (test) {
    test.expect(4);
    test.equals(rpn.compute(prep("1 2 +")), 3);
    test.equals(rpn.compute(prep("1 2 3 + +")), 6);
    test.equals(rpn.compute(prep("1 2 + 5 6 + +")), 14);
    test.equals(rpn.compute(prep("1 2 3 4 5 6 7 + + + + + +")), 28);
    test.done();
};
```

The prep function just splits the provided string into an array:

```
function prep(str) {
    return str.trim().split(/[ ]+/);
}
```

You can repeat this for all the operators your calculator supports (subtraction, multiplication, and division), and even write some additional ones for decimal numbers:

```
exports.decimals = function (test) {
    test.expect(2);
    test.equals(rpn.compute(prep("3.14159 5 *")), 15.70795);
    test.equals(rpn.compute(prep("100 3 /")), 33.333333333333336);
    test.done();
}
```

So far you've only used the `test.equals` assertion to verify that values are what you expect. Nodeunit uses a module from `npm` called *assert*, however, and there are many other possibilities, as shown in Table 13.1.

Table 13.1 **Testing Assertions**

Method	Tests
`ok(value)`	Tests whether or not `value` is true.
`equal(value, expected)`	Tests whether `value` is expected (shallow test with `==`, not `===`).
`notEqual(value, expected)`	Makes sure that `value` is not the same as expected (shallow, using `==` only).
`deepEqual(value, expected)`	Makes sure that `value` is expected, inspecting sub-values if required, using `==`.
`notDeepEqual(value, expected)`	Makes sure that `value` is not expected, inspecting sub-values if required, using `==`.

Method	Tests
strictEqual(value, expected)	Tests for equality, using the === operator.
throws(code, [Error])	Makes sure that the given code block throws an error. You can optionally tell it what kind of error you're expecting.
doesNotThrow(value, expected)	Makes sure the given code does not throw an error (optionally, of the specified type).

So, you can now add a new test to make sure that the calculator rejects empty expressions:

```
exports.empty = function (test) {
    test.expect(1);
    test.throws(rpn.compute([]));
    test.done();
};
```

When the tests fail, nodeunit tells you loudly, giving you both the condition that failed and a full stack trace of calls that led up to that failure:

```
01_functional.js
✘ addition

AssertionError: 28 == 27
    at Object.assertWrapper [as equals] [...]tests/node_modules/nodeunit/lib/types.
js:83:39)
    at Object.exports.addition [...]tests/01_functional.js:9:10)
    (etc)
(✔) subtraction
(✔) multiplication
(✔) division
(✔) decimals
(✔) empty

FAILURES: 1/17 assertions failed (5ms)
```

You can then look in your code to see which test is causing the problem and analyze the problem or regression.

Groups of Tests

You can add groups of tests, as follows, which also allow you to add setUp and tearDown methods, which will be called before and after (respectively) all the tests in the group, as follows:

```
exports.group1 = {
    setUp: function (callback) {
      callback();
    },
    tearDown: function (callback) {
      callback();
    },
```

```
    test1: function (test) {
      test.done();
    },
    test2: function (test) {
      test.done();
    },
    test3: function (test) {
      test.done();
    }
};
```

In the above group, the order in which the functions would be called is:

```
setUp → test1 → test2 → test3 → tearDown
```

Note that for the setUp and tearDown functions you have to call callback in order to continue.

Testing Asynchronous Functionality

Because you do so much asynchronous programming in Node.js, many of the tests are also asynchronous. Nodeunit is designed with this in mind: your tests can take as long as they want to run and be as asynchronous as they want, as long as they call test.done when they're finished executing. As an example, write a couple of asynchronous tests right now:

```
exports.async1 = function (test) {
    setTimeout(function () {
        test.equal(false, true);
        test.done();
    }, 2000);
};

exports.async2 = function (test) {
    setTimeout(function () {
        test.equal(true, true);
        test.done();
    }, 1400);
};
```

Running this test module provides the following output (note that the runtime is roughly the combination of the two tests run serially):

```
hostnameKimidori: functional_tests marcw$ node_modules/.bin/nodeunit 02_async.js

02_async.js
(✔) async1
(✔) async2

OK: 2 assertions (3406ms)
```

API Testing

Functional unit testing is very important to make sure that your code and functions work properly, but you also want to test how your APIs work as a "black box" from the outside. Does your API do the right thing given various inputs? Does it return the correct errors when you try to do things you should not be allowed to do?

To write tests for this, you are going to look at the *Mocha* testing framework, along with an important assertion framework called *Chai* that integrates seamlessly into Mocha.

Before you start, you'll want to install Mocha globally so you can use the `mocha` command to run your tests. On Mac or Linux machines, you'll need to run:

```
sudo npm install -g mocha
```

whereas on Windows machines, you'll want to run a `cmd.exe` with administrator permissions and just run:

```
npm install -g mocha
```

When this is done, go to the folder of your preferred version of the photo-sharing application, either the MongoDB one from Chapter 8 or the MySQL one from Chapter 9. It doesn't actually matter which one you run; you're doing black box testing, so what's running internally within the application is less important!

Clear out the database (either by deleting the *data/* folder for MongoDB or by rerunning *schema.sql* with the `mysql` command line utility), and then run the server:

```
node server.js
```

Each time before you rerun your tests, you'll want to clear out the database as above so you can be sure to run the tests in an artifact-free environment.

Now you can start to edit a file called *chaitest.js*. Put the following code in it:

```
var chai = require("chai"),
    chaihttp = require("chai-http"),
    mocha = require("mocha");

var agent = chai.request.agent("http://localhost:8080");
var expect = chai.expect;
var sid;


chai.use(chaihttp);


describe("Server Testing", function () {
        it("Should get nothing from /v1/albums");
        it("Should fail to add an album");
        it("Should register a new user");
        it("Should login a user");
});
```

All the code before the `describe` function sets up your testing environment—you include Mocha and Chai, along with the Chai HTTP framework that will allow you to make requests to your server. You set the server and remember the agent so you can re-use this in your tests.

Finally, you describe your tests. You've created a group called "Server Testing" and then added four tests to it that do the specified things. Run this with:

```
mocha chaitest.js
```

You should see:

```
Server Testing
  - Should get nothing from /v1/albums
  - Should fail to add an album
  - Should register a new user
  - Should login a user


0 passing (6ms)
4 pending
```

None of your tests are passing because they don't do anything yet. Let's fill in the first to get */v1/albums.json* and verify you get nothing back:

```
it("Should get nothing from /v1/albums", function (done) {
  agent
    .get("/v1/albums.json")
    .end(function (err, res) {
      sid = res.headers['set-cookie'].pop().split(";")[0];
      expect(res).to.have.status(200);
      expect(res).to.be.json;
      expect(res.body.error).to.be.null;
      done();
    });
});
```

This is your first introduction to how Chai works in Node.js—it almost feels like you're writing regular English sentences! You'll see this as you work your way through all the Chai examples in this book and anywhere else you search on the internet: they always feel very natural to write.

You save out the *session-id* that you get back from your photo albums server here because you need it to do requests after you're logged in, then you check a few things about the response (that you got *200* back, that it's JSON, and that it's empty).

Finally, you call the `done` function, which is how Mocha knows that you're done with the test, and it can evaluate everything to see how you did.

For the next test, you'll want to be sure that you get *403* back from the apps when you try to add an album without being authenticated:

```
it("Should fail to add an album", function (done) {
  agent
    .put("/v1/albums.json")
    .send({ name: "testing2012", date: "2012-12-1",
            title: "Testing album", description: "So awesome"})
    .end(function (err, res) {
      expect(res).to.have.status(403);
      done();
    });
});
```

Here you use the send method to add POST data to the request. When you get back *403*, you can be sure that unauthenticated people cannot add albums, which is the desired behavior.

Next, you create a user and login:

```
it ("Should register a new user", function (done) {
  agent
    .put("/v1/users.json")
    .set("Cookie", sid)
    .send({ display_name: "marcwan",
            email_address: "marcwan@a.com",
            password: "abc123" })
    .end(function (err, res) {
      expect(res).to.have.status(200);
      expect(res.body).to.be.object;
      expect(res.body.error).to.bc.null;
      expect(res.body.data).to.be.object;
      var user = res.body.data.user;
      expect(user.display_name).to.be.equal("marcwan");
      expect(user.email_address).to.be.equal("marcwan@a.com");
      expect(user.password).to.be.undefined;
      done();
    });
});

it("Should login a user", function (done) {
  agent
    .post("/service/logintest")
    .set("Cookie", sid)
    .send({ username: "marcwan", password: "abc123" })
    .end(function (err, res) {
      expect(res).to.have.status(200);
      done();
    });
});
```

Not surprisingly, you PUT the new user request, verify that the results are valid, and then login afterwards using the POST. Note that you are now passing the *session-id* (which you store in the global variable sid) into each request via the set method with the Cookie.

There is an interesting thing above, and that is that you do not call */service/login* to log in to your server in the second test above. This is because */service/login* redirects to */pages/home/login* after a successful login. But this is not what you want for your tests. You just want to know that your login has succeeded, so this is one case where it will actually make sense for you to create a new API just for testing that basically does the same thing as the regular login API but without the redirect. So you created the */service/logintest* API to help with this. It is pretty common to see the addition of testing-only versions of code when testing large systems.

Finally, now that you're logged in, you can verify that you can add an album, as follows:

```
it("should add an album", function (done) {
  agent
  .put("/v1/albums.json")
  .set("Cookie", sid)
  .send({ name: "testing2012", date: "2012-12-1",
          title: "Testing album", description: "So awesome"})
  .end(function (err, res) {
    expect(res).to.have.status(200);
    done();
  });
});
```

Now that you're logged in, the *add* will work.

Summary

Testing your Node.js apps and scripts is both simple and fast with many of the available testing frameworks available via npm. In this chapter, I showed you not only how to use *nodeunit*, a popular TDD framework, to test the synchronous and asynchronous portions of your applications but also how to use *Mocha* and *Chai* to perform full API-level testing of your JSON servers.

With this knowledge tucked under your belt, you've come to the end of your tour of Node.js. I hope that I've been able to convey some of the reasons why Node.js is so unbelievably exciting and fun to develop with and encourage you to type things and play with the platform as you've been reading along.

Sit down and start to write some code. If you have an idea for a website, start putting together some pages and APIs for it. If you do mobile development, think about the ways in which you can deliver a server to mobile customers and figure out how to use Node to do that. Even if you're just looking to script some things on a server, play around and start writing code today. The only way to get better at programming on any platform is to just use it.

If you run into problems, don't forget that the Node.js community is extremely active and helpful. With so many helpful and motivated members, it's certain you'll be able to meet many like-minded users and get all the resources and help you need to build interesting, useful, and fun applications.

Index

M

T